MILITARY REGION 2

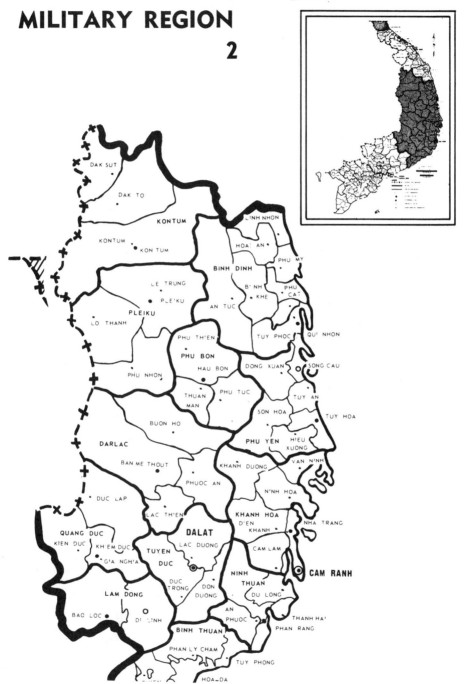

DAK SUT

DAK TO

KONTUM

KONTUM

KON TUM

LINH NHON

HOAI AN

PHU MY

BINH DINH

LE TRUNG

PLE'KU

BINH KHE

PHU CAT

PLEIKU

AN TUC

LO THANH

PHU TH'EN

TUY PHOC

QUI NHON

PHU BON

DONG XUAN

SONG CAU

PHU NHON

HAU BON

THUAN MAN

PHU TUC

TUY AN

SON HOA

TUY HOA

BUON HO

PHU YEN

HIEU XUONG

DARLAC

BAN ME THUOT

KHANH DUONG

VAN N'NH

PHUOC AN

N'NH HOA

DUC LAP

LAC TH'EN

KHANH HOA

QUANG DUC

DALAT

D'EN KHANH

NHA TRANG

KIEN DUC

LAC DUONG

KH'EM DUC

TUYEN

CAM LAM

G'A NGH'A

DUC

DUC TRONG

DON DUONG

NINH THUAN

CAM RANH

LAM DONG

DU LONG

BAO LOC

DI LINH

AN PHUOC

THANH HAI

BINH THUAN

PHAN RANG

PHAN LY CHAM

TUY PHONG

HOA-DA

A Distant Challenge:

THE U.S. INFANTRYMAN IN VIETNAM, 1967–1972

A Distant Challenge:

THE U.S. INFANTRYMAN IN VIETNAM, 1967–1972

Edited by
INFANTRY MAGAZINE

Reflections by
LTC ALBERT N. GARLAND, USA (RET.)

THE BATTERY PRESS
NASHVILLE

dedication

...to the American ground soldier
from Concord Bridge to Vietnam

Copyright © 1983
by
THE BATTERY PRESS, INC.
P.O. BOX 3107, UPTOWN STATION
NASHVILLE, TENNESSEE   37219   U.S.A.

Third in the Vietnam War Series

ISBN 0-89839-071-0

PRINTED IN THE UNITED STATES OF AMERICA

Foreword

Historically, there are few exceptions to the rule that wars on foreign lands are fought for the purpose of acquiring those lands as part of a political or economic empire. Vietnam was one such exception.

Indeed, history may judge that American aid to South Vietnam constituted one of man's more noble crusades, one that had less to do with the domino theory and a strategic interest for the United States than with the simple equation of a strong nation helping an aspiring nation to reach a point where it had some reasonable chance to achieve and keep a degree of freedom and human dignity. It remains a fact that few countries have ever engaged in such idealistic magnanimity; and no gain or attempted gain for human freedom can be discounted.

Although in the end a political default, it is now clearly evident that there was an ironic strategic dividend to our presence in Vietnam; namely the impact of the American military "holding the line" for ten years against communist pressures on Southeast Asia thus provided for the Asian countries (Philippines, Malasia, Singapore, Indonesia and Thailand) a shield and hence a breathing spell toward development of greater political maturity and self confidence as nations. It encouraged Indonesia in 1966 to throw out the Russians and, as time passed, unhappy events in Indochina showed to the people of Southeast Asia the real ugly face of communism and the inadequacy of the communist system. Consequently, the countries of Southeast Asia now seem to be staunchly a part of the non-communist world.

The military quite clearly did the job that the nation asked and expected of it, and I am convinced that history will reflect favorably upon its performance.

This book is a valuable record of the U. S. Infantryman's persistence, ingenuity and sacrifice in answering the distant challenge of communism in Southeast Asia.

FOREWORD

The worn and tired attitudes of a decade ago are now almost history. A sensible approach to the Vietnam War era and toward those involved has emerged. As truth overshadows perceptions, facts are overwhelming emotions.

W. C. WESTMORELAND
General, United States Army (Retired)

April 1983

Contents

1969

1970

1971–1972

A Distant Challenge:

THE U.S. INFANTRYMAN IN VIETNAM, 1967–1972

1967

THE SQUEEZE

U.S. forces, supported closely by aviation and artillery assets, initiated operations to put heavy pressure on the enemy. Enemy manpower was slowly whittled down by decisive operations; his weapons and food caches were seized, blunting many planned raids and offensive actions. Increased air strikes made his supply routes difficult to use.

During the year, troop strength reached a peak of 490,000 servicemen in-country. Increased manpower permitted U.S. forces to enter the field for longer periods of time—expanding their offensive combat capabilities.

Combat action included Operation Junction City, the largest operation of the war, where U.S. troops in War Zone C, north and west of Saigon, formed a giant horseshoe enclosing 250 square miles of enemy held territory.

Heavy fighting characterized the operation, and large stores of ammunition, weapons, clothing, food, documents and utensils were confiscated. Heavy enemy casualties were inflicted in 81 days of operations — eliminating the VC stronghold in War Zone C.

Subsequent action included Task Force Oregon's Operation Wheeler in Military Region 1; the Mobile Riverine Force's Operation Coronado V in the Delta; Operation Bolling, conducted by the 173rd Airborne Brigade and elements of the 1st Cavalry Division; and Operation Shenandoah in Bing Duong Province.

Late 1967 saw the introduction of a helicopter especially designed for ground support — the Huey Cobra. This gunship, with advanced weapons system, slim silhouette, high speed and maneuverability, began combat operations in 1st Aviation Brigade units.

The year closed with the rumblings of the largest battle of the war. Action evolved around the enemy's attempted takeover of Dak To and the infiltration route along 312 north of Pleiku. The ensuing battle inflicted casualties to both sides, but the enemy paid a much greater price for his attempt; there were 1,641 known enemy dead.

During the year the Infantry's additional role of teacher and ambassador began to come to the forefront; American and South Vietnamese forces fought the North Vietnamese and Viet Cong elements throughout South Vietnam. By years-end U.S. troop strength was greater than that of the Korean conflict.

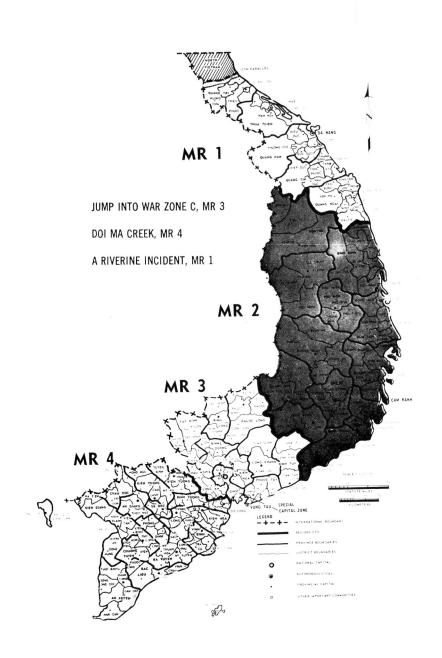

JUMP INTO WAR ZONE C, MR 3

DOI MA CREEK, MR 4

A RIVERINE INCIDENT, MR 1

Chapter 1

Carrying the Momentum

Jump Into War Zone C

Colonel Robert H. Sigholtz

In the mid-morning hours of February 22, 1967, a task force from the 173d Airborne Brigade jumped into history by making the first United States combat parachute assault in the war against the enemy in South Vietnam — and the first such assault since the Korean War. I commanded the task force which put nearly 780 Sky Soldiers under silk over War Zone C near the Cambodian border, long a Viet Cong redoubt. Below them lay drop zone "Charlie" — 1,000 by 6,000 feet of dried rice paddies deep in enemy-controlled territory.

Within an hour after the start of the parachute assault, an Infantry battalion — with artillery, heavy equipment, control teams, and support elements — was on the ground, deployed to secure the drop zone and ready for combat as Operation Junction City got underway. To both men and the planners, the combat jump was a success.

Formed on Okinawa in 1963, the 173d had undergone extensive airborne, guerrilla and jungle warfare training on Taiwan, Korea and Thailand before moving to South Vietnam in May 1965 — the first US ground combat unit committed to the war. Steeled in combat since then, the men of the 173d were eager for the chance to prove that a combat jump could be successful in Vietnam.

In October 1966, the 173d was directed to prepare a battalion-size task force for a possible parachute assault operation. The 2d Battalion, 503d Infantry, was selected as the key element of the task force, and moved to the South Vietnamese Infantry School at Thu Duc to begin training. Joining the battalion was Battery A, 3d Battalion, 319th Artillery with six 105mm howitzers; an engineer squad; a military police squad; a radio research team; an interrogation team; elements of the 173d headquarters as a brigade tactical command post; and combat support elements from the brigade's support battalion.

The training was intense, and emphasized the mental as well as physical conditioning required for airborne operations. Refresher airborne training was a major ingredient. While the men had completed the basic airborne course at Fort Benning, a majority had never participated in an airborne exercise. A routine training jump was made, and then, on November 6, 1966, the task force made a mass tactical jump with full combat loads. A portion of the heavy equipment organic to the task force was also dropped. This full dress rehearsal was the climax to the training phase, and after it was over the task force moved back into the field to conduct normal search and destroy operations against the Viet Cong. In January 1967, after one more week of airborne training, the task force was ready.

On February 11th, the official word came down: the task force would make a combat jump. Stressing surprise and speed, the operation called for the task force to conduct a combat parachute assault into War Zone C some five kilometers south of the Cambodian border to secure the brigade headquarters, a heavy equipment drop zone, the fire support base, and to block the enemy's escape routes into Cambodia. Once set, the other two battalions of the brigade would make a heliborne assault into an adjacent area to join the task force in blocking the enemy escape routes.

Because of security, only the battalion S3 and myself did the initial planning. Later, the principal staff officers and company commanders were briefed on the operation, but were not told when or where the operation would take place. Both groups were instructed not to reveal any information concerning the operation to their staffs or units.

On February 20th, final coordination was effected and that night the order was published. The next morning, the men and equipment of the task force were marshalled at and restricted to Camp Zinn, the 2d Battalion's base camp. There, for the first time, the official word was put to the troops — to a man, the word was received with great jubilation. Even now, though, the exact location of the drop zone was not revealed. Aerial photographs of the drop zone were distributed, but without coordinates.

Out on the field, the heavy equipment and supplies needed to support the task force were being rigged for heavy drop. This included the 105mm howitzers and 2,400 rounds of 105mm ammunition, four ¾-ton trucks, five ¼-ton trucks, one ¼-ton trailer, six M274 Mule vehicles, four 4.2-inch mortars and 746 mortar rounds, six 81mm mortars and 1,500 mortar rounds, 416 five-gallon water cans, 18,000 sandbags, 746 cases of C-rations, 115,700 rounds of 7.62mm ammunition, 1,440 grenades for the 40mm M79 launchers, 1,000 fragmentation hand grenades, and 500 smoke grenades.

For the operation, 23 C130 aircraft were available — 13 for personnel and 10 for heavy equipment. The size of the drop zone and operational plan dictated how the aircraft were to be loaded: the drop zone was 26 seconds long and would require two passes to put all personnel into the drop zone. Each C130 would carry 60 men and would be crossloaded to put the men of each company on the drop zone in the approximate area of their assigned sectors.

On the morning of February 21st, the task force S4 drew all of the air items needed for the operation; these were issued from a central location and fitted that afternoon. For the remainder of the day, refresher training was given with troops wearing the equipment. Mock door exits and parachute landing falls were the order of the day. That night, the air items were secured in the company mess halls.

The problem of manifesting was simplified by using the "shoe tag" rather than the manifest sheet. The shoe tag consisted of four equal sections and each section contained the man's name, rank, serial number, and chalk number. The jumpmasters received the first part of the tag, the loadmasters part two, the battalion S1 part three, while the men retained part four. Last minute changes in chalk assignments were made quickly and easily by removing the individual's part from one chalk and transferring it to his newly assigned chalk; no erasures or additions were required.

The entire task force spent the night in the marshalling area; and on the morning of February 22d, at 0530 hours, they were transported directly to the waiting aircraft. Once again, each man was fitted with his parachute and combat load; once again, each man was checked thoroughly by the jumpmasters.

Prior to station time, all jumpmasters were given their final briefing. At this time, they were issued aerial photographs of the drop zone with coordinates and the latest weather data, the first time that the exact location of the drop zone had been announced.

All was ready. Each man was trained and equipped, ready both mentally and physically. All equipment had been prepared and rigged. At 0825 hours, the aircraft began their takeoff.

At 0900, the green light flashed on in the lead plane and the sky above Drop Zone Charlie began to fill with parachutes. By 0910, the last of the 778 Sky Soldiers in the task force was on the drop zone. During this 10 minutes, as each man hit the ground, he grabbed his weapon and combat gear, and moved to his designated assembly area. Colored smoke, colored helium balloons, and colored tape on each man's helmet assisted the task force in rapidly assembling on the ground and identified each man with his unit and sector. It was imperative that all units react rapidly in clearing and securing the drop zone, for the airdrop of supplies and heavy equipment was scheduled to commence 30 minutes after the first man exited the aircraft.

Right on time and target, the loaded C130s began their heavy drops. Drag chutes pulled jeeps, trucks, mortars, and howitzers

from the tail of each plane, and giant canopies lowered this vital equipment to the ground without mishap. Immediately thereafter, more planes appeared over the treetops at low altitude, leaving in their wakes brilliant clusters of colored parachutes over the drop zone. For the first time in combat, the cargo was being dropped by the container delivery system, which uses colored parachutes to denote the contents of the container swaying beneath it. It was a perfect drop. Everything landed in a drop zone the size of a baseball field without mishap.

Before and during the equipment drop, the rifle companies of the task force moved to their assigned sectors along the perimeter of the drop zone to prevent the enemy from placing observed fires on the area. The fire support base and brigade tactical command post were rapidly secured. Little resistance was encountered, and this was primarily sniper fire. Mortar and artillery crews raced to their weapons and readied them for firing.

By 1000, the first part of the task force's mission had been completed — all men and equipment of the battalion were on the ground and deployed, the brigade command post was set up, and the fire support base was established. But the job had just begun. Now the task force began to patrol the area, conducting search and destroy operations, soon to be joined by the other battalions of the 173d Airborne Brigade. Together, they would block the Viet Cong from reaching the refuge on the other side of the Cambodian border as Operation Junction City swept through War Zone C.

The success of this parachute assault shows that the airborne concept still has a place in modern warfare. It shows that large numbers of troops and heavy equipment can be delivered quickly and accurately with a minimum number of aircraft.

The spirit and professional enthusiasm demonstrated by the men of the task force during the training for and conduct of the jump into War Zone C made this combat parachute assault a success.

Doi Ma Creek

Major Frank J. Phelan

The 3d Brigade, 9th Infantry Division moved into Long An Province during February and March 1967. Long An is bounded on the north by Saigon, on the west by the Plain of Reeds, on the east by the Saigon River, and on the south by Dinh Tuong and Go Cong Provinces. The most populated province in the Republic of Vietnam, it is the commerce center of the rice-rich Mekong River belt, the portal to Saigon from the south and the location of a series of enemy communication lines to the lower Delta and the capitol, Saigon.

The 3d Brigade was assigned the mission of conducting a consolidation operation throughout Long An Province with emphasis on Rach Kien, Tan Tru, Binh Phuoc Districts, the area around Tan An, the province capital, and to open Highway 4, the main route of commerce between Saigon and the Delta. Code named "Enterprise," the operation was aimed at defeating organized enemy forces, eliminating enemy infrastructure and conducting pacification operations. The enemy traditionally had a strong hold on Long An and moved his guerrilla bands, local and regional force companies, and main force battalions through the area with impunity.

The 3d Battalion, 39th Infantry had been conducting operations in Rach Kien District for a short time prior to the 3d Brigade move and had established a fire support/patrol base (FS/PB) in the village of Rach Kien. In early March, the 2d Battalion, 60th Infantry was moved to Ben Luc, on Highway 4, to temporarily operate in that area until its scheduled move to Tan Tru District, some 14 kilometers to the south, at a later date. During the second week in March, the brigade headquarters moved to the outskirts of Tan An to establish their base near the province capital and the airstrip. On March 15, 1967, the 5th Battalion (Mechanized), 60th Infantry displaced from the 9th Infantry Division forward operational base at Dong Tam to the district of Binh Phuoc which, although the battalion operated throughout the northern Delta, became their primary area of operations.

The 5th Battalion (Mech) was organized as follows:

Headquarters and Headquarters Company
    Reconnaissance Platoon (Mech)
    Heavy (4.2-inch) Mortar Platoon (Mech)
    Antitank (106mm RR) Platoon
    Ground Surveillance Platoon
    Communication Platoon (Mech)
    Medical Platoon (Mech)
A Company, 5/60 (Mech) Infantry
B Company, 5/60 (Mech) Infantry
C Company, 3/60 Infantry (attached)
B Battery, 2/4 Artillery (direct support)
3d Platoon, C/15 Engineers (direct support)

During the first weeks in Binh Phuoc, the 5th Battalion's operations resulted in many small contacts and two company-size battles. During this period the battalion placed special emphasis on night operations utilizing squad to platoon-size patrols. This brief period soon proved to have been sound training. By mid-April, the battalion's experiences had hardened the troops and tested the commanders, and the morale was high due to several successes the unit had experienced during this period.

On April 16, 1967, the 5th Battalion was conducting limited operations in the vicinity of Binh Phuoc. The attached Company C, 3d Battalion was operating southeast of Binh Phuoc village. At 1230 hours the brigade operations officer reported that the 3d

Battalion, 39th Infantry had made sharp contact with an estimated enemy battalion in their area of operation near Cau Long Son. He ordered the 5th Battalion to alert one company for airmobile redeployment to reinforce the 3d Battalion. After a quick review of his dispositions, 5th Battalion's CO determined that his Company C, currently committed to a non-critical sweep and reasonably consolidated for pick-up, would be alerted. In addition, since the move was by helicopter, it was more reasonable to commit a straight Infantry company.

A short time later, the brigade command group arrived at the 5th Battalion's CP (Binh Phuoc) with instructions to make the move as soon as the helicopters arrived. Company C, now ready on a PZ, was ordered to conduct an airmobile assault. Their mission was to sweep south through the woodline below the LZ in an effort to make contact with any enemy elements attempting to withdraw to the northwest, and then establish a blocking position in the vicinity of the junction Doi Ma Creek and route 227. The brigade command group coordinated a short artillery preparation of the landing zone and gunships escorted the troop carrying helicopters into the LZ.

After making an unopposed landing, Company C moved south as planned. Minutes later the lead elements made contact with an enemy squad attempting to escape the 3d Battalion's encirclement. Employing rapid fire and movement, the company eliminated the enemy without sustaining any casualties. The company then continued to move south without further contact and reached their blocking position shortly after 1700 hours.

Meanwhile, the 3d Battalion (minus) was still engaged in a violent battle against a frantic enemy who was using all means to break contact, but by 2200 hours the action subsided to only sporadic contacts. The battalion remained in position throughout the night in order to sweep the battle area at sunrise. The remainder of the night was characterized by frequent enemy probes against the friendly positions in what apparently was either an attempt to find a gap in the encirclement or a feint to cover enemy egress in another area.

At approximately 1700 hours the same day, the 5th Battalion was alerted to move to the village of Rach Kien, with one additional rifle company, for prepositioning and quicker reaction for influencing the battle in progress. Company A was left to secure the battalion's fire support base and the Reconnaissance Platoon was to conduct patrol operations around Binh Phuoc. Battery B, 2/4 Artillery (DS) was moved to Ben Luc, to reinforce the artillery fires already within range of the battle. The battalion (minus) departed their base and closed at Rach Kien at approximately 1900 hours. Upon arrival, Company B coiled in the village while the command group coordinated with the commander and staff of 3d Battalion. During this situation briefing, the CO, 5th Battalion was notified to remain in the village and not to proceed into the battle area until ordered. However, the 5th's CO thought that an immediate move into the area of contact would greatly assist the 3d Battalion in containing and destroying the enemy, as well as achieving better positioning for subsequent operations. The request for immediate employment was denied because of a known enemy minefield enroute to the battle area, the only area through which APCs could move to enter western Rach Kien District. The minefield, plus darkness, would make the move extremely hazardous. Weighing the risk involved against the benefits, 5th Battalion's commander made a second request to deploy into the battle area.

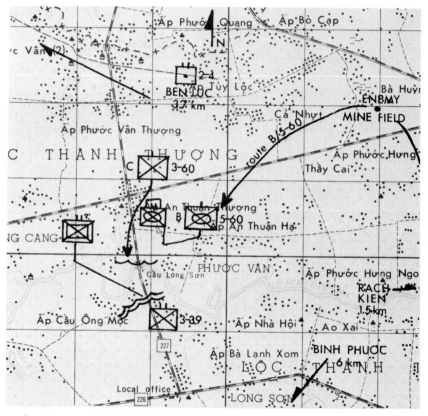

It was now 2100 hours. The 5th Battalion (minus) set out after carefully planning its route through the mined area. The force of one rifle company mounted in 18 M113s and the command group mounted in two M113s and one M577 set out in single file formation under strict light discipline. By 2200 hours the unit had moved through the minefield without incident. (It is interesting to note that at a later date this battalion sustained APC losses when moving through the same mined area during daylight).

While enroute, the battalion commander received instructions to link up with the 3d Battalion and resume control of Company C, 3d Battalion, 60th Infantry. Upon link up, the battalion's mission was to block to the south, patrol aggressively to preclude enemy egress to the north and prepare to conduct a sweep the following morning. After arrival and link-up, the battalion deployed as ordered and began planning for the next day's operation.

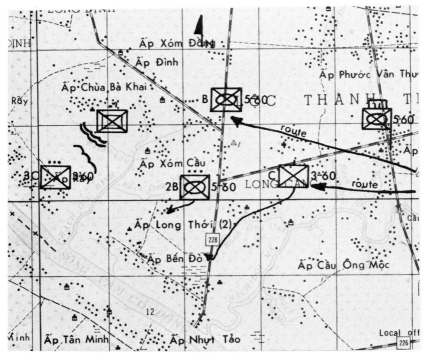

On the morning of April 17th, the battalion set out to sweep the area west of the previous day's contact. The plan called for Company B, with APCs, to conduct a sweep west-southwest through the woodline and streams near Ap Xom Cau. Simultaneously, Company C minus one platoon was to sweep southwest and turn their sweep northwest upon reaching the southeastern end of Ap Ben Do at route 228. The remaining platoon from Company C was to conduct an airmobile assault into an LZ just northeast of Ap Ray at the same time as Company B's arrival at its start point.

The platoon's mission was to conduct a search of the vegetated area north of the Rach Ong Binh and along the Rach Sau. H-hour was set for 0705 hours.

At 0700 hours the helicopters arrived to pick up the first platoon of Company C. They touched down in the LZ at H-hour without benefit of an artillery preparation. Moments later, as the platoon reorganized for their search, they came under heavy fire. The enemy, located along the Rach Sau, had obviously been surprised. The platoon leader, experienced and in complete control of his unit, employed fire and maneuver and attacked into the woodline. Gunships arrived within minutes to support the platoon. Moving directly into the Rach Sau, the platoon swept both banks and the stream bed itself. In the stream they engaged a frantic squad-size enemy force. The enemy was using reeds to breathe below the water's surface while attempting to disengage to the southeast. Within minutes enemy bodies bobbed to the surface of the now red water. The platoon continued southeast in a meticulous search of the woodline and the stream.

Meanwhile, Company B arrived at its start point at H-hour. The company commander's plan was to drop-off the 1st platoon at the start point and have them sweep west along the creek while the 2d platoon was to sweep south along the creek in that area. The 3d platoon and company headquarters was to move to Ap Chau Ba Khai, search that area and then sweep south. The APCs, with drivers and track commanders, were to be used to screen and block along the outer edges of the woodlines. Upon arriving at the start point the 1st platoon dismounted from their APCs and proceeded west into the woods. As they entered the woods, the platoon leader was shot and later died enroute to a hospital. The platoon, now under command of the platoon sergeant, attacked the enemy position and destroyed it. After a quick reorganization, the platoon continued west. For this unit, the remainder of the day was typified by brief engagements with small enemy elements. Each time they eliminated the resistance from what appeared to be a series of enemy pickets conducting a delay-type action. By mid-afternoon they had reached the stream junction and linked up with the 2d platoon.

The 2d platoon searched the woodline and stream throughout the day, with small sporadic contacts. As it was later discovered, their presence in this area forced the enemy into killing zones for the remainder of the company.

Upon reaching Ap Chua Ba Khai, and following notification of the 1st platoon's initial contact, the Company B commander turned the APCs of the 3d platoon and Company Headquarters south and headed into the gap between the platoon of Company C operating along the Rach Sau and his 2d platoon in the woodline to the east. As this force headed south, they observed a large

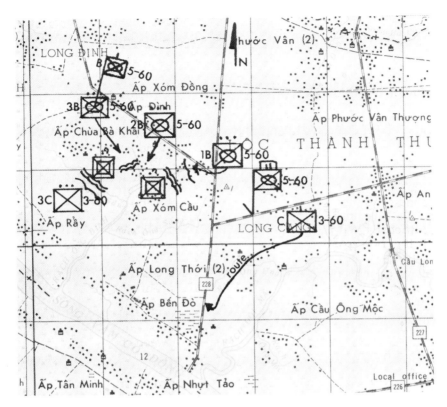

cluster of small haystacks. As they closed with them the hay-stacks began to move. Each stack was an enemy soldier trying to conceal his attempt to break out from the impending encircle-ment. In the words of the company commander, "It was a hay day." Employing the .50 caliber and M60 machineguns mounted on the APCs, the company (minus) conducted a mounted attack directly into the fleeing enemy. Across the open field and paddy dikes they pursued the enemy. After insuring the destruction of that enemy force and thoroughly searching the area of contact, the 3d platoon and company headquarters moved back to Ap Chau Ban Khai and swept that area with no results.

At H-hour of this same day, Charlie Company, minus one pla-toon, moved out in a sweep of its assigned area. Moving west, the company searched the area along the Rach Ong Ung and by 1000 hours reached route 228 without incident. But, based on the assessment that the battalion's current contact north of the Rach Ong Binh was an enemy unit of company-size, it was determined that C Company should continue its sweep into Ap Ben Do with one platoon moving southwest while the remainder of the com-

15

pany continued south along route 228. The company commander chose to place himself between and to the rear of his two platoons. Making a very deliberate and careful approach, the company began its sweep.

Concurrent with the evolution of events in the Bravo Company sector and following consultation with the 5th Battalion and 3/39 Infantry COs, which was no longer in contact, the brigade commander placed all available artillery and gunships in direct support of the 5th Battalion, requested an air alert of fighter-bomber sorties in close air support of the 5th and moved the 2d Battalion, minus one company, into a blocking position southwest of the Vam Co Dong River. The 2d Battalion was to be reinforced and assisted by Vietnamese river assault craft. This blocking force was in position by approximately 1130 hours and by 1400 the 3d Battalion had concluded its sweep along Doi Ma Creek and was extracted to its base at Rach Kien, leaving a small stay-behind force to survey the former battle area.

Around 1100 hours, Company C, now moving southwest towards Ap Ben Do, began receiving heavy fire from the woodline to its front. The enemy was deployed on line in bunkered positions along the northeastern edge of the woodline. During the initial volley of fire, Charlie Company sustained two casualties and moments later a company medic was killed attempting to reach the wounded. Due to the open terrain and excellent fields of fire afforded the enemy in Ap Ben Do, Charlie Company was unable to maneuver effectively, despite several desperate tries on the part of the company commander. A medical evacuation helicopter attempting to get to the wounded was shot down, adding two additional casualties. The battalion command group landed at Charlie Company to make an on-the-spot assessment. By this time Company C's artillery forward observer, demonstrating great courage, had moved forward and was directing the fire of two batteries of 105mm artillery on the enemy positions approximately 300 meters to his front. The artillery, firing a linear concentration to cover the target, was only marginally successful in neutralizing the enemy.

Gunships were then employed, again with limited success. Two airstrikes came on station and met with greater success in silencing the enemy. The battalion requested six more airstrikes to attack in succession and divided the linear target in half, directing the aircraft on the southern half while the battalion artillery liaison officer massed all available artillery on the northern half of the target. In this way the artillery was able to concentrate its fires in a smaller area and be more effective. With careful coordination between the artillery, the forward air controller and the fighter pilots, this system proved successful and fire superiority was achieved. At this time a second dustoff was called in and the wounded were evacuated.

Assessing the enemy's firepower and frontage to be that of a dug-in battalion, the 5th Battalion's CO decided to rely on artillery and air support to gain the upper hand and then maneuver against the enemy position. Since the remainder of his battalion was committed to operations in Binh Phuoc, he requested an additional rifle company to assault the woodline. The request was approved and Company B, 3d Battalion went under the operational control of the 5th Battalion. Realizing the unprotected posture of Company C, the battalion commander ordered B/5 to release four APCs from the 1st platoon. These APCs moved immediately to Company C's position and, upon arrival, came under the control of Charlie Company.

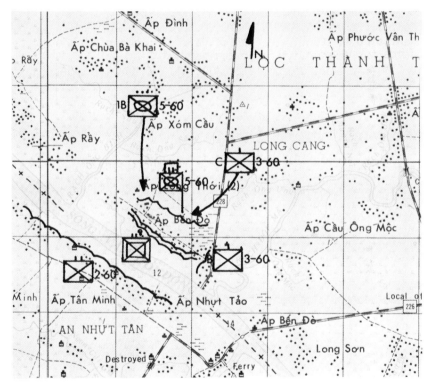

The APCs arrived at approximately 1200 hours and elements of Company C, under the control of a platoon leader, mounted the vehicles. Still under fire, this ad hoc mechanized unit assaulted the northern end of the enemy position. With all machineguns firing they closed to within 100 meters of the enemy and destroyed several positions. By now, Charlie Company had managed to move its right flank closer to the contact while the left flank remained in its original position, placing small arms fire on the objective. Charlie Company was now running low on ammunition and a resupply was flown in by helicopter. One of the APCs was disengaged and used to distribute the ammunition along the company line and the few casualties sustained so far were evacuated to a safe PZ for pick-up by dustoff.

By 1400 hours Company B, 3d Battalion was airborne and enroute to join the battle. Upon landing they would attack northwest into the woodline. By doing this, the battalion would hit the enemy on a flank and from a different direction. Following a short, violent artillery LZ preparation, Bravo Company, 3d Battalion landed and pushed toward the objective with a two-platoon front. The company walked artillery about 100 meters forward of their point while Charlie Company ceased all small arms fire. Plagued by a maze of boobytraps and sustaining casualties, the assaulting company was making very slow progress.

Anxious to complete the sweep before dark and having neutralized the enemy, the battalion CO decided to give Company B, 3d Battalion a limit of advance and move Company C into the northern part of the objective. This attack was executed with

minor resistance and by 1700 hours the entire objective had been swept. In Ap Ben Do alone, 73 enemy KIA were found. This fact, coupled with the equal successes of Company B, 5th Battalion and the 1st platoon of Company C to the north of Rach Ong Binh, indicated that a large portion of an enemy battalion had been destroyed. The 5th Battalion, 60th Infantry suffered 11 casualties and consolidated for the night, leaving stay-behind forces in Ap Ben Do and Ap Chua Ba Kai. The night passed without incident. The enemy had been defeated.

A Riverine Incident

Lieutenant Colonel Richard E. Mack

In the early morning light, during a torrential downpour, the river looked anything but friendly as the South Vietnamese regiment established its command post across from the small mining village of Nong Son. And even though it had yet to fire a round from its position at point I, an artillery platoon had to be moved because of the rising water. The river had overflowed, water lay deep in the adjacent paddy lands, and the streams feeding the river flowed deep and swift. No roads capable of supporting any sort of vehicular movement existed beyond point I.

The South Vietnamese regimental commander had considered these problems earlier and had acquired two M3 assault boats with outboard engines, some stout hemp rope, and the idea of picking up sampans from either friendly or Viet Cong sources. With as few as four sampans, for example, he could move one of his battalions across the river in about five hours.

Because of the rain, it appeared that the planned heliborne movement of the 3d Battalion from point J to point E would have to be cancelled. This unit, after landing, was to conduct a search and destroy operation to compress an estimated VC battalion against the river and the 1st Battalion.

The 1st Battalion, moving from point I with one company east of the river and the remainder of the battalion on the west side, reported its progress to be slow and difficult. The battalion was going to have considerable trouble in negotiating the smaller streams and flooded areas that lay ahead of it while still retaining enough stamina to engage the VC in the jungles around Hill 404. Resupply, as well as the evacuation of the wounded, would be difficult at best, particularly if the bad weather continued and helicopters could not support the operation.

Fortunately, a short break in the weather permitted the 3d Battalion's heliborne operation to go off as planned. Contact was light initially and for the next two days, as elements of the battalion patrolled in three directions west of Hill 350. Then the battalion turned on Hill 350 itself. The 1st Battalion's actions, meanwhile, had varied from constant sniper and squad harassment to company-size activity as the battalion neared the Hill 350-Hill 404 complex.

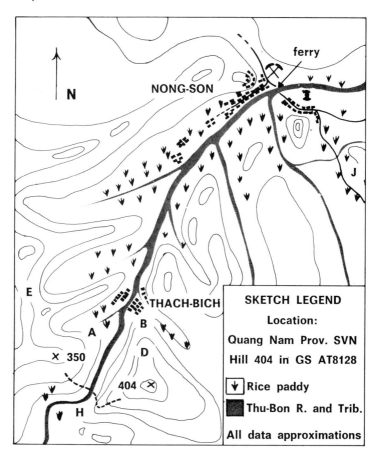

It rained and it rained, and the river rose and rose. By this time, though, the regiment had acquired a number of sampans (from various sources), two motorized coal barges (from the coal mine) capable of carrying about 50 tons, and a runabout with a questionable looking 40-horsepower outboard engine (also from the coal mine). And it was becoming more and more apparent to the South Vietnamese regimental commander that the success of his operation was dependent upon coupling his meager boat resources to the band of water that stretched out to his battalions.

The VC, of course, had almost perfect terrain over which to conduct a delaying action, and they appeared at first to be protecting Thach Bich, which had been a center of local VC activity. A segment of the Ho Chi Minh trail that branched off into southern Quang Nam province traversed this area, an indication that the VC might have established a supply point at Thach Bich and were concerned with getting out as many supplies as possible.

On the fourth day, the bulk of the 1st Battalion crossed to the east side of the river and joined its one company which had been operating there, an action that was prompted by increased contact with the Viet Cong. Six sampans were used to cross the battalion minus in two-and-a-half hours; three men were lost, drowned when one of the sampans was swamped by the strong current.

After the 1st Battalion had consolidated on the east bank, the battalion commander moved his companies into Thach Bich, uncovering a sizable quantity of ammunition, weapons and medicine. The VC had been protecting a supply base, but had pulled out before they could be hurt. The 1st Battalion then continued its movement, fully expecting to meet increased VC resistance as the companies drew closer to Hill 404.

Events lived up to expectations for, in a scurry of events, a VC mine was detonated, and an estimated VC company located at point D began hitting elements of the 1st Battalion at point B with mortar, automatic weapons and small arms fire.

Considerable Viet Cong activity was also noted near point H, with several sampans observed crossing the river at that point; suspicions were also aroused because of the scarcity of any population in the area.

Friendly artillery fire directed on point H caused some casualties, but an airstrike requested against points D and H could not be flown because of the bad weather conditions. A light aircraft managed to slip into the valley between the hills and the pilot reported many sampans under the ledges at point H and considerable movement on the trails leading from the river to the hills.

An attack by the 1st Battalion against Hill 404 was halted by intense, well-aimed fire from the dominating height; a company sent to ascend the west side of the hill came under fire not only from Hill 404 but also from Hill 350 across the river.

To maintain their pressure and mobility, the battalions needed to be resupplied, and to have their wounded and sick evacuated — both battalions reported having a number of men who were running high fevers. The battalions also needed a resupply of mortar ammunition so they could take the sampans at point H under fire; almost all of the mortar ammunition they had started with had been expended.

All of this, of course, called for transportation. And the make-shift river flotilla that had been collected over the past few days provided the answer. The assault boats, for example, made excellent squad patrol craft. They were low, had sufficient speed, and could carry a South Vietnamese squad; the boats could also be used as fast evacuation craft for three or four men.

The motorized coal barges were slower, but each could carry five days of supply for a battalion, plus 15 to 20 men and an improvised crew. Each barge was armed with two machineguns and a mortar, the latter mounted in the cargo hold on top of planks covered with rubber shock mats which had been taken from jeeps. In effect, then, the barges became a poor man's Monitor.

The runabout became the command boat. Speed was its major asset, and it could be used to evacuate the most seriously wounded.

On the fifth day of the operation, the flotilla went operational and proceeded toward Thach Bich with badly needed supplies; the lead barge carried supplies for the 1st Battalion, the other, for the 3d Battalion. After unloading at the village, the lead barge was sent forward to a position about 1,000 meters from point H. Using line of sight observation from the barge, the mortar crew began firing. Some VC fire returned from point A was soon neutralized by the barge's two machineguns and fire from individual weapons carried by the men on the barge.

The second barge did not unload on the west bank, for the South Vietnamese regimental commander had decided to concentrate his effort first against Hill 404 and to move two companies from the 3d Battalion to the east side to support the 1st Battalion's attack. After transporting the two companies across the river and partially resupplying them, the second barge moved to support the lead barge in pounding the VC at point H and along the trails leading from there up both hills.

As the day waned, the two barges were withdrawn to Thach Bich for security reasons. There, one was loaded with wounded and the more serious fever cases and departed for point I. On the jungle slopes leading to the top of Hill 404, the better part of the two South Vietnamese battalions deployed and then attacked. The remnants of a VC company, hastily preparing to withdraw, were caught and further decimated. On the trails leading from the hill to point H, and at point H, the effects of the mortar fire from the barges were easily discernible. Dead bodies and parts of sampans littered the area.

For several more days the operation continued; the weather showed little improvement. Most assuredly the operation would have been called off if the South Vietnamese had not found a new friend — the previously unfriendly river.

It really does not matter where a river is located —- what does matter is its mobility potential. I know one thing — I am now a believer!

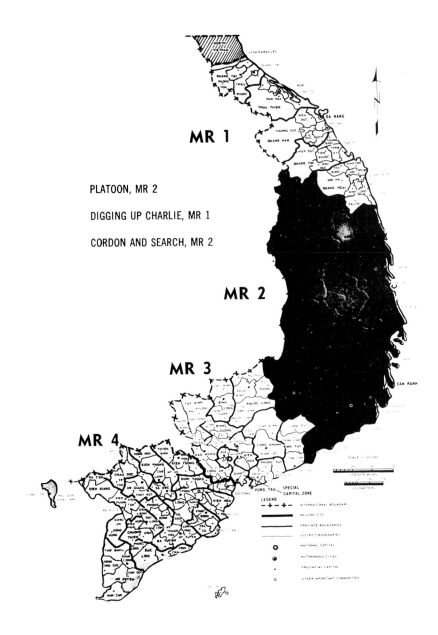

PLATOON, MR 2

DIGGING UP CHARLIE, MR 1

CORDON AND SEARCH, MR 2

Chapter 2

Searching for the Enemy

Platoon

Captain Robert F. Radcliffe

The first light of dawn streaked the eastern sky as members of a US rifle company from the 1st Cavalry Division (Airmobile) stirred in their night defensive position. Stand to was complete and the CO had dispatched local security patrols. All personnel were rolling up their gear, eating breakfast and preparing their equipment for the day's operations. The CO had requested a CH47 to lift out the company's rucksacks, allowing the men to move unburdened during the day. Platoon sergeants and squad leaders supervised the loading of the cargo slings for that extraction. The men soon fell to the mandatory task of cleaning weapons as the platoon leaders moved to the command post to receive the CO's order.

The CO began his operations order in a manner the same as many other days in this area of operations. His platoon leaders, professionals in terms of ability if not in length of service, listened intently. They realized that this order resulted from countless manhours of diligent work to provide the necessary information and intelligence.

Situation — the CO began his order using the established format to ensure that all information and planning would be presented in detail. The platoon leaders recorded all that was said.

Enemy situation — the CO presented the intelligence estimate of the enemy's capabilities. This knowledge in turn became a mandate governing the size of elements and manner in which they would conduct operations. "No intelligence of company-size or larger enemy units."

Friendly situation — the information so vital to the platoon, which must be reinforced in the event of heavy contact, was given. "Company A will be conducting reconnaissance-in-force 3,000 meters to the south." Mission and concept of operations — the time-honored format was followed.

When all questions had been answered and the essential coordination between elements completed, the platoon leaders returned to their platoons with the mission for the day. Squad leaders soon assembled and pads and pencils again appeared. The platoon leaders presented their operations orders and, in turn, squad leaders briefed their squads. The dissemination cycle was complete.

All preparations having been completed, the platoon was ready to move out. As a last measure the preoperation inspection for unsafe conditions and forgotten equipment was conducted. The RTOs made an initial communication check with the CP and sent the message, "Alert all OPs, Three Six is moving out."

From the company's position on a low ridge the third platoon slipped unseen into a small draw running south. There were easier ways to move south; the higher ground was more open, but enemy eyes probably would not observe the platoon on this more difficult route. The men grimly struggled through the dense undergrowth following the trace of a small stream. Each wondered if this would be one more day of fruitless and exhausting searching for the elusive enemy. The platoon moved under dense overhead cover for an hour. The distance covered was short, perhaps 900 meters. But there was good reason not to hurry. In this environment all the senses assume as much importance as sight. The platoon leader, noticing that the point squad was tiring, changed the order of march. The point squad leader, a veteran of many patrols, remarked while moving to the rear, "There's no sign, Lieutenant." However, the platoon leader already knew, because he was fourth in order of march where he could rely on his own senses.

The terrain opened up to the front and the platoon cautiously approached a small rice paddy area dominated by a low rocky hill. The lieutenant dispatched the point team to recon the area, after bringing the number one machinegun forward to provide covering fire if necessary. The point team soon signaled all clear and the platoon moved out of the thick undergrowth toward the low hills.

Securing the hill without incident, the platoon took a quiet, watchful break. The platoon leader used this time to pinpoint his location on the map, and a situation report was sent to the CO. Subconsciously, each man relaxed a little. They shared similar feelings as each in his own way thought, "If we didn't find them under cover by that stream, they're not here." The enemy was not there, but he was very nearby.

Twenty minutes later the platoon moved out, crossing a saddle to a second low, rocky hill. These low hills were relatively open and for the first time this day, sight was the most valuable sense. From the second hill the platoon moved east down a nose. After a hundred meters of open terrain the point signaled that they had reached a tangled, impenetrable dropoff. The platoon leader gave the order to reverse direction, moving back to the crest of the hill to begin the search for a new route.

Suddenly, there is movement. A man in grey is running away from the platoon, where no friendlies should be. "VC!" someone cries, and the men drop behind rocks and fire a dozen rounds. As he pulls the trigger of his M16, the platoon leader sorts the hundred thoughts which race through his mind. He fires because he sees the enemy, and few are the men who actually see the enemy in this kind of war. Having found the enemy, the platoon guides itself by a new framework of rules — rules governed by the fundamental concept to destroy the enemy by fire and maneuver at a minimum cost to friendly forces.

Success or failure from this point on depends upon the state of training of the platoon and upon how swiftly and how decisively it is led. This greatest responsibility of leadership falls on one man, the platoon leader. He allows himself a fraction of a minute to reflect. The first question is, "Do we pursue?" He hears again the operations order. Enemy situation — "No intelligence of company size or larger units." A squad leader volunteers the comment, "Sir, I think we can catch them." The lieutenant makes the decision to pursue. This decision is based on available intelligence, but the confidence of his men is equally important.

By now the enemy has disappeared to the south. Decisions and orders come naturally now. Experience in combat and training in places far from Vietnam make it so. The RTO makes the spot report to the CO and sends coordinates for artillery, should it be needed. By now the platoon, running hard, has covered the ground to the area where the enemy was sighted. But the enemy is gone and no blood is found. The pursuit continues as the platoon moves down a finger running south. Soon dense vegetation channelizes the platoon into a draw running southeast.

Is this so bad? "Wouldn't a fleeing enemy also take the path of least resistance?" Then, as if to reinforce the thoughts of the platoon leader, a pith helmet is found, obviously stripped from the running enemy by a low branch. The pursuit continues without contact and doubts once again assail the mind of the platoon leader, "Could we have missed them? Are they armed? Is this a trap?" But these doubts are put aside by the feeling of confidence in three factors: faith in intelligence, capabilities of supporting arms, and ability to reinforce. The platoon leader sends a message to the CO requesting that the balance of Company A move to cut off the enemy and prepare to reinforce if necessary. A few minutes later he sends new coordinates for the artillery to lay on. Constantly, the squad leaders check their men's preparedness for contact. A grenadier is instructed to load cannister. Machinegunners load 100-round belts and loaders stand by. Weapons are taken off safe.

The platoon grimly moves on as the undergrowth yields to a small valley and a stream flanked by rice paddies. Low trees on the stream banks conceal the water and the platoon leader passes the word to the 1st squad, "Check the stream." As the squad fans out on line moving toward the stream, there is a sudden burst of automatic fire and the report of an M79-fired cannister round. The grenadier dives to the rear, crying, "VC!" As he attempts to reload, a rifleman fires a long burst to cover him. Contact has

been regained and the platoon's reaction is swift and resolute. The machineguns open fire on the stream bed as the platoon leader moves to the 1st squad.

A grenade is thrown and explodes — the squad then enters the stream bed. As the squad moves downstream the machineguns shift their fire. All actions transpire with incredible swiftness as reactions, made sharp by long hours of training, take hold. Working downstream, firing as they move, the 1st squad finds a dead VC on the stream bank, a result of the covering fire. A French 9mm submachinegun (SMG) is captured. Five meters away a second VC is killed before he can fire his 7.62mm modified SMG. The initiative is ours. The enemy is down and will not fire again.

A few meters further, a third VC is found wounded and is captured. A Thompson SMG, map case, and pair of binoculars attest that this is the leader of the enemy group. The squad flushes the stream bank 50 meters further down with negative results. The platoon leader emerges from the stream bed and organizes 360 degree security. A report is sent to the CO, "Two

VC KIA, one VC WIA, three weapons captured." The CO replies, "Battalion wants the prisoner." The medic is already working on him as the platoon knows the value of intelligence. Another burst of M16 fire is heard and a fourth VC with a French 9mm SMG is killed as the second sweep of the battlefield pays a dividend.

Silence falls. Only the sound of the approaching medevac ship containing the S2 and an interpreter breaks the stillness. Pride and exhilaration are shared by all members of the platoon. Today they have defeated the enemy in close combat. In the minds of the platoon's leaders there is a brief moment of pride in the knowledge ·that their decisions and actions were correct. But brief it is, for they know that the war continues and it is their responsibility to ensure their men are ready.

In subsequent debriefings, the men of the platoon who fought in this action attributed their success to several points which serve as the salient lessons learned. The most significant occurrence to the men of the platoon was their undetected approach to the area of contact. This was made possible by using a more difficult but concealed route and by rigidly enforced noise discipline. This made possible the contact with the enemy, whose early warning measures failed.

A second point cited was the ability to conduct a hard pursuit after the initial contact. This was possible because the platoon was traveling without its rucksacks which had been extracted earlier in the day. Also, because of a complete preparation phase, the members of the platoon had an excellent understanding of the mission. They had confidence in supporting arms and the ability to be reinforced should they need it. In short, all men were well informed regarding the conduct of the operation. Consequently, the platoon assumed an aggressive attitude upon contact.

A third factor was that the platoon leader and his subordinate leaders enforced a rigid SOP regarding the maintenance and cleaning of equipment. Inspections were conducted prior to all operations to prevent the possibility of accidents and forgotten equipment. Squad leaders supervised their men constantly during movement. As a result, there were no malfunctions or equipment deficiencies of any kind during the firefight.

The fourth consideration was the spirited and aggressive manner in which the platoon closed with the enemy. This was a direct result of high morale and confidence of the platoon, in one another and in their leaders.

Lastly, the members of this platoon had no doubts as to why they were in Vietnam. Armed with this understanding and the knowledge that they were members of the most powerful and best-prepared army in the world, they were psychologically ready to meet the enemy. It was this preparation that ultimately led to their victory.

Digging Up Charlie

Major Ben G. Crosby

Have your sitreps been interspersed with too many "negative results" lately? Has your unit made contact, only to have the VC disappear before your eyes? Do you conduct sweeps without success? Perhaps you need to do some hole hunting.

The history of our hole hunting really began back in May 1967 when the 2d Battalion, 35th US Infantry, as part of the 3d Brigade Task Force, 25th US Infantry Division, operating in the Duc Pho area of the coastal plain, soundly defeated the 60th VC Battalion in open combat. The battle ended the organized resistance of enemy units and since then only isolated small contacts have developed.

Soon after the battle and somewhere in the enemy's higher level, someone made the decision to concentrate their efforts on anti-sweep operations — inflicting a few casualties at relatively long range and disappearing without making close contact. This tactic was implemented by the enemy about the middle of June and was used quite successfully against us for several weeks. We countered this enemy move with ambushes in which one rifle company would divide into 10 ambushes that operated without resupply or any assistance for three days. This was only partially successful, although we killed some enemy and captured some weapons. During the three-day ambush program, though, it became apparent that the enemy was not moving as we swept through these areas. Obviously, we were walking right over him.

Our break came on July 10, 1967 when Captain Larry Hicks, the Company A commander, captured an NVA soldier in one of our most troublesome spots; the enemy soldier had been slightly wounded by an M79 fragment. Unfortunately for his comrades, he led us to our first hole. When he pointed the tunnel out to me, I couldn't believe my eyes. I could see only a small pile of leaves next to a bamboo clump. I thought surely this Charlie was only stalling for time. But then I studied the pile, and slowly I began to see the slight outlines of a small square about 18 inches on a side and to notice a small depression around the edges of this square looking as windblown as Nature herself could make it.

Larry looked at it and exclaimed, "I'll be damned." There it was. Now, plain as day, we could see the outline of the square in the pile of leaves. One of Larry's soldiers raked back the leaves, exposing a wooden door of the same dimensions, and our first "hole reduction team" went to work with its M16s. We killed two from that hole and soon found another that also contained two enemy. Before the day was out, Company A had killed eight, detained one, and had five weapons to its credit, all within an area measuring 250 by 250 meters.

Field Day

The next day was equally successful in an area adjacent to that of the previous day's contact. Lieutenant Colonel Tiller, the battalion commander, took the other company commanders and platoon leaders over to the area where Larry Hicks was having a field day. They carefully studied the holes and the area, admiring Company A's precise technique and results. ·Then the battalion went to work. The race was on. Ever since, the battalion has been digging out Charlies at a fantastic rate, although we soon found out that a need existed for a detailed study of the different types of holes and the techniques required to reduce them.

We found that there were three main types of holes, and that these could be classified more by their location than by their construction. By far the most common was the under bamboo hole, easily and quickly camouflaged and characteristic of all the holes found in the Duc Pho-Mo Duc area of Vietnam. The entrances to the hole differed widely, as did the techniques of camouflage. Most of the entrances were located within the edge

of a bamboo clump or just outside the edge, and the hole cover or trap door contained the camouflage material. Some had pieces of cut bamboo affixed to the door itself. The edges of the door itself fit snugly into the entrance. Many other entrances were covered only by the door, which was camouflaged by spreading leaves, rocks, and other materials over the top. Another characteristic common to all these small tunnels was the air hole, usually made from a hollow piece of bamboo three to four inches in diameter and inserted into the tunnel and camouflaged on the surface.

Air Hole

The air hole was the only telltale indicator of the second type hole, the beach hole. This hole differed from the bamboo hole in that it was in the sand and was normally constructed from cut timbers; it did not depend on the bamboo roots to add rigidity to the roof. Naturally, the entrance to a beach hole was impossible to locate, for it was often buried under a foot of loose

sand, but it could be detected by finding the breathing tubes. Some air holes were a continuation of the bamboo frames that made up the local fisherman's lean-to, while other air holes could be exposed by pulling up the cacti plants that grew along the sand dunes on the beach. The enemy was clever in hiding these breathing tubes and we had to be just as clever in locating them.

The third type of tunnel, the least common, was the water entrance type. This tunnel might be located near a small stream or beside an old bomb crater that was filled with water. These holes usually had no lid and depended on the natural growth along the stream bank to hide the entrance. Sometimes the entrance was completely submerged, but not always.

No matter the type of hole, the slogan "Find 'em-fix 'em-fight 'em-finish 'em" is as true as the day it was first promulgated. Unfortunately, many units fail to put the sequence in proper order. During several of our operations we fixed and fought, only to learn that we had nothing to finish. The unmatched success of our battalion lay in finding the enemy through the deliberate search technique before we attempted to fix or fight.

The one true indicator of success is the actual number of enemy killed or captured and the number of weapons seized. During the period July 10th to August 10th, our battalion killed 386 enemy, detained 77 VC suspects, and seized 158 weapons, while suffering only 12 US soldiers killed in action. The high kill-ratio and large number of weapons captured had been a result of locating the enemy within his hiding place. Once the enemy was located, the job was relatively simply, for the enemy had fixed himself by choosing a small tunnel in which to hide. The enemy, dependent only on his expertise at passive camouflage, had no choice but to be killed or captured — the defense of a small hole against an American rifle squad was a difficult if not impossible task.

The key to a successful search was the application of common sense to the situation in Vietnam. We assigned a rifle company a small search area, never larger than a 1,000 meter grid square, based on intelligence reports or past actions. The company then painstakingly searched every square meter of the assigned area. There was no time limit to complete the task, but we were able to capitalize on the natural curiosity of the American soldier in developing our techniques of deliberate search.

Locate

The first and foremost technique was the art of locating the hole. Visual indicators often disclosed the general area of the hole but not its precise location. Worn places on the bamboo that the enemy had used as hand-holds were good visual indicators. Another was a small trail, much like a game trail, through the brush into a bamboo clump. Easily seen, although not a sure sign, was cut bamboo. Frequently the enemy would dig holes under partially harvested bamboo clumps.

A good visual indicator, too, but difficult to detect, was a slight depression in or around the bamboo clump. This depression often marked the location of a trap door, and the depression itself usually collected leaves and trash that aided in the camouflage of the hole entrance. The surest of all visual indicators was the ever present air hole. Once located, these bamboo breathing tubes always revealed the tunnel below.

Indicators

Once the individual soldier achieves success in locating the enemy he will almost be able to smell them. There is a certain sixth sense about locating the enemy, although more often than not it is knowing where to look and what to look for. The specific indicators are what to look for: in the corners of hedgerows, in the corners of villages, and in the corners of trails or trenches. The enemy often hides in these corners, for he can see from them while not being seen. Additionally, hiding in a corner allows the party who puts the finishing touches on the camouflage to escape undetected. While the enemy is aware of the danger in establishing a pattern, he still must have a location that provides him with observation as well as concealment. So look for an OP that allows him to move undetected into or out of an area.

The technique of deliberate search that we successfully employed centered around the rifle squad. The squad was divided into a security team and a search team, with the curious going to the search team and the less curious to the security team. Needless to say, these positions had to be rotated after a period of time because the thorns in the bamboo clumps wreaked havoc on hands, arms and uniforms. Each platoon assigned the squad a search area and it in turn started a systematic search along the hedgerows and bamboo clumps. Meanwhile, the security element moved toward the limits of each search area. Once a hole was discovered, the security element surrounded the area while the searchers cleared away enough brush to allow the comparatively large American soldier to operate within the confined space. Then hole reduction began.

Simple Process

Reduction of the hole was a simple four-step process, beginning with a soldier firing one or two magazines from his M16 into the trap door. This had a tendency to discourage enemy grenadiers from getting too close to the door. After getting the enemy's attention with a magazine or two, various US and Vietnamese expressions would be shouted into the hole exhorting the enemy

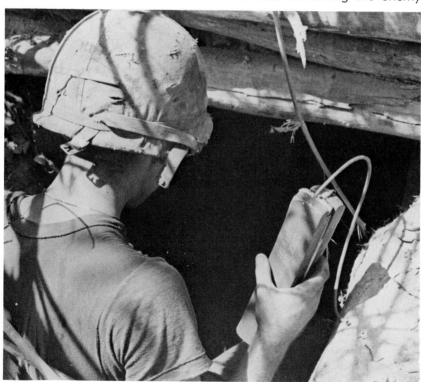

to come out or be killed. Sometimes he would give up without a fight, thereby saving his life and also freeing us from the task of excavating the tunnel for weapons and documents. When all else failed and the "hard core Charlie" remained within his

self-created tomb, a few strategically placed grenades usually reduced both the tunnel and Charlie to rubble.

Frequently, the M16 fire would open a hole large enough to allow the insertion of a grenade. If not, a grenade could be placed on top of the trap door or the door removed from a distance with a rope. This reduced the effects of any attached boobytrap. Sometimes an air hole would be enlarged and a grenade pushed through it, an action particularly effective against a stubborn enemy who hid behind a grenade baffle.

The last step was the sending in of a tunnel rat to insure that all weapons and documents had been recovered. The holes had to be thoroughly searched, for the enemy had small compartments built into his holes to hide weapons and ammo. Obviously, it was far better to capture the enemy, because he could frequently lead us to another hole containing items of interest. In any event, capture will save you the time wasted digging out the hole for weapons and documents.

Caution

After the hole had been searched, we destroyed it with explosives — if it had not already been destroyed in the four-step process. A caution to remember is that the enemy's defense is to toss out a grenade when everyone is standing around the hole and attempt to escape from another exit to the tunnel. Many of these holes have two entrances, so naturally the best defense against the grenade tosser is the dispersion of your forces and alert security men who fire into the hole before the grenade or Charlie comes out.

The success of any hole hunting operation depends entirely on the skill of the searchers. Accordingly, your best men should be used first. As soon as your unit finds success in hole hunting, everyone will desire to be a searcher. But success usually is short lived, and frequently the unit's enthusiasm dwindles to a low ebb. The operation will only be successful if the officers and non-commissioned officers lead the way in the search for holes and maintain in the searchers an enthusiastic approach to the mission.

The results of a successful search operation can be amazing. During our search of an area just north of Duc Pho, we uncovered two enemy company commanders, the S3, the executive officer, and a first sergeant from the 97th VC Battalion. Further to the north, we killed the XO of the 1st Company; the CO of 3d Company; and the battalion commander of the 38th VC Battalion. In still a different area, the village chief, the district finance chief and several other members of the infrastructure were literally unearthed from their hiding places. Of more than 350 enemy we killed in one month, a substantial number had been either members of the infrastructure or cadre of the VC units. These losses hurt the enemy doubly: many of the weapons seized were crew-served, including machineguns, recoilless rifles and rocket launchers.

Deliberate search techniques are easily taught and quickly learned. The emphasis, of course, is placed on where to look for the enemy: a location that provides him with observation, cover and concealment and a route of escape. Then the soldier learns what to look for: the indicators — a game trail, worn and cut bamboo, an air hole, human feces, a depression, fresh food, a lone individual. All trigger a mental alert in the curious American soldier and tell him that the enemy is not far away.

The four-step reduction process provides a simple means of effectively combating the enemy with minimum friendly casualties. This type of "on the scene" training was presented to selected members of the 196th Light Infantry Brigade, a part of Task Force Oregon, by the 2d Battalion, 35th Infantry. In a matter of only two weeks, the 196th had located over 300 of these holes. The success of their operation resulted from good leadership and a knowledge of proper hole hunting techniques.

Cordon and Search

Captain Phillip L. Blake

A certain Chinese gentleman of some renown once wrote a statement, now often quoted, to the effect that in an insurgency the people are like the sea, and the insurgents must be like the fish that swim in the sea. Having learned from experience that our opponents in Vietnam tend to follow the teaching of that erudite Chinese, we have made many attempts to keep fish away from the sea. But might it not be more profitable, at least occasionally, to jump into the sea and pluck out the fish?

The place is a small hamlet in the Bong Son plain of Binh Dinh Province in the central highlands of the Republic of Vietnam. The time is about 0330 hours in early June 1967; it's still a couple of hours until dawn. This hamlet is the home town of a platoon of Viet Cong irregulars and they come here whenever possible to rest, resupply and visit their families. After dusk last night they slipped into the hamlet to spend a night at home. They felt so safe from enemy attack that they didn't bother to put out local security. To avoid detection by US scout helicopters making first-light recons, they will leave before dawn and return to their base camp in the hills.

Shortly before 0400 hours a light sleeper among the VC detects movement outside the hamlet and goes out to investigate. Suddenly, a rifle shot and a scream of pain are heard. Now the entire hamlet erupts with frenzied activity. The women, children, and old men run into their protective shelters. Some of the VC try to exfiltrate the hamlet, but are either shot or driven back by fire from their enemy outside the hamlet. Now the VC realize that they are surrounded, and they also know that they are surrounded by US troops, since the firing came from M16s, M60s and M79s. Not only are they trapped, but the hamlet is now being illuminated by artillery illumination rounds. Their only hope is to conceal themselves in their carefully prepared hiding places. The Americans are usually impatient, inexperienced in searching, and can't speak Vietnamese, so they won't interrogate the women and old men to find out where the VC are hidden.

Shortly before dawn the VC, scattered throughout the hamlet in their hiding places, detect the movement of troops into the hamlet. Those VC who are in a position to do so can also see that there are still troops all around the hamlet but that the troops who have entered are systematically and thoroughly searching every nook and cranny and skillfully questioning the civilians,

doing so in Vietnamese. In reality, these men are members of the RVN National Police Field Force, paramilitary policemen especially trained to search, interrogate and fight if necessary.

Cordon and Search

Soon the policemen are pulling VC out of camouflaged tunnels and caves, and on occasion, when they find a group of well-armed and well-fortified VC, call on the US troops for assistance. By the end of the day the VC platoon can be dropped from the S2's files — its members are either dead or captured. As for allied losses, there are four US soldiers and one RVN policeman slightly wounded, from a total troop involvement of two US rifle companies and one NPFF platoon of about 60 men.

This was but one of a number of typical and successful cordon and search operations conducted by the 1st Battalion, 12th US Cavalry during the spring and summer of 1967.

The basic ingredients of the cordon and search operation are the same as for any offensive action: thorough planning, close coordination and aggressive execution. The cordon and search is much like a raid, but it also employs many of the principles of the night attack. Planning begins several days in advance of D-day, when the hamlet to be hit is selected because of an agent report, intensive VC activity in the area or simply because no allied troops have been in the area for some time. The battalion commander, S2, S3, and fire support coordinator make an initial reconnaissance in the CO's C&C helicopter. At the same time, the S2 gets aerial photographs of the objective hamlet for distribution to the company commanders. When a basic plan has been formulated, the company commanders are assembled for a warning order.

Planning

Any number of rifle companies might be used, of course, but usually the number to be employed will depend on the size of the hamlet and the anticipated enemy strength.

The warning order should actually include most of the elements of an operations order so that the company commanders can make useful reconnaissances on their own and can begin making their plans. The company commanders may make their reconnaissances in the C&C ship, but a more secure way is to go two at a time in a pair of scout ships at dawn and dusk, as though making routine first-light and last-light flights. During these flights the company commanders decide and agree on the exact points on the ground where their flanks will make contact with each other — the company coordination points. This is an extremely important part of the preparation phase, because it insures that there will be no gaps in the cordon and that each company will know specifically where each company on its flanks is located. For this reason, easily recognizable terrain features should be selected for coordination points.

Normal fire support coordination is arranged, to include planning for the use of illumination. Flare ship illumination is best, because there's no danger to the troops from falling cannisters. But flare ships cannot normally be used until actual contact has been made with the enemy, so if it is planned to have the cordon in place by 0400, for example, then that is the time planned for the initiation of illumination. If the VC are alerted and try to escape before the cordon is completed, however, the illumination is begun at that time.

Other supporting elements that are usually requested are armed helicopters and scout ships to assist in securing the perimeter of the hamlet, and, of course, the NPFF. If it is anticipated that extensive tunnels or boobytraps will be encountered, engineer or EOD support should also be requested. Usually the riflemen, equipped with some demolitions, will be able to handle either of these tasks, but there's nothing like an engineer bulldozer for destroying large bunkers.

After dark on the evening of D-1, the companies move into their assigned positions no closer than 2,000 meters to the objective on their respective sides of the hamlet.

If the route from the night position to the cordon line is a difficult one, it should be checked by a small patrol a day or two in advance; but the patrol must not move within sight of the hamlet. This reconnaissance will also help the company commander determine how much time to allow for the move. Timing is important, because if a unit arrives too early it runs a greater risk of being discovered before the other units are in position; if one arrives late there will be a large gap in the cordon until it is in position. Ideally, all units should arrive just a short while before H-hour. We found that it usually took about an hour to an hour and a half after arriving at the hamlet to move a company into position and to link up with the flank companies. Therefore, we normally began movement at about H-3 hours.

Preparation

Moving into the cordon position is much like movement into position for a night attack, but without guides. This is where aerial photographs prove their value. A thorough advance study of the photographs by the company chain of command will prevent a lot of fumbling around in the dark on D-day. A rifle company, if it uses its weapons platoon as a fourth rifle platoon, can be expected to cover a sector of the cordon line about 1,000 meters long. The troops are placed in pairs, about 20 to 25 meters apart, and should take advantage of whatever natural cover and concealment is available; rice paddy dikes are excellent for this purpose.

Pyrotechnic devices should be carried by all platoons to mark the cordon line for flare ships and armed helicopters, and VS17 panels can be used after dawn.

Skillful Execution

We found that the VC, or sometimes the NVA soldiers, would start trying to exfiltrate about 20 minutes after H-hour, and would often keep trying until about BMNT. If contact is light and sporadic, the NPFF platoon can move in, after arriving by Chinook at dawn, to begin searching and interrogating. But if the enemy is in strength and stubborn, a real fight may develop and there will be no immediate need for the NPFF.

After the enemy in the hamlet has been neutralized, another search should be conducted to insure that all weapons, equipment and documents have been found. Then all bunkers, tunnels and other hiding and fighting positions should be destroyed. It may be necessary to leave a company or two at the hamlet for

several days to accomplish these tasks, and the men should be reminded to be especially watchful for boobytraps while looking for tunnels and caches.

Every type of operation must have some disadvantages. As with any night operation which involves several companies, a cordon is difficult to coordinate so that all units arrive at the right place at the right time. Moving an entire company at night is tricky and involves a rather high degree of risk. Also, a unit in a cordon position at night is vulnerable to attack from the rear. Finally, this operation tends to be rather exhausting, and therefore I'd advise not more than two cordons per week per company. Actually, none of these drawbacks are serious, and the harmful effects of them can be reduced by thorough planning and skillful execution.

A variation of this tactic that can be used is to move to the objective by helicopter. Using this technique, the companies are air assaulted close to the hamlet on their respective sides and rush into position as quickly as possible. American units can accomplish both the cordon and the search, but it is usually preferable to use the NPFF for the search. Whatever variation is used, if it fits the situation and if sound fundamentals are used, the cordon and search operation can be a resounding success. Charlie will literally be caught with his pants down. '

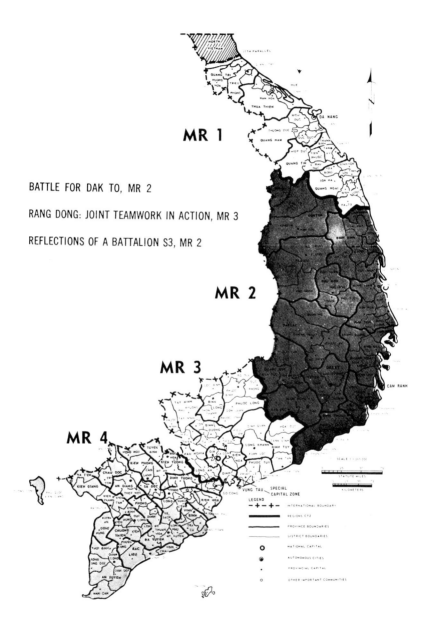

BATTLE FOR DAK TO, MR 2

RANG DONG: JOINT TEAMWORK IN ACTION, MR 3

REFLECTIONS OF A BATTALION S3, MR 2

Chapter 3

Getting It Together

Battle for Dak To

Major George P. Long, III

On November 19, 1967, the 1st Battalion, 12th Infantry was operating just north of the Me Wal Plantation, approximately 15 kilometers north of Ban Me Thuot. Late in the evening the battalion commander received word that the battalion was to move from their present location to Dak To, to assist in the fighting that was going on in that area. The next morning, the battalion began breaking down its fire support base in preparation for the move by CH47 and UH1H aircraft to the East Ban Me Thuot airfield. The equipment was then palletized for C130 movement to Dak To. The first lift, with Companies A and D on board, got off around 1300 and arrived around 2030 hours on the 19th. It was after dark when we landed at Dak To and, of necessity, the runway was lighted by fire barrels filled with five gallons of diesel oil and gasoline. I was met on the ground by Lieutenant Colonel Birch, the battalion commander, who informed me that Companies A and D had already been lifted by helicopter to the 173d Brigade FSB and were opcon to them. The 173d Brigade FSB was approximately 15 kilometers to the west of Dak To. I was told to take command of the task force and prepare to conduct a supporting attack on Hill 875 in the near future.

On the 21st I made three separate aerial reconnaissances and was able to get quite close to Hill 875 and see the 503d Airborne locations, our landing zone and the surrounding countryside. During a coordination conference with the battalion commander of the 4th Battalion, 503d Airborne, I was informed that we would combat assault into an LZ on the south side of Hill 875. Artillery fire support and airstrikes would be placed on Hill 875 and controlled by the 2d Battalion, 503d Airborne, which was in position on the north slope of Hill 875. The 4th Battalion was preparing to relieve them since they had taken rather heavy casualties. Our task force, the 1st Battalion, 12th Infantry, was to conduct a supporting attack on the south slope of Hill 875. We were given a limit of advance about 300 meters due south from the crest of the hill. Mobile Strike Force (MSF) 26 was already on the ground and was to prepare and secure an LZ for our combat assault. Immediately following the combat assault, MSF 26 would opcon to TF 1/12.

That evening extra ammunition was issued to Alfa and Delta Companies along with 25 LAWs for use against the bunkers we had been told were located on Hill 875. During the early morning hours of November 22d, my command group moved by helicopter from Dak To to join A and D Companies, which were still located at the 173d Brigade FSB. Final fire coordination was made with the 173d and TF 1/12. I had decided to let Delta Company lead the assault, followed by the TF headquarters group and Company A. Just prior to the lift off we were ordered to make maximum use of tac air and artillery once we had located the enemy positions. The purpose of this "locate and back off" tactic was to reduce casualties, since taking the hill itself was of little significance.

At 1100 hours the first lift of Delta Company departed. Almost immediately, the flight began to receive small arms and automatic weapons fire from the ridges to the east and south along the route to the LZ. Several ships were hit, but only one was disabled and it managed to return safely to the 173d Brigade FSB. By the time Delta Company and task force headquarters got to the LZ and established contact with MSF 26, fire from the ridges had become so intense that the lift could not be completed until gunships and artillery silenced some of the enemy fire, which took about an hour. As Alfa company began to complete their move, another ship was hit, but made it to the LZ. The aircraft had lost its tailrotor and couldn't leave the LZ, which reduced it to a tight, two-ship LZ. During the completion of Alfa Company's lift, Delta Company moved to a small knob about 300 meters in the direction of Hill 875. The task force now moved up the south slope with

Company D deployed and in the lead, followed by the TF head-quarters group and Alfa Company. The MSF was to secure the LZ until the downed helicopter could be evacuated.

The terrain on the south slope of the hill was double canopy jungle with a heavy undergrowth, and visibility was limited to 75 to 100 meters. A trail ran directly up the crest of the slope to Hill 875 and apparently had been used by the enemy for resupply. The temperature was around 85 degrees and quite humid.

As we were moving, Delta Company discovered 30 unoccupied bunkers with overhead cover. The smell of decaying flesh was everywhere, but we didn't stop to explore further or dig up any of the bunkers. Suddenly, there was an explosion, either an enemy mortar round or a boobytrap, and five personnel had to be evacu-ated. The wounded men were moved to the rear of our column where they received first aid while we began enlarging an opening in the jungle for the medevac helicopter.

The Mobile Strike Force notified us that the downed ship had been evacuated and they were moving to catch up with the TF, when 82mm mortar rounds began impacting in their vicinity. There were no casualties. Delta Company continued to move up the hill, but with limit of advance in order to avoid being completely separated from the rest of the TF, which was preparing an LZ for the medevac. Delta Company reported they had reached their limit of advance and were receiving shrapnel from the 1,000 and 750-pound bombs being dropped by the Air Force on the crest of the hill. At this point the entire TF was halted, its location reported and a perimeter defense established for the night.

That evening we were briefed on the next day's operations. Air and artillery strikes would begin again at first light and would be followed by a coordinated ground assault, beginning at 1100 hours. The plan called for TF 1/12 to assault from the south in a supporting role while elements of the 503d assaulted the crest of the hill from the north. The morning of the 23d began with heavy air and artillery strikes being fired as planned, and the TF continued to receive shrapnel from the ordnance which was impacting as close as 150 meters; however, no casualties were sustained. Alfa Company and the Mobile Strike Force had the mission of cutting another landing zone on the south side of the perimeter, to allow the evacuation of four wounded that we still had with us from the previous day, and for resupply. At 1100 hours Delta Company crossed the line of departure in the assault. Alfa Company was held at the line of departure to be committed in support of Company D, if required.

Immediately after crossing the LD, Company D received sporadic fire (60mm mortar rounds or rifle grenades), which resulted in one man wounded. The company continued to move without heavy opposition and reported link up with 503d elements at the crest of Hill 875 at 1125 hours. Company D was now opcon to the 503d and Company C, 1st Battalion, 12th Infantry conducted a combat assault into the LZ we had used the preceding day, to become a part of TF 1/12. The composite force of Alfa Company and MSF 26 returned to link up with Company C and obtain water from the stream. At 1600 hours, a resupply ship bringing rations and ammo in for the Mobile Strike Force crashed while attempting to land. The crew managed to get out by themselves except for the pilot, who was pinned in his seat. He was unconscious and seriously hurt. The ship burst into flames and it was only through the efforts of two members of Alfa Company, who broke the windshield, that the pilot was removed just as the flames enveloped his chair. During that operation, rounds from the machineguns and other ammo inside the ship were cooking off. The pilot and crew were subsequently evacuated although the ship was a total loss.

About 1700 hours the Thanksgiving Day meal was flown in with about 20 five-gallon cans of water. Company D was forced to eat a Thanksgiving meal of C-rations since they were on Hill 875 and the 173d did not have enough rations to go around. After our meal, we received instructions to assist the 503d in policing the battlefield and then assume control of the entire Hill 875 complex. The 503d began withdrawing around 1100 and had completely evacuated the hill by 1500 hours. Alfa Company and the command group moved to the top of Hill 875 to join Delta Company and assume control of the perimeter. Company C and the Mobile Strike Force occupied the former TF positions, about 300 meters down the hill. During the police of the battlefield, numerous weapons and equipment were found and evacuated.

That evening our battalion commander arrived on Hill 875 to assume command and I returned to the battalion trains area. The next day, November 26th, the battalion left Hill 875 and began other operations further to the west.

Rang Dong:

Joint Teamwork in Action

Lieutenant Colonel John A. Bender
Major Cecil E. Bray

Captain McNaughton, the company commander, took a smoke grenade from his belt, pulled the pin and tossed it in the middle of the road. As the green smoke billowed out, he took the handset of his radio, "Red Dog, this is Zebra Six. Land your lead on my mark, over." "This is Red Dog, I identify green." Captain McNaughton watched as the black dots in the sky made a slow arc toward the smoke.

He looked around at his command: a US rifle company reinforced with an ARVN platoon. Battle-dressed troopers, seven men to a group, stood at the ready, to race toward the choppers before they touched the ground. Within a matter of seconds, the Hueys lifted off. The company was headed for a suspected enemy location.

After a five-minute flight south, the Hueys began their descent. Before the choppers touched the ground, the troopers were off and running. Moving quickly, the seven-man groups formed into squads and platoons. McNaughton gave the signal, and they moved off to begin a methodical search of the target area.

A thousand meters later a shot rang out, followed by a burst from an automatic weapon. Men dropped to the ground. Captain McNaughton reached for the radio handset and waited.

"Zebra Six, this is Lead. We've found 'em. 'Bout a squad, dug in, over."

Almost immediately he received a report from Sergeant Smith, US advisor to the Vietnamese platoon.

"Roger, hold up and return fire. Break, Zebra Two, swing right; Zebra One, flank left. Three stay put."

Captain McNaughton turned to his artillery FO, "Give me fire on that area but watch out for the platoon trying to flank the camp." The company sealed off the flanks of the camp and pounded the enemy positions with artillery until the VC fire gradually diminished, then stopped. The artillery FO then shifted the fire to the back trails leading out of the camp. The platoons swept into the base camp.

There was no resistance as the search turned up six dead VC, four weapons, documents, rice, medicines, and a tunnel system. Blood trails led out of the camp toward the river.

Circling high over the battle area in a command and control helicopter, the battalion commander told his artillery liaison officer to put fire on the VC fleeing across the river into the bordering district. For the past 10 years, the VC had enjoyed freedom of movement in this area, and across that river was his sanctuary. There would be many more eagle flights into this area, but the district boundary would no longer provide him safety.

Sampan

Sergeant Holland, the squad leader, sat up with head cocked to one side. Off in the distance was a faint putt-putt sound of a motor. Moving quietly and quickly he checked his men. When he returned to his position, he put his hand on the machine-gunner's shoulder. They waited as the putt-putt grew louder.

Slowly a sampan moved along the shadows of the near bank. Sergeant Holland waited. Then he tapped the machinegunner on the head. "Now!" he whispered. The gunner opened fire, triggering the ambush.

It was all over in a matter of seconds. There were shouts, two shots from the sampan, a splash — then silence. Cautiously, a Popular Forces soldier and an American GI moved to the edge of the stream. Lying in the sampan were two VC bodies and one weapon. The men pulled the boat into the nipa palm.

The squad returned to its silent watch. Within two hours, another sampan approached from the opposite direction. The scheme was repeated. The results — one VC killed and one Chinese machinegun captured.

Back at battalion headquarters, the operations sergeant posted the results. Each night there were 15 such ambush patrols scattered throughout the area.

County Fair

The lead platoon leader came to a halt. He signaled to his squad leaders. Squads moved out in predesignated directions. Crouched silently in a sheltered location, the command group waited as the company commander, Captain Shoemaker, listened to the radio. The other platoons executed similar actions. The first, then the second, and finally the third radioed in, "Kilo Six, this is Three. We're in position." Captain Shoemaker nodded to his radio operator who relayed to the battalion TOC that the hamlet cordon was complete. Stillness returned to the area as all movement ceased, and the company settled down to await the morning's light. This was to be a county fair operation.

At the first light, the battalion S2 and S5 moved towards the cordoned-off hamlet. The county fair would last from two to four days, depending on the size of the hamlet, for it would be a concentrated effort to gather intelligence and strengthen the ties between the Vietnamese people and their government.

As soon as they entered the hamlet, the S2 and a special team of Vietnamese and US intelligence personnel went to work. Their first hours were spent screening every individual in the hamlet by interrogating and checking family registration records and ID

cards. Simultaneously, under control of a special Vietnamese force, a thorough house-to-house search for contraband and illegal documents was conducted. The S2 interrogated VC suspects or confirmed VC. Gradually, innocent civilians were weeded out and allowed to return to their homes. Interrogation reports stacked up. The S2 and his staff began the tedious task of compiling and analyzing the bits and pieces of information.

Civic Action

The civic action group looked like a band of gypsies as they moved into the hamlet. Composed entirely of Vietnamese soldiers and civilians, with the exception of the battalion S5 and his driver, the group would live in the hamlet until the operation ended. So the group's personnel were loaded down with personal gear, pots, cooking units, and foodstuffs; they carried sacks of rice and other food to feed the villagers while the village was being searched house-by-house; and they also carried posters, a movie projector and mobile sound equipment. During their stay, they would stage a musical-propaganda drama show, hold games and give goodies to the children. Special Chieu Hoi material had been printed to give to the families whose husbands and sons were VC.

There was much to be done in too-few days. The battalion surgeon started holding sick-call for the villagers, while the S5

made arrangements with the hamlet chief for an open house discussion between the hamlet elders, the district chief and the battalion commander. At the meeting, the hamlet chief mentioned several projects which the soldiers could help the people work on.

The next three days were a whirlwind of activity: soldiers helped some of the hamlet men construct six wooden foot bridges and repair roofs on five houses; the battalion surgeon treated over 150 patients; the Vietnamese information specialists distributed over 1,000 items of printed materials and held informal discussions with the people; food staples were presented to the hamlet chief, and he distributed them to especially needy families. A complete census of every man, woman and child was taken. And last but not least, the people were entertained and were taught patriotic songs, children's songs and games.

On the morning of the fourth day, the S5 waved a farewell to the groups of people gathered around his jeep and started back to battalion headquarters. He would return in a few days to check on the hamlet. The S2's intelligence files and the happy smiles of the people indicated a job not finished — but one just begun.

Clue

Captain Roache, the company commander, watched as men unloaded the ration truck and carried the daily rations into the company field kitchen set up in a small Vietnamese building. Days before, he had been ordered to move his mess hall into the hamlet, but he felt the move just caused extra problems he could do without. As he watched, his interpreter approached. "Sir, the hamlet chief has man who know dead VC."

"The one who tried to throw a grenade into the CP area?" asked Captain Roache.

"Yes, sir," he answered.

Captain Roache called the battalion S2 on the phone. "John, we have a lead on that VC we killed the other night. — yeah. The one with the .45 pistol. — OK, I'll meet your people at the hamlet chief's office."

Informant

When he reached the hamlet chief's office, Captain Roache was surprised to discover the hamlet police chief was the informant. They had become quite friendly during the past weeks and had frequently eaten together at both the chief's house and the mess hall. In fact, the police chief usually spent a couple of hours every day around the CP.

When the battalion S2 and his interrogator arrived, the police chief told them he knew the VC who had been killed. He had known him years ago before he had joined the VC and knew where the widow lived now. Finally, he asked for a map and pointed out positions where he was positive at least two VC platoons were located.

The information was cross-checked by the intelligence center. It appeared to be valid. The many friendly helping acts of the company, culminating in the simple act of moving the mess hall into the hamlet, had assured the police chief that the troops were to stay. As a result, he had given information that he otherwise would have been afraid to give. That evening, an eagle flight was planned.

The above incidents are not unrelated. They all occurred in one thoroughly planned military operation.

The fundamentals of counterinsurgency are not original or unique, and experts have long known that successful operations must include population and resources control, environmental improvement and sound tactical operations founded on extensive gathering of and rapid reaction to intelligence. What is unique, though, was the special application of these fundamentals in a joint US-Vietnamese operation called Rang Dong.

Mission

In Rang Dong, two Infantry battalions (one American and one Vietnamese) conducted joint military operations within and around one military district. This joint task force had a two-fold mission:

- To destroy the local VC forces and the VC infrastructure.
- To conduct extensive civic action operations.

The two battalions also assisted the district chief in training the local Regional Force and Popular Force (RF/PF) personnel. It was anticipated that after the two battalions had eliminated the strong local VC forces, the newly trained RF/PF would take over the defense of the district and the battalions could be gradually withdrawn.

Although the joint aspect of Rang Dong was without precedent, the key factor in insuring success was the cooperation and coordination between ARVN and US Forces in support of the Republic of Vietnam Rural Development Program. Since part of this program's goal in each district is to reestablish government control and project the image of a strong government, the district chief should be responsible for all operations of both military forces and civilian agencies. After some initial maneuvering, both US and Vietnamese battalion commanders agreed to provide direct support to, and act under the operational control of, the district chief. This was designed to impress upon the Vietnamese people that the district chief was responsible for providing security, improving the standard of living and providing governmental services to the district.

56

Teamwork

To assist the district chief and the two battalion commanders, special resources were made available for the operation. The US civilian agencies of JUSPAO and USAID were directed to provide as much support as possible, and both US and Vietnamese psywar and civil affairs units established priority support. In addition, US and Vietnamese military and civilian intelligence agencies agreed to provide specially trained personnel and equipment.

The thoroughness of the joint planning was illustrated by the establishment of a local central committee within the district to control and coordinate all military and civilian resources. Called the area support coordination committee (ASCC), it had the district chief as the chairman. Its membership consisted of the Vietnamese and American battalion commanders and representatives of the civilian and military intelligence agencies. It was recognized that final success depended on complete coordination and cooperation between all military and civilian agencies.

Before the operation could get under way, certain problem areas had to be solved. The first area tackled was to establish a good working relationship between the US and the Vietnamese. US per-

sonnel were cautioned that the Vietnamese would resent being made to feel they would be under US command or operational control. It was emphasized that this was to be an equal partnership between the Americans and Vietnamese, civilian and military. Therefore, the utmost diplomacy was required to establish good rapport even before the district ASCC could be formed.

Until Rang Dong, large Vietnamese or American units had only infrequently operated in the district, and it was important to show the people that cooperation and comradeship existed among the two battalions and the local Vietnamese authorities. Therefore, in the initial meetings between the district chief and the two battalion commanders, it was decided to divide the district into two tactical areas of operation, one for each of the battalions. Subsequently, as mutual trust was further established, both battalion commanders agreed to exchange and integrate units.

Throughout the entire operation, one US Infantry company operated with the Vietnamese battalion and one Vietnamese company worked with the US battalion. This concept was further carried out by exchanging platoons, while local defense force personnel were integrated into both battalions. The rotation of units established a warm personal relationship among the battalions and local defense forces and vastly improved mutual trust and confidence.

At first it was decided that in addition to the district chief, his US advisor, the battalion commanders, and the representatives of the intelligence community and civilian aid agencies, the ASCC would consist of the S2s, S3s, and S5s of the two battalions, the local defense forces chief, the district police chief, and the chiefs of the Vietnamese Information Service and Chieu Hoi program. But it was soon apparent that the committee was too large and cumbersome. The ASCC was then broken down into a primary committee consisting of the district chief, his US advisor, the two battalion commanders, the US advisor to the Vietnamese battalion, and usually the battalion S3s. The remaining personnel were divided into two subcommittees: intelligence and civic action. The members of the primary committee met daily to plan future operations and critique past actions.

Security

The initial efforts of the ASCC were directed towards eliminating and neutralizing VC forces and reestablishing security in the area. To accomplish this, the ASCC realized that it must have the cooperation and assistance of the local populace by assuring the people that the GVN/US forces could and would protect them from the Viet Cong. Without this feeling, little or no assistance could be expected from the people.

To establish an immediate atmosphere of security, heliborne eagle flights and cross-country search and destroy operations were made on all known or suspected local VC base camps and supply caches. Simultaneously, squad and platoon-size ambush patrols were set up throughout the district.

Intelligence

After several days, the area of operations was extended beyond the district borders. By coordinating with neighboring district officials, operations were mounted several thousand meters into their districts. Artillery free-fire areas were created to destroy long-established base camps and staging areas which existed in the buffer zones just outside the district borders.

After the first three days of tactical operations, sufficient security had been established in most areas to permit the intelligence and civic action personnel to start their operations.

Any tactical operation is only as good as its intelligence. This is especially true in counterinsurgency operations where there is considerable difficulty in identifying the enemy. In a war where the support of the people means the difference between success or failure, a counterinsurgency force's ability to distinguish friend from foe is critical. Therefore, in addition to providing tactical information, the counterinsurgency intelligence agency must be able to weed out innocent civilians. The Rang Dong special intelligence force was tailored to meet this requirement.

The district combined intelligence center was as unique as Rang Dong itself; in many respects, it was the hub around which tactics and civic action revolved. It was more than just an intelligence gathering and processing agency — it was a small, self-contained operations center and tactical unit.

Center

Eighty percent of the personnel in the center were Vietnamese; the remaining 20 percent were intelligence personnel from the US battalion's S2 section, the American advisors to the Vietnamese working in the center and the US battalion's reconnaissance platoon. The center was divided into several highly specialized sections, and in addition to the usual S2 personnel, there were interrogators, translators, order of battle specialists, photographers, fingerprint specialists, National Police Field Force (NPFF), and intelligence personnel familiar with the local situation.

Civilian intelligence personnel were also part of the team, while the US reconnaissance platoon acted as a mobile security force for the center.

In the beginning, the only intelligence immediately available came from local district sources, and the battalion's first combat operations were based on this intelligence. In time, though, the center was able to establish its own intelligence network to reinforce the existing sources.

The first fresh intelligence was developed as a result of the initial county fair operation. During the county fair operation, the target hamlet was completely sealed off just before dawn, and no one was allowed to enter or leave. At first light, intelligence specialists and interrogators began their work. The district police provided security inside the cordon for the National Police Field Force as the latter conducted a house-to-house search.

Identification

While the house-to-house search went on, the people were processed by interrogators who had a blacklist of known and suspected VC personnel. At the same time, the district police checked family registration records and identity cards, looking for persons without ID cards or in possession of forged or out-

dated cards. All suspected and confirmed VC were taken to the combined intelligence center compound.

Here the VC suspects were put through an intensive interrogation period to determine their innocence or to gain additional information. All suspects with civil offenses — lack of an ID card, draft dodging or illegal papers — were processed, given

proper papers, and turned over to the district police either for disposition or to be returned directly to their hamlet, as decided by the district chief.

Information gathered was processed and analyzed by the intelligence center and disseminated to all interested intelligence agencies, both US and Vietnamese. Intelligence of tactical value was sent direct to the ASCC to assist in operational planning.

The center, in addition to its intelligence gathering and processing role, also conducted several special tactical operations. For that purpose, the US reconnaissance platoon, the NPFF, district police and some intelligence specialists were organized into a special mobile intelligence collection agency called the "Mobile Strike Force." The strike force's operations were conducted usually at night and after curfew, usually between 2400 and 0500 hours. Using the intelligence center's blacklist and the S5's list of families with members who were VC, the strike force conducted raids on individual homes or groups of houses in a hamlet. It attempted to surprise VC members who had sneaked back to visit their families, to uncover clandestine night meetings and to apprehend suspects who may have been absent at the time a county fair operation had been conducted. During the day, the strike force set up mobile road blocks and checkpoints on main and back roads to check ID cards and search for contraband.

Civic action was perhaps the easiest of the three fundamentals to implement during Rang Dong. It was the first time that a Vietnamese tactical unit had become extensively engaged in civic action, and this had been one of the fundamental reasons for conducting joint battalion operations. It was hoped that the natural inclination of US troops to conduct civic action would influence the Vietnamese troops to do likewise.

The county fair operations were basically public relations programs to introduce the troops into an area, to explain the purpose of the operation, and to gain the willing cooperation of the people. Two days after the US battalion had conducted the first county fair, the Vietnamese battalion conducted its first county fair with the assistance of the US S5. Subsequent county fairs were conducted independently by each battalion in its own operational area, with the exception of a joint operation dictated by the large size of one hamlet. Based on the success of the county fairs, the RF company commander conducted a county fair on his own in a village within his area or responsibility

Like the combined intelligence center, a special civic action group was organized specifically to support Rang Dong operations. It, too, was composed principally of Vietnamese personnel. The US personnel consisted of the battalion S5 section and the district USAID representative who assisted in the planning and support of the civic action.

The Vietnamese were all specialists provided by the Vietnamese government — civil affairs specialists, psywar specialists, civilian information specialists, medical personnel, Chieu Hoi cadremen, ARVN security soldiers, and an assortment of entertainers. These were divided into two equal groups, one for each of the two Infantry battalions.

The civic action group conducted a complete population census in each hamlet, counting the number of families and the number of people in each family. An informal survey was also conducted to determine what was actually required by the villagers. Plans were then made to return to the hamlet to accomplish more sophisticated projects which would have a lasting impact.

The civic action group initially concentrated on small-scale self-help projects that could be accomplished in a short time — foot bridges were repaired, small culverts put in, and minor repairs to schoolhouses accomplished. And in one five week period, the US battalion surgeon treated over 1,100 patients, while his Vietnamese battle surgeon treated the same number.

From the wait and see attitude, to willing cooperation, to the final act by the villagers of volunteering both assistance and information, these are the steps in the growth of a nation.

When the hamlet police chief volunteered information, it resulted in the discovery of one of the largest VC base camps in the area, the death and capture of several VC, and a sizable cache of weapons, ammunition and demolitions. This was one of the critical phases in the operations within the district.

Documents uncovered in the base camp resulted in the discovery of additional base camps in the same area. At about the same time, a VC tax collector was captured in a hamlet after one of the villagers pointed him out to a US soldier. In another instance, the strike force acted on a tip from an informer and raided a house. The force captured a complete VC cell and members of another. Gradually, incident gave rise to incident in a snowballing effect.

What sparked the act of volunteering? What encouraged the hamlet police chief to come forward at that moment with the vital information?

Was it one of the successful eagle flights? Or an ambush patrol which captured a supply sampan loaded with weapons? Or the death of an important VC? Or the sight of two soldiers helping a farmer repair an irrigation ditch? Or the improved and helpful attitude of the Vietnamese soldiers towards the people? Or the sight of a unit mess hall moving into the hamlet, which signified permanent security for the area? It was probably a combination of all these acts woven into the framework of security which Rang Dong provided.

There was one additional, irrevocable sign of movement forward: When that young Vietnamese captain, commander of an RF company, planned and executed his own successful county fair operation without any prompting or assistance, this signaled progress.

This incident alone stands as testimony to the validity of Rang Dong. For it provides the US with the means of working itself out of a job through joint support of the increasingly successful Rural Development Program.

Reflections of a Battalion S3

Lieutenant Colonel Garold L. Tippin

One of the enemy's favorite battlegrounds was the fortified village. This usually consisted of several hamlets prepared with extensive fighting positions, trenchworks, connecting tunnels, and spiderholes. The fighting bunkers often had five to seven feet of overhead cover and could take a direct hit from a 155mm howitzer round. The bunkers were placed to cover avenues of approach and were interspersed throughout the village, with tunnels connecting the bunkers and trenches, thereby allowing the enemy to disappear and reappear firing from another location. Trees, shrubs and even the earth itself were reshaped to conceal these positions.

At first glance, there seemed to be no logic or method to these defensive works. But upon closer investigation, one could find an intricate, well-planned defensive position that took advantage

65

of existing cover and concealment, natural barriers and avenues of approach into and within the village.

The enemy elected to use a hamlet or a village as a battleground for one or more reasons:

• He expected to inflict enough casualties on US troops during the attack to justify his making a stand.

• He knew that the US soldier does not like to fire upon villages and populated areas.

• The village offered the enemy a labor source to prepare the fortifications.

• In the open valleys and coastal lowlands, the villages contained a great deal of natural cover and concealment.

• The hamlets in a village were usually spread out and their arrangement offered many avenues of escape.

The enemy's usual plan of battle followed the same pattern:

• He would allow US troops to get as close as possible before opening fire, usually 15 to 25 meters. The purpose of these hugging tactics was to get the US soldiers so closely engaged that they could not effectively use artillery and tactical air support.

• The enemy felt that if he inflicted several casualties in his initial burst, the US soldiers would become involved in trying to get the wounded back to the rear for evacuation. He believed that when the US troops started worrying more about getting their wounded buddies to safety than about the battle, they would become easy targets; in this respect, he was correct.

• Another facet of his battle plan was to fight viciously until dark; then, using the cover of darkness, he escaped by using one of his many preplanned escape routes, carrying off his dead and wounded, their weapons, and even empty cartridges. We captured numerous enemy documents which either condemned or commended certain units for the police of the battlefield. On one occasion, after an 18-hour battle, there was one particular bunker from which an LMG had been firing; after the fight and upon checking the position, not one empty cartridge case could be found. At other times, enemy dead were found, and lying by their side were large tin cans filled with empty cartridge cases — they had been ready to move out when our fire caught them. The enemy also knew that we placed great emphasis on body count and weapons. Our men, like all soldiers, were intent on making the enemy pay a heavy price for each friendly casualty. The enemy felt that he had won a psychological victory if he could remove his casualties, leaving a sterile battlefield for our men to find, especially if he had inflicted some casualties on us.

The enemy liked to initiate his actions in the late afternoon, for this gave him several hours to inflict as many casualties as he could prior to escaping after dark. He did not have enough ammunition to conduct a sustained defense, nor could he be resupplied as well as our men could.

To keep the enemy from getting away, all escape routes had to be sealed off. This was indeed a difficult task, and, in fact, was usually beyond the capability of one rifle company. The impulsive company commander who attempted to use his platoons to maneuver and flank a fortified village soon found himself in deep trouble, and the same was true if he tried a frontal assault. He might succeed in taking the position but his losses would not be worth the effort. His best course of action was to immediately call in blocking fires to the rear of the enemy position and to use his unit to fix the enemy and give his commander an appraisal of the situation.

Predicament

At the village of Dien Troung 4, Quang Ngai Province, on May 22, 1967, Company A, 1st Battalion, 35th Infantry, 4th Infantry Division, found itself in such a predicament. At 0600 the company was approaching the village from the west when it began to receive automatic fire. As the company commander maneuvered his 1st and 2d platoons to the left to come in on the village

from the north, both platoons became heavily engaged in the open rice paddies and could not move. Then the 3d platoon and the company command group moved across Highway 1 and entered the northwest corner of the village. They, too, were stopped by intense enemy fire. The company command group spent the next four hours pinned down in a peanut patch. Much later — some 32 hours in fact — and only after a liberal use of gunships, 13 airstrikes, 2,000 artillery shells and three more rifle companies, the village was taken and the enemy defeated. It took four of those hours for the company, under gunship support, to break contact and withdraw so that the artillery and aircraft could soften up the village.

The blocking of enemy escape routes was the battalion commander's problem; he had the capability of committing additional maneuver elements into the rear and flanks of an enemy position.

Between April and September 1967, the 1st Battalion, 35th Infantry took part in seven major battles involving fortified villages, resulting in some 371 enemy soldiers killed. All of these actions were similar in the way they began and ended. The one major difference was that the battalion learned from each battle and applied those lessons in subsequent battles.

The Pattern

Each time the action began with the involvement of one rifle company. From this, the pattern was the same: the enemy allowed the friendly troops to get into the village and usually within 15 to 20 meters of a fighting bunker before they opened fire. Each time the battle began with the US rifle company getting several men wounded and pinned down in the open. As the unit would delpoy it would encounter more enemy positions, and it was not long before the entire company was involved in the firefight. In the early stages, the battle would go pretty much according to the enemy's plan.

But then, gunships would be sent to the battle areas, and while they did not have a great effect on the bunkers, they did an outstanding job of suppressing enemy fire — and they can fire accurately within 15 to 20 meters of friendly troops. Under this suppressive fire, the closely committed units would back off, taking their wounded with them and would take up positions to fix the enemy. The full brunt of artillery and tactical air would we brought down on the positions, while other companies would be moved into blocking positions around the village.

In all seven actions, all three rifle companies of the battalion were ultimately committed. Once the area was ringed off, all available fire support was used; in addition, during the night, "Spooky" C47s with Gatling guns were used and the area was kept in continuous illumination as the friendly troops on the ground pressed in close and maintained a heavy volume of small arms fire into the enemy positions.

Willpower

On several occasions, the enemy fought viciously, and only four prisoners were taken in the combined battles. There is no doubt that some of the enemy escaped, because following each battle, blood trails and sandal tracks could be found leading out of the villages.

One factor that the enemy completely overlooked was the dogged determination, bravery and fighting ability of the US Infantryman. Several captured enemy documents revealed that the enemy had been told that as soon as several casualties had been inflicted on US troops in the initial stages of a fortified village action, the US troops would panic and withdraw. The enemy had a lesson to learn, because our men did not panic and run — they withdrew only on order, in an orderly fashion, and only in order to use their air and artillery support. In all cases, their casualties were taken back with them. When the time came to go back, they went without hesitation and closed on the enemy positions like the well-trained, professional fighting team they were.

The Fortified Village

A thorough, organized search had to be conducted in the occupied villages, because the enemy had a tendency to go underground and hide in his numerous concealed spiderholes and tunnels. It was imperative that the village be searched inch-by-inch, with particular attention paid to wells, livestock pens, hedgerows, and bamboo groves.

The use of CS riot-control gas could not be overlooked when fighting in a fortified village, and, on one occasion, the battalion made a night attack with gas masks following an aerial CS attack. The ship made a low pass on the windward side of the hamlet and dispersed about 250 CS grenades. This was followed by 20 minutes of artillery fire, about one-half of which saw VT fuse fired into the enemy positions. Behind a walking barrage of artillery fire, one company moved forward, and once inside the hamlet, lit up the area with flareships. Eighteen enemy were killed while no casualties were suffered by the friendly troops.

The use of CS in such an action depended upon several factors:
- The availability of dispensing devices.
- Wind direction and location of friendly units.
- The availability of masks for the ground unit.

It was generally recognized that to conduct guerrilla warfare successfully the enemy must have control of the people, for it is with the people that the enemy acquires his food, intelligence and labor force. Our primary mission was to cut off the main force VC and NVA units from the population. Without the support of the people and faced with defeat if he tried a pitched battle in the lowlands, the guerrilla would be forced to move back into the mountains and ultimately "die on the vine" or be tracked down and destroyed by our units.

Hearts and Minds

But an area could be secured only when the government won the hearts and the minds of the people. And to properly secure an area, several preliminary steps had to be taken:
- The NVA and main force VC units had to be defeated and driven into the hills. In other words, they had to be cut off from the population.
- The VC infrastructure had to be broken, and in order to do this, the local force VC and VC cadre had either to be killed or captured.
- Once these two steps had been accomplished, the Vietnamese government could begin to pacify the people and win them over to its cause, while US and allied forces moved into the hills to hunt down and destroy the remaining NVA and main force VC units.

In our area, we had been successful in step one; breaking the VC infrastructure, however, was a difficult task, a war of hide-and-seek and of trying to outwit the enemy in his own backyard. In the populated lowlands this involved conducting numerous village search and clear operations.

Methods

The methods of search that we employed varied with the situation:
- Deliberate cordon and search was used when the specific mis-

sion of the unit was to conduct an exhaustive search of the target village. In this method, troops were positioned before daylight in ambush locations to cover all exit routes from the village. Then, at daylight, a psyops team — if one was available — would begin to broadcast instructions directing the people to gather at a particular location in or outside the village. One platoon would then enter the village to check for an enemy force. If a psyops team was not available, one platoon would enter the village, round up the people, and direct them to a central location. The remainder of the unit would remain in the blocking positions around the target village. On more than one occasion following the psyops broadcast or a unit moving forward, VC soldiers fled from the village, only to be shot down or apprehended by the cordon units. While the people were being questioned the village would be given a thorough search.

• Modified cordon and search. Here, again, two different methods can be used. In the first one, blocking forces would move into position before daylight to cordon off the village, but would leave one side of the village unguarded. At daylight, an additional unit would be air assaulted into the open side and would move toward the village. This technique was used when it was believed that there were armed enemy in the village; the objective was to give the enemy the choice to stay and fight or withdraw into our ambush units. The enemy liked to fight on his own terms and usually the airmobile assault, preceded by an artillery preparation and fire from gunships, would cause him to take the easy way out. This operation usually required two or more rifle companies.

The second method was used when natural barriers — lakes, beaches, open rice paddies — were on one or two sides of the village. These features acted as either a barrier or offered excellent observation from the air, thereby doing away with the requirement for a complete cordon around the target village. If the village was near a beach and the people had boats with which to attempt an escape, it was a simple matter of prior coordination to have one or two Navy Swift Boats on station. In this operation, the blocking forces would be positioned before daylight around that part of the village not bordered by the natural obstacle. Psyops broadcasts were used when desired, and aerial reconnaissance played an important role.

One of the finest examples of a modified village search and clear operation was conducted by our sister battalion — the 2d Battalion, 35th Infantry — on August 8, 1967. This action took place at An Ba hamlet, Nghia Han District, Quang Ngai Province, a 13-hour battle that started with a report from a Hoi Chanh (VC returnee). The battle was an outstanding example of the use of armed reconnaissance helicopters and gunships working in conjunction with ground elements.

- Area cordon and search. This method was used when a large area or several villages had to be searched. The blocking ambush forces would be positioned at one end and on the flanks of the target area, while the sweeping forces would drive into and search the villages to push the enemy soldiers into the blocking ambush positions. To be successful, the blocking ambush positions had to be placed between the suspected enemy and his sanctuary and they had to be occupied without our forces being detected. Two or more rifle companies were usually employed in this operation.

- Normal village sweep. This was used when units moved through a village conducting a search but not in conjunction with blocking forces. This was the least productive and least desirable method of searching a village, and was used both as a show of force and as an intelligence gathering means. The sweeping forces looked for large quantities of rice, bunkers and positions, or indications of recent enemy use. We were forced to use this method many times but only because of a lack of troops. If a unit on this type of operation could obtain the use of aerial reconnaissance aircraft to work in conjunction with its sweep, its chances of success were greatly increased.

Terrain

It was desirable to conduct village search operations in cooperation with the local Vietnamese authorities, for once the people were rounded up, only Vietnamese personnel could do any sort of intelligence questioning. We found that the National Police were ideally suited and trained for these population control activities.

There are really two wars in Vietnam — one that is fought in the coastal lowlands and valley plains, the other than is fought

in the mountainous jungles. In some areas, units would be operating in one environment one day and in the other the following day. Our methods of operation differed sharply in each.

Jungle fighting is not new to US soldiers, nor does the enemy have a monopoly on jungle know-how. US units adapted well to jungle fighting, and when we operated against the NVA along the Cambodian border we found that they had as much difficulty operating in the area as we did. The prisoners we captured were, as a rule, undernourished, emaciated and sick with malaria. They stated that almost everyone in their units had malaria and many had died from it.

In the jungle, landing zones were few and far between, trails few and narrow. Navigation was difficult and units in many cases were limited to jungle trails. Flank security was difficult to attain, visibility was down to between 20 to 30 meters and forward movement was limited to 300 to 500 meters per hour.

The most difficult problem in fighting the enemy in this terrain was in finding him, for this is where he built his fortified base camps and located his bunkers on ridges and in the heads of draws, in hopes that a US platoon or company would blunder into the area. The enemy habitually emplaced his fighting positions to fire down a valley or ridge, and, as in a fortified village, he realized that our tactical advantage lay in our artillery and air support. So, again, he liked to use hugging tactics, and we had the problem of finding and fixing him without having our units engaged and shot up at close range.

Reaction Time

In the jungle, where LZs were limited, reaction time was reduced to the cross-country mobility of units on the ground, and commanders continually had to consider this factor when they wanted to reinforce small units locked in heavy contact with the enemy. When contact with large enemy units seemed probable, we found it safe to keep our rifle companies within one to three hours of each other.

Our rifle companies operated as a unit with their platoons within 15 to 30 minutes of one other, and with security elements covering the main body, front, flanks, and rear. Too often, company commanders overlooked flank and rear security because of the difficult terrain. Admittedly there were times when it was impossible to have flank security because of the heavy jungle vegetation; in this case the unit moved in a single file, with the point element preceding the main body by about 200 meters.

A rifle company stopped every so often to send out patrols in all directions. Not only was this a good security measure, it was also a good method of search in the jungle. Special emphasis had to be paid to the rear. On the border, the NVA developed a habit of having a small reconnaissance party following our units to keep tabs.

Buttonhook

There were a couple of ways we used to combat this technique — one was by dropping off a small ambush patrol, a procedure that paid dividends for us on several occasions. The other method was to have a patrol buttonhook, move off the trail, double-back some distance, and then move back along the trail. In mountainous terrain, and if it were at all possible, a company commander kept one or two platoons on the high ground, so that if need be they could maneuver down on the enemy.

When firm contact with the enemy had been established, the ground commander had to be careful not to overcommit his unit. Rather, he concentrated on fixing the enemy with his forces and immediately employing his supporting fires. Following extensive artillery and air bombardment, the commander maneuvered his elements to determine the effect of his supporting fires, any additional support required, and to destroy the remnants of the enemy force. The deciding factor in many of these battles was the immediate application of firepower.

On normal operations, it was a good policy for a company to halt at about 1600 hours to give the men sufficient time before dark to prepare their night defensive perimeter. Digging in was an absolute must. At the very least, individual prone fighting positions were prepared. Security in the form of OPs and LPs was another cardinal rule. For some reason, this was a difficult thing to get commanders — especially new commanders — to do. They seemed reluctant to put out two or three men 100 to 200 meters from the company perimeter.

Claymore

One of the finest weapons in a jungle perimeter was the claymore. The hand grenade lost much of its usefulness in the thick jungle, and a lot of men were wounded by their own grenades when they hit a tree limb or bush. The same was true of the M79 grenade launcher. But the claymore was an aimed weapon, just like a rifle, and therefore could be carefully sighted in to cover the desired target area.

Some men tended to put the claymore out too far for fear of being injured in the backblast. But the enemy had a habit of sneaking up to our perimeters and turning the claymores around. To counter this, the claymores were placed close enough to be observed and we also found it effective to rig the claymore with a tripflare or anti-intrusion device.

A claymore could be detonated safely by placing it just outside the foxhole against the berm. In fact, we found it a good idea to emplace one there just in case. Another good rig for a claymore was up in a tree, with the business end aimed on a slant toward the ground. While the locations for claymores and tripflares were selected before dark, ideally they were not emplaced until after dark.

Mortars

Whenever possible a company cut an LZ within its night perimeter. Of course, this was a must if the unit expected to be resupplied. Our units liked to bring in their 81mm mortars, not only for close-in fire support but also to provide immediate illumination.

Medical evacuation was another problem. In the jungle, only emergency cases were evacuated at night. Too, since LZs in the jungle were limited, many wounded or injured personnel could be evacuated by means of a hoist rigged on a medical evacuation ship. Our units kept an emergency rig of a rope and parachute harness, and while we used this rig only twice, on both occasions the men were saved. The problem with this rig was that the individual could not be lifted all the way into the aircraft but had to dangle 15 to 30 feet under the helicopter.

In the jungle, too, most of the meeting engagements with the enemy were at a distance of from 15 to 20 feet, and in this terrain, our point men liked to carry the shotgun. It was an excellent close-in weapon, especially when a point man turned the corner of a trail and ran head-on into a couple of enemy soldiers.

It is well to keep in mind that in the jungle all natural LZs are probably hot and mined, and that the enemy will try to keep all possible landing zones under observation by small elements. Some enemy units, in fact, had a primary mission of ambushing prospective LZs.

The best method we found to secure an LZ in this type of terrain was to move a rifle company in on foot to provide security for the following elements. When this was impossible because of the tactical situation, preparatory fires were carefully planned and coordinated. Ideally, tactical air, artillery, and gunships would be used. In these preparatory fires, not only would the LZ and the immediate area be hit by supporting fires, but also the likely avenues of approach into the area and likely enemy assembly areas some distance from the LZ.

Ambush

One of the weakest tactical areas in Vietnam was the ambush, and too many commanders felt that the night belonged to the enemy. This was nonsense. The reason our units were not adept at ambushes was simply that the units did not use the proper techniques. The principles of patrolling and ambushing as taught in the Ranger course are tried and tested, and if unit commanders would apply those techniques, their ambushes would be successful. Many of the so-called "new techniques" used in Vietnam are simply bad habits into which units have fallen.

Oftentimes, a unit would try to accomplish too many missions at the same time. A rifle company, for example, cannot operate all day and then be expected to conduct ambushes at night. But this is exactly what happened in many units. As a result, a rifle platoon would move to its ambush position, organize a perimeter defense, and the men would go to sleep, leaving only a few on guard. This was not an ambush, but it was called that. To conduct a proper night ambush, a unit must have rest and time to prepare.

Another problem area was patrol preparation. Few units applied the proper troop leading steps. A patrol leader must be given time to prepare, and, if at all possible, he should make a ground reconnaissance. Some commanders seemed to feel that a ground reconnaissance would compromise the ambush site. A small reconnaissance patrol, well camouflaged and taking great pains to remain undetected, had little chance of being discovered. And if it was seen, the enemy had no way of knowing what it was doing. Those fresh enemy tracks in the stream bed might go undetected if a unit moved only after dark. Too many ambush patrols simply moved out and finally ended up saying, "Well, this looks pretty good, let's set up here."

Security

Another common error was the failure to establish proper security at the ambush site. In a linear ambush, security had to be emplaced at least 100 meters up and down the trail from the kill zone, and rear security put out beyond hand grenade range. Many leaders were reluctant to put out those security elements because they felt they were endangering their men. In reality if a leader failed to put them out, he endangered his entire patrol. The security elements provided early warning, and one procedure we used was communications wire strung from the security to the main body; when the enemy approached, the security men simply tugged the wire. The security element must allow the enemy to pass its position to get into the kill zone. The element then cut down any enemy soldier who attempted to flee the ambush site. Using a claymore with the security element for the purpose of hitting the enemy soldiers as they fled also worked well.

Mistakes

Another problem was men falling asleep. No matter how much rest the men have received, some of them are going to doze. Communications wire strung along the position and wrapped around each man's wrist was one way to alert all of them to the enemy's approach. Here again, leadership was the answer: "The patrol members will stay awake if the patrol leader makes them stay awake."

Many times ambushes were properly planned, well laid, and correctly positioned only to fail because of some small mistake on the part of the unit commander. The most common mistakes were:

• Springing the ambush too early and before the enemy arrived in the killing zone.

• Poor noise discipline, talking, shifting positions, and slamming of weapon bolts.

• Not enough firepower in the initial springing of the ambush.

• Failure to have escape routes covered by claymores and artillery fires.

• Failure to provide for illumination in conjunction with springing the ambush and with sweeping the area.

We considered the ambush one of our primary weapons, particularly at night. When the brigade moved into the Duc Pho area in April we became involved in four months of heavy contact with the NVA and main force VC units. Eventually, they were forced back into the hills, leaving behind a large number of dead and prisoners. During the last two of those four months, most of the battalion's kills were made as the result of night ambushes. The enemy had to come down out of the hills to get his rice and intelligence and he relied heavily on night travel.

A Variety of Ambushes

There were several unique kinds of ambushes, other than the usual ones that were employed: stay-behind, claymore, anti-intrusion, and tripflare.

In some areas the VC habitually followed our units, keeping tabs on them and feeling that the safest area was the area US troops had just vacated. It proved to be a good practice for us to occasionally drop off a squad to set up a stay-behind ambush. The ambush element had communications with the main body, which did not get so far ahead as to be unable to return and assist the ambush element if necessary.

One of the most effective weapons to employ in an ambush was the claymores, and the ambush site was always selected to

take the greatest possible advantage of the claymore's capabilities. For greatest effectiveness, the claymores were located about 20 meters from the trail. Each claymore was sighted in to insure a thorough coverage of the killing zone and to make certain that the fire fans overlapped. To get a simultaneous detonation, they were rigged in a daisy chain using detonating cord. Claymores were also used to cover escape routes from an ambush area and to help provide flank and rear security to the ambush unit.

The anti-intrusion device with the tripwire area covered by claymores could be an extremely effective small ambush. The tripwire was spider-webbed across the trail, high enough so that small animals would not set it off, with the triggerman positioned a safe distance from the killing zone. Care had to be taken in putting in the device because the wire was fragile and easily broken. The claymores were carefully sighted in and camouflaged, and a company often rigged this device for use by the rear security element. In two nights, four enemy soldiers were killed by this method as they approached one of our ambush patrols from the rear.

One type ambush that had some success in Vietnam was the tripflare ambush. The site selected was always within friendly artillery or mortar fires, which were adjusted into the target area. The tripflares were clandestinely set throughout the target area, preferably along trails habitually used by the enemy and from then on it was a matter of keeping the area observed. When a flare was tripped, artillery or mortars were immediately called in, while the area was also laced with friendly small arms fire.

The two types of ambushes used most successfully were the linear ambush and the inverted "L" ambush.

Litterbug

In Vietnam, our soldiers were a major part of the enemy's supply system. The US soldier by nature, was rather wasteful, a trait that carried over from his civilian life. He tended to discard anything he considered extra and the idea of policing the battlefield was distasteful to him. Rather than take the time to cut up a C-ration can he would either throw it away or bury it; the unfortunate fact was that the can might be returned to him later in the form of a boobytrap.

The enemy, by contrast, was a scavenger. He made use of practically everything he found on the battlefield and his scavenging teams habitually searched our old campsites. The amount of US equipment found on enemy dead and prisoners could be startling, running the gamut from weapons and ammunition to bottles of insect repellent. Almost every enemy soldier killed or captured by our battalion during a four-month period carried a bottle of US Army issue insect repellent.

The enemy had three main sources of supply: supplies carried overland through Laos and Cambodia and then into Vietnam; supplies carried in by sea from North Vietnam; and supplies captured from US and allied troops. Major efforts were made to stem the first two sources, but there was not enough being done about the third source.

Statistics

During Operation Baker, from April 19, 1967 to September 20, 1967 our battalion compiled some interesting statistics:

• One hundred and seventy-four US grenades were recaptured, not counting those found rigged as boobytraps. Too often the individual US soldier either failed to secure the grenades properly or simply left them lying at his position when he moved out.

• One hundred and seventy-two boobytraps were located; of these, 35 were found the hard way — we had 32 men killed and 70 wounded. During this operation, we attained a 14 to 1 kill ratio over the enemy. Of particular note was the fact that 75 percent of our casualties during this period resulted from enemy mines and boobytraps.

• Twenty-four of the enemy's boobytraps were homemade explosive devices constructed from discarded US C-ration cans.

• Thirty-five enemy boobytraps used captured US hand grenades.

• Four enemy boobytraps used captured US claymores; five used US M16 antipersonnel mines; 12 used 155mm artillery rounds; eight used 250-pound bombs rigged as boobytraps; seven were boobytrapped 105mm howitzer shells; six were boobytrapped 81mm mortar rounds; four were boobytrapped 5-inch US naval gun shells; and some 18 other homemade explosive devices used powder from US artillery shells and other miscellaneous material.

• During a two-week period in September 1967, when the battalion had the mission of securing Highway 1, 10 enemy antitank mines were discovered on the road. Most of these had been rigged for electrical detonation by using parts of discarded US AN/PRC-25 batteries.

These statistics are revealing, for they give an indication of just how much we unwittingly contributed to the enemy's war effort.

Policing the immediate battlefield and campsite was not enough. We found a large number of dud bombs and artillery shells in our areas of operation, and in the same time frame mentioned above, we located and destroyed seventy-six 250-pound bombs, two 500-pound bombs, 50 CBU bomblets, and 189 artillery and mortar shells. This amounted to a lot of potential boobytraps that the enemy did not get. With this large number of duds, we soon found it necessary to train several men in each platoon in demolition techniques, and it soon became policy for each unit to carry explosives and to blow duds in place.

Basic Load

As with all other US units, the individual's basic load was a problem. It was not unusual to see a rifle company moving out on an operation with men carrying 50 to 60 pounds of equipment. The individual soldier usually carried his weapon, a double basic load of ammunition, two to four grenades, two canteens of water, and three to four C-ration meals. These were the essentials. When one added to this a pack, one claymore, smoke grenades, and a few other "nice to have" items, the soldier was bogged down to the point that his mobility was greatly decreased, and

after a day's walk he was physically exhausted. Every pound that a man carried reduced his ability to react and impaired his fighting ability.

One method that we used in normal day-to-day operations when we knew that the units would be resupplied each day was to pick up the individual packs and extra equipment each morning and return them to the unit with the evening resupply. This allowed the units to maneuver during the day with only their combat load. This procedure depended upon the mission and the availability of landing zones and aircraft.

The individual soldier's load must be tailored to the operation and limited to essentials. Commanders must carefully consider each item carried and designate each soldier's load in terms of the unit's mission, the length of the operation, means of resupply, time of resupply, availability of water, climate, and terrain.

We found that the basic and advanced individual training centers in the US were doing an outstanding job. The new men who arrived in Vietnam were well trained in the fundamentals of soldiering and, surprisingly, they seemed to know what to expect. It was clear that they had been thoroughly oriented on the war and the country.

When they first arrived they were apprehensive and a bit frightened, which is only natural; but when it came to soldiering, they were consistently better than we had hoped for.

Emphasis

There are, however, some areas where additional emphasis should have been placed:

• Nowhere in any other war has rifle marksmanship been more important than in Vietnam. This is a small unit war where fast and accurate shooting makes the difference. In this respect, the individual soldier has a tendency to fire too much automatic fire, thereby decreasing his accuracy and wasting ammunition. Emphasis should be placed upon well-aimed, semiautomatic fire — volume does not replace accuracy.

• The majority of our soldiers tended to shoot high at night. This is an old problem that can only be overcome by additional training and emphasis.

• The M16 rifle is an ideal weapon for jungle warfare; it is lightweight, has a rapid rate of fire and the individual soldier can carry a large amount of ammunition. But the weapon cannot take the rough handling that the M14 and the M1 could, and it requires a great deal of maintenance. In most cases, it had to be cleaned three times a day, while nine times out of 10, weapon malfunctions were due to poor maintenance procedures. And many of the new men seemed to lack the urgency of caring for their weapon. On March 3, 1967 a long range reconnaissance patrol made contact with six enemy. All six of the enemy escaped unharmed, and the patrol's position was compromised because, of the five members of the patrol, only one could fire his weapon. On checking out the incident, we found it was plain and simple negligence: poor weapon maintenance.

• Some units in Vietnam have found that darkness can be a friend to those who know how to use it, and that the enemy does not have a monopoly on night operations. More emphasis should be placed on night training, because the only thing that will give men the confidence to work efficiently at night is night training and more night training.

• In Vietnam, the problem area in leadership was at the most crucial level: the squad. There were simply not enough experienced junior NCOs available, and over half of the squads in Vietnam were commanded by Specialist 4s. Many of these men were good squad leaders, but most of them had come to Vietnam straight from AIT and they lacked a broad military background. To improve the caliber of junior NCOs and to provide them with additional leadership training, most divisions and brigades in Vietnam organized NCO schools. Our battalion organized a monthly small unit leaders combat training course, and the subjects taught in the course were based on the needs of the battalion, with emphasis on practical work, on leadership, and on the role of the squad leader. The school was a success and was well received by the students. After a soldier had been in a couple of firefights and with the realization that other men might soon be looking to him for leadership, he was eager to learn all he could as fast as he could.

No military unit can be overtrained. In keeping with this thought, we required our firebase company to spend at least one-third of its time in training, leaving another third for tactical operations and the remainder for firebase defense improvements. Most training requirements were selected from post-action critiques involving the company commander and his platoon leaders, or the battalion commander, his staff, and the company commanders. We found these post-action critiques to be valuable aids in improving the combat proficiency of the battalion.

1968

TET AND THE AFTERMATH

Undoubtedly, this was the most eventful year of America's participation in the Southeast Asian conflict. It produced the most savage series of enemy attacks, the most brutal fighting and a strong glimmer of hope for an honorable end to the conflict.

As January neared its end, an offensive was beginning near the DMZ where a string of artillery, rocket and ground attacks were unleashed on Allied posts all along the buffer zone. Khe Sanh and neighboring Lang Wei were hit hard, beginning a three-month drama that would focus the eyes of the world on a small Marine garrison in the rolling hills of the Laotian border country.

The most violent time of the year was the Communists' winter-spring offensive—tabbed the "Tet Offensive" by servicemen and the news media. It began midway through a declared 36-hour Lunar New Year's truce when rockets began slamming into Da Nang Air Base.

Wild street fighting subsequently broke out in the peaceful seaside resort of Nha Trang and Communist sappers breached the security of the U.S. Embassy grounds in Saigon. Street fighting raged in all eight major cities and at least 30 towns and provincial capitals.

The North Vietnamese virtually occupied Hue. They assassinated more than 1000 civilians in that city alone. They held half of Kontum, and terrorist slaughter was reported everywhere. Foreign missionaries were slain, and anyone who had worked for the Americans was marked for murder or torture.

That's how it began; in some sections of the country the ensuing fighting raged for several weeks. Fighting continued in Saigon until mid-February when sporadic resistance was eliminated in the suburbs of Cholon and around the Phu Tho racetrack.

Who won the battle of the Tet Offensive? It is a hard question to answer. Certainly, the Communists were deprived of every major goal, with the exception of publicity. It certainly was no military victory; 27,706 enemy soldiers died in the Tet fighting. For this, the Communist high command had not one single prize to show.

On May 3, there was an announcement the world had been waiting for: the United States and Hanoi agreed to begin preliminary peace discussions in Paris. On the following night, however, the enemy began simultaneous shelling of 119 cities, towns and villages in the Republic—perhaps, forecasting the coming frustrations of peace negotiations.

The last half of the year saw a switch in combat accent away from the cities and back into the countryside.

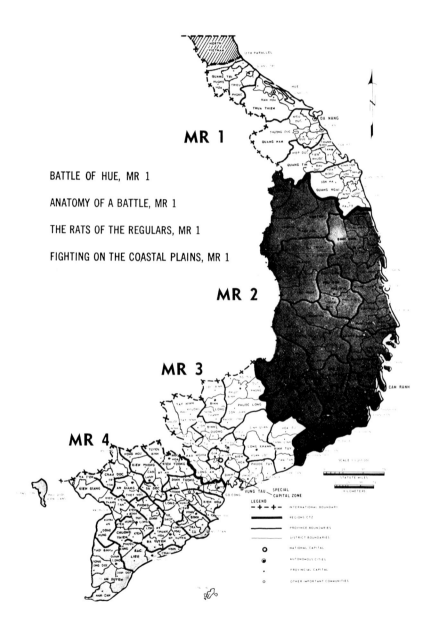

MR 1

BATTLE OF HUE, MR 1

ANATOMY OF A BATTLE, MR 1

THE RATS OF THE REGULARS, MR 1

FIGHTING ON THE COASTAL PLAINS, MR 1

MR 2

MR 3

MR 4

LEGEND
- + - INTERNATIONAL BOUNDARY
━ ● ━ REGIONS CTZ
━━━ PROVINCE BOUNDARIES
─── DISTRICT BOUNDARIES
○ NATIONAL CAPITAL
◉ AUTONOMOUS CITIES
• PROVINCIAL CAPITAL
○ OTHER IMPORTANT COMMUNITIES

Chapter 4

The Tet Offensive

The Battle of Hue

Captain George W. Smith

Hue, the ancient Imperial capital city of Vietnam, lies a hundred kilometers south of the 17th Parallel. It has a population of nearly 140,000, making it the third largest city in the Republic of Vietnam. The headquarters of the 1st Infantry Division, Army of the Republic of Vietnam, was in the northern corner of the Citadel of Hue.

The Citadel, or Imperial City, is the walled-in portion of Hue, sitting on the north bank of the Perfume River, and the barrier around the Citadel formed a 2,500 meter square. The outer stone wall was one-meter thick and five-meters high and was separated from the inner wall by dirt fill. The distance between the walls varied from 75 meters to 17.5 meters.

Within the Citadel was the palace area where the ancient emperors of Vietnam lived and in which some are buried. Hue was generally regarded as the most beautiful city in South Vietnam and was popular as a tourist site. In fact, during the last week of January 1968, thousands of visitors began arriving in Hue to celebrate Tet — the Vietnamese Lunar New Year and holiday of holidays — with their friends and relatives.

A cease-fire truce between North and South Vietnamese forces had gone into effect at 1800 hours, January 29th, but that very night, the enemy struck in many areas of South Vietnam with their largest offensive of the war. Hue was not one of those areas. At 0945 the next morning, though, the Tet truce in South Vietnam was officially terminated because of the truce violation and the 1st ARVN Infantry Division in Hue went on 100 percent alert.

First Lieutenant Nguyen Thi Tan, Reconnaissance Company Commander of the 1st Division, and 36 men were on a river and area surveillance mission four kilometers southwest of Hue during the night of January 30-31. At 2200, a Regional Force (RF) Company to their east was attacked by a large enemy force. Lieutenant Tan radioed information about enemy positions, strengths, and equipment to division headquarters as elements of at least two enemy battalions filtered past his position during the night — all headed toward Hue.

At 0340 two salvos of enemy rockets, launched from the mountains to the west of the city, flew over the company's position towards the Citadel and the whole city erupted in flames as the intense fighting broke out in all sections. The battle of Hue had begun.

Attack

The enemy drove two battalions, the 802d and the 800th, into the Citadel toward the 1st Division's headquarters. But as the latter unit approached the Hue city airfield at 0400, it ran into the 1st Division's reaction force, the all-volunteer Hac Bao, or Black Panther, Company.

Captain Tran Ngoc Hue, Hac Bao commander, positioned his men on the eastern side of the runway, facing west, and as the 800th NVA Battalion crossed the airfield it was met by a fusillade of M72 LAW rounds, breaking up the attack and creating a panic. The 800th was then diverted to the south, 1,000 meters short of the 1st Division Headquarters, after losing 30 men killed to the Hac Bao.

Meanwhile, the 802d NVA Battalion had pentrated the 1st Division compound and had occupied the area of the medical company. First Lieutenant Nguyen Ai, a member of the G2 section, gathered up 30 staff personnel, mostly clerks, and assaulted the enemy penetration. Though shot through the shoulder, Lieutenant Ai and his makeshift platoon killed five NVA soldiers in the compound and another 40 as they tried to flee to the west. An attack on the main gate was also repulsed.

By daylight, the enemy occupied the entire Citadel except for the corner that contained the division compound; identified as the 6th NVA Regiment, the enemy soldiers had established a blocking position with the 806th Battalion outside the northwest corner on Highway 1, the main reinforcing route from the north, and the red and blue Viet Cong flag flew from the Citadel's flagpole.

Defeat

Meanwhile, across the Perfume River to the south, the MACV compound was under attack from elements of the 4th NVA Regiment. Following a rocket and mortar attack, the 804th

Battalion with highly trained sapper personnel (demolition experts), tried to assult the compound but was thrown back by a hail of grenades and small arms fire. Enemy bodies found the next day revealed that the NVA unit had planned to overrun the compound and destroy it with explosives.

By daylight, the enemy controlled the entire Hue area except their two prime objectives — the 1st ARVN Division headquarters and the MACV compound. On the friendly side, plans were put into effect to get reinforcements to those two areas, and Brigadier General Ngo Quang Truong, Commanding General of the 1st Division, issued orders to his 3d Regiment, the Vietnamese 1st Airborne Task Force, and the 3d Troop, 7th ARVN Cavalry to move to the Citadel. At the same time, two companies and four tanks from the 1st Battalion, 1st US Marine Regiment at Phu Bai were also dispatched as a reaction force.

First Lieutenant Tran Van Minh, commander of the 3d Troop, 7th Cavalry, received the order early in the morning of 31 January to move his unit to Hue Citadel; he was told that the headquarters of the 1st Division was under attack and that the situation was serious. At 0920 his unit and the 7th Airborne Battalion departed their base camp, 17 kilometers north of Hue, and proceeded south on Highway 1. Four hundred meters short of the Citadel the enemy attacked the convoy with an estimated two battalions, and although Minh tried three times to break through he could not and he was forced to request additional help. The 2d Airborne Battalion was dispatched from the Quang Dien subsector and on the fourth attempt, these reinforcements made the difference.

Convoy

Early the following morning, February 1st, the convoy entered the division headquarters by the northern gate, although the units in the convoy had suffered numerous casualties. Too, the 3/7 Cavalry had lost four of its 12 armored personnel carriers.

The 2d and 3d Battalions of the 3d Regiment then moved east along the north bank of the Perfume River to the Citadel where they spread out along the southeast wall, unable to enter the walled city. The 1st and 4th Battalions of the 3d Regiment, which had been on operations southeast of Hue when the enemy's Tet offensive began, were completely surrounded by enemy forces and had to fight their way back to the city.

Captain Phan Ngoc Luong, commander of the 1st Battalion of the 3d Regiment, after breaking the enemy encirclement, had maneuvered his unit eastward under constant harassment to the coastal outpost of Ba Lang. During an emergency resupply mission on the way to the outpost, Captain Luong had had to call in air-strikes on the enemy to allow his troops to retrieve the ammunition. On February 1st, the battalion boarded Vietnamese mortorized junks and arrived at division headquarters at 1500.

Surrounded

Major Nguyen Huu Lu, commanding officer of the 4th Battalion, 3d Regiment, had found his unit totally surrounded by the 804th NVA Battalion on the morning of January 31st, and it took the unit four days of continuous fighting to break the enemy encirclement and reach the MACV compound. By February 4th, only 170 men from the battalion had managed to get to the compound.

Meanwhile, the two companies of US Marines from the 1st Battalion, 1st Regiment and four tanks that had moved north from Phu Bai during the morning of January 31st, had run into the 1st Battalion of the 4th NVA Regiment, first at the An Cuu Bridge

site on Highway 1 and then again only 700 meters south of the MACV compound. The Marines finally arrived at the compound at 1420 but only after suffering many casualties.

Both of the Marine companies then crossed to the north side of the Perfume River and attempted to enter the Citadel, but were thrown back as the enemy, firmly entrenched between the Citadel walls, kept up a heavy volume of fire. The Marines returned to the MACV compound and together with the rest of the battalion, which joined the next day, proceeded to enlarge the friendly perimeter on the south side of the river. To accelerate the expansion, the 2d Battalion of the 5th US Marine Regiment from Phu Bai reinforced the 1/1 Battalion on February 2d.

Sweep

On February 1st, the 2d and 7th Vietnamese Airborne Battalions, together with the 3/7 Cavalry and the Hac Bao Company, swept toward the west and recaptured the airfield. On the same day, one-half of the 4th Battalion, 2d Regiment was airlifted from Dong Ha to the Citadel where it deployed south of the division headquarters. The next day, the rest of the 4/2 Battalion, a company from the 3/1 Battalion, and the 9th ARVN Airborne Battalion were airlifted into division headquarters. While the 9th Airborne Battalion joined its sister units near the airfield the 1st Battalion, 3d Regiment went into position along the northwest wall.

During the first few days, the three airborne units reported killing over 200 of the enemy in the vicinity of the airfield, and on February 4th the 1/3 Battalion took the An Hoa Gate and the northwest wall and pushed toward the western corner. The 4/2 Battalion also made good progress on the eastern side of the Citadel, and moved about halfway before the enemy resistance stiffened. Casualty figures on the 4th revealed that 693 enemy had been killed in the Citadel and to the northwest on Highway 1.

On the 5th, the airborne task force was redeployed along the northeast wall and the 4/2 Battalion took up positions by the airfield; on the following day, the 4/2 Battalion drove all the way to the southwest wall and set up its CP on the breastwork. But on the night of February 6-7th, the enemy attacked this position six times and forced the battalion off the walls. At one time during the night the enemy came over the walls from the west with grappling hooks, and the 4/2 Battalion had to fall back, finally reorganizing near the southern end of the airfield.

Remnants

On February 5th, too, the 4/3 Battalion managed to cross the Perfume River and assault the south gate of the Citadel seven times, although it was never able to enter the city. Eventually, the remnants of the unit took up positions adjacent to the 2d

and 3d Battalions of the 3d Regiment just outside the southeast wall and along the Perfume River.

On the 6th, the 1/3 Battalion attacked and secured the western corner of the Citadel wall. Then, during the early morning hours of the 7th, the six-span bridge, the last overland link with the two battalions of US Marines on the south side of the Perfume River, was destroyed.

Unable to penetrate the Citadel from the south, the three battalions of the 3d Regiment (the 2d, 3d and 4th) were put aboard Vietnamese junks and transported by water to the division headquarters on the 7th; they were then deployed to the airfield area the next day, relieving the 4/2 Battalion.

Some days before, on February 3d, to be exact, First Lieutenant Nguyen Hoa, commanding officer of the 2d Troop, 7th Cavalry, had been ordered to move his unit from Quang Tri to the Hue Citadel. But the 2/7 Cavalry and the 1st Regiment, 1st Division were then hotly engaged in the provincial capital city and Lieutenant Hoa could not extricate his unit for deployment in Hue. On February 6th, though, he did break out of the city and began moving south on Highway 1 with 15 armored personnel carriers and one company of Infantry from the 2d Battalion, 1st Regiment.

Breather

Stopping at Camp Evans that night, the convoy started out the following morning for Hue. About 12 kilometers north of the Citadel, the convoy cut east and then south across rice paddies and entered the division headquarters at 1700; it had traveled all the way without any enemy contact and without any .50 caliber ammunition. The units were then rearmed and deployed to the airfield area, thereby giving the 3/7 Cavalry a breather.

The weather for this first week of fighting — overcast and chilly — had enabled the enemy to move men and supplies into the Citadel without the threat of allied air power. On February 7th, though, the Vietnamese Air Force managed to drop twenty-four 500-pound bombs on the soutwest wall for the first large-scale aerial bombing; enemy casualties soared to over 1,200 killed.

By the end of the first week, an intelligence estimate placed two enemy battalions within the Citadel; one in the southwest, the other in the southeast. A third enemy battalion remained outside the western corner to block Highway 1, and the enemy still maintained his capability of resupplying in large quantities from the west.

The general picture during the next week February 7th-12th indicated a well-dug-in enemy offering stiff resistance and with little headway being made by the ARVN forces. The enemy, infiltrating fresh troops each night, continued to probe the 3d Regimental positions near the airfield.

A company of US Marines from the 1st Battalion, 5th Regiment, reinforced with five tanks, arrived by boat at division headquarters on the night of the 11th, and on the following day the rest of the battalion arrived and took over the southeastern portion of the city, relieving the airborne task force.

Fresh Units

The 1st and 5th Battalions of Vietnamese Marines from Task Force Alfa arrived on the 12th with six 105mm howitzers and were deployed to the southwestern portion of the city; these green beret troops had been fighting in Saigon during the early part of the enemy's Tet Offensive.

Both of these fresh units had the mission to sweep toward the southeast wall, a distance of about 1,000 meters, but the enemy, during the previous days, had taken advantage of a heavy overcast and a lull in the ARVN offensive to strengthen his positions in the Citadel with new men and supplies. Consequently, on the 12th, when the battle was renewed by fresh troops on both sides, the same savage street fighting took place that was so reminiscent of the first few days.

The 3d Regiment and the 2/7 Cavalry first contended with the enemy salient west of the airfield, but on the 14th, the enemy broke out of this salient and cut off the 1st Battalion of the 3d Regiment in the western corner. The Hac Bao Company and the 2/7 Cavalry eventually broke the encirclement two days later.

Vital Gate

On the 14th, the 1/5 Battalion of US Marines attempted to take a vital gate on the northeast wall but was thrown back by a well-dug-in enemy; the Leathernecks did succeed the next day as artillery and 200 rounds of five and six-inch naval gunfire softened up the position. Air strikes by VNAF, US Marine and US Air Force bombers increased on the 14th and 15th, with most of the ordnance being delivered along the southwest wall.

The Vietnamese Marines, moving cautiously in the southwest, killed 39 enemy on the 15th and captured a valuable schoolhouse only a block from the Palace; found in the classrooms were 22 weapons eighty 60mm mortar rounds, and 10 grenades. It was also learned on the 16th that the commanding officer of the enemy forces in the Citadel had been killed and that his replacement had immediately requested permission to withdraw his troops from the city; permission had been refused and he had been told to defend in place. By now, very costly harassing artillery and naval gunfire made enemy movement difficult at night, especially to the west of the city.

Vice President Nguyen Cao Ky flew to Phu Bai on the 16th to receive a status report on the battle, and promised General Truong additional support, expressing his confidence for total victory in Hue. That same day, the 4th Battalion of the Vietnamese Marines arrived in the Citadel. They were dispatched to the western corner on the 17th and were given the mission of sweeping down the southwest wall to cut off an enemy infiltration route. The resistance was tough, however, and after two days the 4th Battalion had gained only 400 meters.

Push

On the 18th the Hac Bao and Reconnaissance Companies moved to the right flank of the US Marines along the northeast wall of the Palace, while the 4th Vietnamese Marine Battalion joined its sister units on the 19th for a determined push to the southwest wall.

On February 21st, the 1st Cavalry Division Airmobile sent four battalions on a sweep through the La Chu area, five kilometers to the northwest, and a suspected enemy regimental headquarters was overrun the following day. The Cavalrymen had four men killed, but the enemy suffered 41 killed and had 23 weapons captured.

Meanwhile, the US Marines, using their tanks and Ontos vehicles, crunched to within one block of the southeast wall. There, after receiving a fresh company for the final push, they reached the southeast wall on the 22d, with the 2/3 ARVN Battalion on their right flank.

At 0630 on the 22d, the NVA, feeling the pressure of the advancing 1st Cavalry Division, launched a massive ground attack through the southwest wall against the 3d Regiment and the 4th and 5th Battalions of the Vietnamese Marines. Eight-inch fire from the 1st Cavalry Division and from ARVN 105mm

howit: for a two-hour period broke the back of the offensive. The Hac Bao Company then spearheaded a counterattack by the 3d Regiment, resulting in 150 enemy killed, while the Vietnamese Marines' counterattack resulted in 48 enemy killed and 23 weapons captured.

The 21st and 39th ARVN Ranger Battalion formed outside the northeast wall, also on the 22d, and began to sweep south on the large island east of the city. These Rangers, part of the MR 1 reaction force, met light to moderate resistance during their three-day operation, killing 55 enemy.

Raid

During the following night, the enemy launched a last-ditch rocket and mortar attack, followed by a ground assault in the western area of the city, but the ARVN artillery answered with over 300 rounds in this area and by daylight the attack had ceased. While this action was taking place, in the southern portion of the Citadel, the 2/3 Battalion conducted a surprise night raid along the southeast wall and seized the area around the main flagpole. At 0500 on the 24th the Viet Cong flag, which had flown for 24 days, was ripped down and the flag of the Republic of Vietnam was hoisted in its place.

At 0730 on the 24th, the 3d Regiment, Hac Bao Company, and the 2/7 Cavalry moved forward to the southwest wall and met only light resistance. By 1025 the 3d Regiment had moved to the wall and secured it. General Truong then issued orders to the Hac Bao Company and 2/3 Battalion to take the Palace, and the units entered it at 1515; by 1700 the Palace had been secured. At no time during the 25-day battle had any artillery fire or airstrikes been called in on the grounds, although the walls surrounding the area had been partially destroyed.

The Vietnamese Marines also began to move, slowly at first, but when the resistance proved light, by nightfall they had swept all the way to the southeast wall. At 0500 on the 25th, after 70 artillery rounds had plastered the southern corner, the last stronghold in the city fell and the Citadel was declared secure. Fifty-six enemy weapons were captured, together with 102 rounds of B40 ammunition, sixteen 60 mm mortar rounds, sixteen 82mm mortar rounds, and 158 assorted grenades.

Intercept

Meanwhile, four battalions from the 1st Cavalry Division had been sitting just to the north and west of the Citadel in perfect position to intercept the withdrawing enemy. These troops killed 152 enemy soldiers, in addition to capturing 96 weapons.

General Truong paid special tribute to his 3d Regiment, which had been in continuous combat for 26 straight days when he said, "They fought long and hard. Many fought without knowing how their families were, always wondering if they were sti'l alive. They were subjected every night to enemy attacks by fresh troops who infiltrated from the west. They did very well."

Late in the morning of February 25th the President of South Vietnam, Nguyen Van Thieu, flew into the 1st ARVN Division headquarters to congratulate General Truong on his victory. The President, a former commanding general of the division, had nothing but praise for the defenders of Hue. When he departed, a feeling of all-was-well spread across the smiling faces of the Vietnamese who now could begin the long process of rebuilding.

Much of the city lay in ruins and many people were homeless. Many days would be needed to search the surrounding areas for weapons, ammunition, and guerrillas who might still be present. But the 1st ARVN Division had won the biggest battle of its life, perhaps the biggest victory in the modern Vietnamese conflict, and one that had involved the most savage street-fighting in the nation's history. Intelligence sources estimate that 16 NVA Battalions, or two divisions, had been committed against Hue. Despite the enemy's best effort, 2,642 of his soldiers had been killed in the battle of Hue, and he would never fully recover from this blow.

Anatomy of a Battle

Major David R. Collins

On the evening of February 3, 1968, Company C, 1st Battalion, 35th Infantry had been ordered to occupy a ridgeline overlooking an ARVN compound and an RF/PF outpost. Both of the installations had been hard hit during the past three days by a regimental-size force of VC and NVA troops. The ridgeline afforded a commanding view of the area north of these two installations, where the enemy was most active. The terrain was flat and densely to sparsely vegetated and populated. It was bounded on the west by an abandoned railroad, on the north by a river, and on the south by a highway along which were located the ARVN/PF units, a Republic of Korea (ROK) marine battalion, and a ROK marine 105mm howitzer battalion. Far to the east was Highway 1, which paralleled the South China Sea. Company C occupied a position on the ridgeline about 300 meters west of the ARVN, along with Alfa Company.

101

The battalion wanted to conduct operations in the area, but first had to obtain brigade's approval and effect close coordination with friendly units in the area. The plan called for the ARVN units and ROK marines to remain in their compounds and act as a blocking force along the highway, which would be the southern boundary. Two companies, Charlie Company, which I commanded, and Captain Charles Chaplinski's Alfa Company, would make initial moves into the area, pushing west to east; Bravo Company, commanded by Captain Donald Reh, would enter the area later and occupy a position to the east as a blocking force. It looked good—there were three howitzer batteries that could fire for the companies and excellent flying weather in case air support was needed. The entire chain of command was enthusiastic about the operation. Every unit was up to strength and spoiling for a firefight.

The next day, following six airstrikes on suspected enemy locations, Charlie Company moved off the ridgeline around 1430. It was to proceed to a small abandoned village west of the railroad tracks and secure a jump-off point for the other two companies the next day. By 1500 the village was occupied, with no enemy contact enroute. The 4th platoon (weapons) was sent to find a night location in a graveyard west of and adjacent to the village; the remainder were to search the village.

A heavy volume of small arms fire broke out to the northeast, in the vicinity of the railroad tracks; 4th platoon took cover and suppressed the fire before the other platoons could engage. There were no friendly or confirmed enemy casualties in the exchange and the platoon proceeded to the graveyard, established a perimeter and started digging in. Each man was required to dig a fighting position each night on the perimeter and the company CP was not excluded. An LP was reconnoitered on the eastern end of the village and fields of fire to the east were cut and cleared with demolitions for the main body. Resupply came by helicopter and included a .50 caliber machinegun. Lieutenant Monty LaFitte, the FO, registered defensive concentrations around the perimeter and the men settled in for the night.

The LP was sent out at dusk and consisted of seven men, including the artillery reconnaissance sergeant. At 2230, automatic weapons fire, and claymore and grenade detonations erupted in the vicinity of the LP. Then we hear the tell-tale "thump thump" of mortars being fired. Someone yelled, "Incoming, incoming, get a hole!" Everyone was in fighting positions before the first round hit. Men on the eastern side of the perimeter were yelling, "LP on the way in!" The mortar attack was accompanied by a heavy volume of small arms and automatic weapons fire from the northeast.

As soon as the barrage lifted, the .50 caliber machinegun opened up to the northeast and M60s opened up all around the perimeter. The automatic weapons fire was suppressed and we started yelling for casualty reports, which were surprisingly negative. First Sergeant Antonio Cartagena advised battalion of the situation and Lieutenant LaFitte started calling in illumination. One of the NCOs then yelled, "Get down in your hole, there's NVA in the perimeter!" He threw an illumination grenade into a hedgerow and killed an enemy soldier. The batttalion commander, Lt. Col. William W. Taylor, was contacted and advised of the situation, including the suspected presence of a sapper squad in the area and a ground attack possibly on the way. A flareship was requested. It was then around 2330. The flareship came on station around 0030 and stayed until daybreak. Throughout the night claymores were detonated toward suspicious sounds and movements, but no ground attack came.

The next morning, February 5th, Alfa Company, which had viewed the action of the previous night, moved off the ridgeline into our position. They coordinated the days' activities; Charlie was to move east across the railroad and secure a foothold in the objective area and Alfa would follow. At this point, the companies would then link up their flanks and push east, with Charlie Company on the north, Alfa on the south. This phase of the operation was to be a thorough search and destroy mission. Bravo Company, at that time to the south, would proceed to a location about 4,000 meters due east of Charlie and have a blocking position set up by the next morning.

Following a detailed briefing for the platoon leaders and a heavy artillery preparation, the company moved out. Everyone sensed a fight and experienced the ⊦nsion that precedes battle. They waited for that opening burst but it never came. There was negative contact. The flanks of the two companies linked up and they moved out on line, as best they could. Dense foliage did not permit a smooth flow into the intial positions they had hoped for, and visual contact between the flanks was hard to maintain. On the search, the two companies located numerous boxed 81mm mortar rounds, 50 pounds of TNT and some plastic explosive, six tons of bagged rice, medical supplies consisting mostly of narcotics, and .50 caliber ammunition. All the items were buried in loose dirt and camouflaged with twigs and dead leaves.

The area had been pounded repeatedly by airstrikes and artillery the preceding days. No one had ever seen an area more thoroughly plastered and the smell was acrid from white phosphorus and rotting vegetation. Late in the day, Alfa Company's 1st platoon, led by Lieutenant Kerry Nogle, killed an NVA attempting to evade. He was in green uniform and carrying a French submachinegun and six grenades. Throughout the day Charlie Company encountered expertly fortified villages and mortar and antiaircraft positions, all fresh but unoccupied. It was getting late and both companies veered off to the south to form a joint perimeter for the night in another graveyard. Graveyards offer good LZs, excellent fields of fire, and the mounds, peculiar to the Vietnamese, offer good protection if hit while digging in.

The company commanders, Chaplinski and I, agreed that a large NVA force had been there quite recently preparing for sustained operations, but had been forced out by artillery and napalm strikes. The NVA had apparently moved north across the river, possibly completely out of the area. The battalion commander concurred. Lieutenant Colonel Taylor wanted to complete a search of the area and move north to pursue. A new northern boundary had to be coordinated all the way to III Marine Amphibious Force headquarters. The companies were directed to resume operations the next day where they had left off and continue eastward toward Bravo Company, which was set to move into position the next morning. During chow Charlie Company received a burst from an AK47 to the north—it had been trailed into its position. It was just harassing fire and no contact developed.

At 0800 the next morning, February 6th, the companies moved out. Due to unfavorable terrain, Alfa and Charlie agreed not to work shoulder-to-shoulder and an east-west trail was picked as the boundary. Charlie Company again would work the northern sector and Alfa Company the southern.

No enemy contact was made by either company. But every village was fortified with bunkers and connecting trenchlines, punji pits and helicopter traps in likely landing zones. These fortifications were virtually hidden from the air. One thing was sure—the enemy knew his business. Bravo Company, then in position, killed three NVA trying to evade across the river. This, it was thought, confirmed that the enemy had moved north and was leaving troops behind to harass, delay, and confuse the pursuing Americans. Late in the day, 3d platoon, led by Lieutenant Joseph Llewellyn, was sent to link up with Bravo, fix friendly positions and get a feel for the terrain. Once more, a joint perimeter was set up with Alfa Company in a large, open, dry rice paddy. Patrols were sent to check out surrounding villages and hedgerows for snipers. They had brief exchanges of fire with NVA moving in again to harass the perimeter. There were no friendly or enemy casualties. Both company forward observers fired defensive concentrations close to the perimeter. The companies dug in for the night and waited for enemy probes, but none came. The night passed without incident.

At around 2100, Colonel Taylor put out a net call outlining plans for the next day. A northern boundary extension had been granted. Bravo would cross the river during darkness and secure crossing sites for Charlie and Alfa Companies. Bravo's reconnaissance party had already found a shallow point in the river. Once Bravo had the crossing site secured and the companies had crossed, Bravo was to move northeast about 3,000 meters, then move north another 1,500 meters. From the crossing site, Charlie would move north about 500 meters, then east 2,000 meters, and from that point veer off towards the north once again for 1,000 meters. Alfa would cross behind Charlie, contour generally eastward along the river for 2,000 meters and move north about 500 meters to a point south of Charlie. When all companies attained these positions, they were to jump off due westward in rapid movement to gain contact and have enough elements available to maneuver and exploit any major contact, with plenty of daylight left to develop it. The sky was slightly overcast, but favored the employment of high performance aircraft. Since a contact with a major enemy element appeared imminent, air support was essential.

At 0500 the next morning, Bravo reached the river. The first platoon across had secured the crossing site for the main body when a firefight erupted. The enemy was firing into Bravo's security platoon from the north, and Bravo was temporarily pinned down. The exchange ended, leaving two NVA killed and no friendly casualties. One of the enemy troops carried an AK47, the other an M14. The remainder of what was estimated as a squad had withdrawn. It was now shortly after first light, about 0600, and Charlie started to move out, led by the 3d platoon which had covered the ground the day earlier. There were no incidents and the crossing site was secured for Alfa. Bravo consolidated and moved out. Alfa moved quickly across and then Charlie moved out. We were making good time; it was shortly after 0700. Bravo and Charlie Companies moved eastward with an aeroscout and a gunship screening to the front. Before a kilometer had been covered Charlie's lead element made light contact with a small enemy force. A brief exchange of fire took place, then the enemy broke contact and moved eastward. There were no friendly or confirmed enemy casualties despite a blood trail. With Bravo on the right flank, Charlie moved eastward quickly, hoping to locate the enemy's main body; another 500 meters and still no contact. The enemy's actions were puzzling. Was he delaying, diverting or setting up a trap? Charlie moved another 500 meters, to the point at which it was to turn north, and again traded fire with a small enemy element. One man was wounded.

Charlie Company was on the eastern edge of a small village and the fire was coming from another village to the east, across 300 meters of dry rice paddy. Gunships were called in to strafe the treeline of the village with rockets and miniguns. Three platoons were deployed on line and entered the village. Again, no enemy KIA. The village was fortified and even included three strands of barbed wire strung on long pickets in front of the trenches. The area was further east than Charlie was to have gone and Bravo company was contacted to inform them of this. Bravo, about 600 meters to the right rear, had just come under fire from a sniper team. Their return fire cracked overhead, and

Charlie withdrew to its last position to give Bravo free fire in the area.

Alfa Company then pulled into position south of Charlie. The S3, Major John Joyce, called and asked if Charlie could control an airstrike 800 meters to the north. We gave him an "affirmative" and as the FAC marked the target, Charlie Company broke for first meal that day, around 1300. The exchanges of fire had eaten up a lot of time, and Bravo was still having difficulty. Two or three sniper teams had inflicted a few casualties and a medevac chopper had gone down in the LZ with a round through the engine. The gunships Bravo was using to ferret out the snipers had flushed out two NVA to the south. They were killed by a rifleman and a grenadier.

Charlie Company waited to see if it could assist Bravo. By 1430 Bravo had taken care of the snipers, but had to secure the downed ship and wait for it to be lifted out. No aircraft were available to retrieve the downed craft. Bravo would have to stay there overnight. Charlie proceeded north, through long rows of huts and thick undergrowth, hoping to flush out some snipers or gain contact. It moved slowly, searching, and at 1600 arrived at its destination.

A hasty perimeter was established to accept resupply, and patrols were sent across a small stream to the west and into a small village to the north. The patrols were to stay out until resupply was complete. In the event the helicopters were sniped at, there would be men on the ground to fix and destroy them. The resupply took place without incident and Charlie Company started digging in for the night. Alfa was at its designated location to the south. Bravo remained southeast of Charlie and due east of Alfa. Defensive targets were fired in close again. The .50 caliber machinegun was test-fired to the east, the patrols brought in, and the night perimeter established.

The next morning, February 8th, the log bird extracted the empty mermite cans, mailbags and the .50 caliber machinegun. Charlie was to search a village to the southwest and then move due west. Alfa Company, to the south, would move due west. Bravo was to proceed to its original objective, placing the company northeast of Charlie. An armored cavalry platoon of five APCs would link up with Bravo, to provide the companies with 15 additional automatic weapons in the event of heavy contact by Alfa or Charlie.

After the five APCs linked up with Bravo at 0830, Company C headed southwest. Artillery was adjusted in the direction of movement to provide immediate adjustment points and two airstrikes, both with napalm, high explosives and 20mm cannon, were to precede us. Charlie moved slowly, methodically searching abandoned huts which were then burned. This tactic denied the

enemy any shelter if he moved into the area after US troops departed.

Two explosions from burning huts shook the rear of the formation, probably boobytraps or dud rounds from the 105s that the enemy likes to store for future use. Before the men of Charlie swung due west, they waited for the airstrikes. It was a little past noon, so they stopped for chow and watched the airstrikes go in. Men looking skyward as the F105s zipped overhead yelled "Keep pushin', baby, keep pushin'." By 1300, the airstrikes were complete, and Charlie moved in to search the village and evaluate the airstrike. The search was thorough, but yielded nothing save a few documents, NVA mess gear and a few uniforms, freshly washed and neatly folded.

On the right flank, an enemy sniper suddenly fired at the point man at nearly point blank range. The point man's ear was scratched as the round whistled past him. The two platoons on the right flank moved forward cautiously and chased two NVA into the underbrush. Further search failed to produce them, and the company moved west, in the enemy's direction of flight. The sweep through the deserted village resulted in no further contact and the airstrike assessments were negative.

It was then 1630 and Company C was well ahead of Alfa company, so we located a good night position in a graveyard west of the village. Observation and fields of fire were excellent. As the first sergeant began to coordinate resupply, the platoon leaders were assembled and debriefed. Maps were taken out and actions for the following day discussed. Every village in the area but one had been checked. The last one, about 1500 meters to the north required movement through a broad field of dry rice paddies and chest-high elephant grass. This village would be the next day's target.

At dusk, three-man teams were sent out about 100 meters from the perimeter to set up tripflares. Resupply had not come. The choppers, busy throughout the day, had run out of daylight. Charlie wanted the .50 caliber machinegun and an 81mm mortar, but did not request it on an emergency basis. Night flying around large NVA units endangers the crew and the lights invite mortar attacks: Charlie did without them. Shortly after dark, male voices were heard about 150 meters away, but they didn't sound like Vietnamese. One of the soldiers whispered, "Sir, they're saying 'American go back, go back home.' " Orders were issued to hold fire; no positions were to be given away. Hopefully, a tripflare would go off where there was an M60 zeroed in, but no such luck. Battalion was informed of the activity—the first of the NVA's psyops programs to be encountered. It was a new experience for everyone. The FO adjusted 105 rounds in the vicinity of the voices, which quieted them. He further coordinated numerous harassing and interdictory targets in and around the adjacent village. A rather uneasy night passed without further incident.

The next morning Charlie was held up waiting for Bravo to get a bit closer. They were limited in route planning because of the APCs and couldn't move as fast as Alfa and Charlie companies. Alfa was held up about 1500 meters south. As Charlie waited, it received mail, C-rations, and ammunition resupply. At 0930, with Bravo making good progress, Charlie Company moved out. Not wanting to cross all the open area to the north, the 2d and 4th platoons would move 500 meters northeast to a treeline. They would wait there while the 1st and 3d platoons linked up with them. We would then move through the trees and light undergrowth, to the objective. The company command group moved behind the 2d platoon, with the lead platoon on the right flank.

As the lead element approached the treeline, sniper rounds cracked from the north into the CP group. The 2d platoon leader was told to move into the trees along with the 4th platoon, so that the two platoons could be used to maneuver towards the fire, while the two left flank platoons, the 1st and 3d, deployed as a fixing force. The movement was rapid and looked good. The two left flank platoons were deployed on line behind paddy dikes which were overgrown with grass. The CP group had started to move with the maneuver element when mortar rounds fell on the left flank. The platoon leader and medic were hit, as well as a few others. More mortar rounds fell as the platoon prepared to move out from under them with its wounded. The machineguns had started firing and the men looked in that direction. No one could believe their eyes. About 250 to 300 NVA were standing in rows, covered with grass from the shoulders up. They were about 30 meters away. Some of them waved and yelled "Hello, GI!"

At this point, the company was deployed in a backward L-shape, and fire cut into the enemy ranks from each platoon. The right flank was in good shape; no casualties, because of good cover and fields of fire into the fully visible enemy from about 100 meters. The left flank was hurt; it was taking the full impact of the enemy's machinegun, small arms, mortar, and now B40 rocket fire. Two NCOs took charge of the left flank and organized the defenses, pulling the wounded to cover behind them. One platoon leader had been killed. Individual soldiers were trying to draw fire as buddies pulled the wounded back. Two soldiers, spotting a large enemy group squatting in the grass on their left, ran to that point and killed 16 NVA. It was bewildering; some of the enemy stood straight up and covered their faces with their hands or turned their heads, waiting to be shot. Others began crawling toward the Americans across a dry rice paddy and were killed. Very few of them fired their AK47s. Some of Co C's troops were yelling profanities at the enemy as they fired. Others were laughing and shouting encouragement to their buddies as the enemy fell. Because the enemy might try to assault the platoons' position, gunships were summoned. Charlie Company had taken six KIA and numerous wounded. Locations were marked with smoke for the battalion commander, now airborne in the command and control ship.

Intense fire cut into the smoke; the NVA knew what was happening. The gunships came up on the company's radio net, confirmed the location, and made a dry run to insure their pattern was safe. Given quick approval, they made rocket runs followed by strafing runs with their miniguns. The enemy soldiers jumped like marionettes as they were hit. The gunships continued until their ordnance was expended and another team came on station. The battalion commander was maneuvering Bravo Company toward the action. It was now eight friendly KIA and 20 wounded. Fire had broken out to the right rear and Alfa, to the south, was maneuvering to engage the enemy in that location.

The right flank was adjusted to cover the rear. Charlie Company was now deployed in an inverted T-shaped formation. Bravo, enroute, had an APC knocked out by recoilless rifle fire and was also in heavy contact. With the aid of artillery and the heavy automatic weapons aboard the APCs, they were slowly breaking through to Charlie's position, literally blasting their way through.

Alfa Company had also met heavy resistance and was stopped about 500 meters to the south, so gunships were diverted to Alfa to help them break through. The enemy at that location was fighting from bunkers. The gunships' rockets did little damage, but helped fix the enemy in place. When the gunships broke station, massive artillery concentrations replaced them.

Suddenly, the battle was over. The enemy broke contact and ran, leaving their dead and weapons behind. Charlie Company suffered 10 killed and 31 wounded. Enemy dead were stacked all around. The mortar that had hurt the left flank had been destroyed when two riflemen had spotted it, had run 100 meters through an open rice paddy, killed the enemy crew, and then carried the tube back to their position. They had been new replacements in their first heavy contact.

The first sergeant had again taken charge of the situation. Firing subsided, save for a few brief exchanges. The action shifted to Bravo and Alfa Companies. Charlie consolidated its position, forming a box-shaped perimeter to protect its wounded and prepare for a counterattack. The men had hurt the enemy badly; those NVA that could, ran. Charlie was never penetrated. Intensive care was given to the wounded, but it still wasn't safe enough for medevac.

Late in the day, Bravo broke through to Charlie's position. Combined, they could easily handle a counterattack. It had done a magnificent job fighting through to Charlie, destroying many enemy personnel and weapons enroute. As darkness approached, Alfa Company broke contact and formed a perimeter to the south. Bravo and Charlie Companies organized a joint perimeter and men from both companies hugged each other. A major enemy unit had been met and badly crippled. Casualty figures were double-checked and the RTO called in a final count of 10 friendly KIA, 33 WIA for Charlie Company. As darkness fell, 70 enemy KIA had been counted on one portion of the battlefield alone. Enemy individual and crew-served weapons were stacked high in a pile. The wounded were in pain but not in critical condition. The two medics left were busy caring for them, as they had all day. All were in good spirits. Medevac was refused, as everyone thought the enemy was still out there, preparing for a night attack. The situation did not favor a night medevac. The night passed but no attack came, because the enemy had broken contact. The next morning, the medevac helicopters took out the wounded. Over 100

enemy KIA and 70 weapons were counted, and assorted maps, field glasses, and other gear were stacked up. Three more NVA were killed trying to recover weapons. The first sergeant, shot in the arm, watched in silence as the wounded were medevaced.

The enemy had been met and defeated, and it was time to lick our wounds and get set for the next meeting we would have with him.

NOTE: In this action below Hoi An, in Miltiary Region 1, on February 9, 1968 during the Tet Offensive, over 200 NVA were accounted for by the men of Company C. The 1st Battalion, 35th Infantry, 4th Infantry Division, was credited with over 300 NVA KIA.

The Rats of the Regulars

Major Joseph M. McDonnell

The 1st Battalion, 6th Infantry (The Regulars) had just rendered a battalion of the 2d North Vietnamese Army Division combat ineffective while participating in a three-day operation south-southwest of the city of Da Nang. Called Operation Miracle, it was conducted by a task force consisting of two battalions of the American Division under the operational control of the 1st Marine Division. With the enemy threat to the city of Da Nang and US and RVN military installations in the Da Nang area alleviated, the battalion was redeployed on February 12, 1968 to Landing Zone Baldy (vicinity of Hoi An, Quang Nam Province, RVN) and placed under the operational control of the 3d Brigade, 4th US Infantry Division Task Force, which was at that time under the operational control of the American Division. The brigade commander, Colonel George E. Wear, had several missions to accomplish, but first and foremost among them was a requirement to maintain contact with and destroy elements of the 2d NVA Division that were now retreating from the lowlands in the central portion of Military Region 1 through the many valley routes to the hills and the enemy base areas in the mountain regions along the Laotian border. To accomplish this mission, the brigade deployed several maneuver battalions in the Que Son Valley and established several forward firebases to block the westerly movement of the enemy.

The 1st Battalion, 6th Infantry, commanded by Lieutenant Colonel William J. Baxley, Jr., was one of the maneuver battalions participating in this concerted effort of Col. Wear's brigade. As a result, the preponderance of the battalion's combat power was deployed to the foothills and mountains west of LZ Baldy along the northern fringe of Que Son Valley. The battalion also had an implied task of securing its operational base area and a specified task of participation in the minesweeping operations and security of Highway 535. Highway 535 was classified open (secure) at that time from its intersection with Highway 1 (vicinity of LZ Baldy) to LZ Ross, approximately 17 kilometers west of Highway 1 in the Que Son Valley. The security of this line of communication was vital to mission accomplishment for two reasons: First, the road provided a land route west of LZ Ross for the movement of supplies to the forward battalions, thus decreasing the blade time of helicopters in a logistical role and allowing for their more effective utilization in the mission of finding and destroying the enemy; and second, the security of this road was essential to the combined US/RVN pacification effort in the area.

The initial modus operandi of the battalion in accomplishing its firebase and road security mission was to task each maneuver company, on a rotating basis, to deploy a reinforced platoon to the battalion base area for a three to five-day period. This platoon would deploy each morning at first light to provide security for engineer minesweeping teams from LZ Baldy to a point midway between LZ Baldy and LZ Ross. An Infantry platoon from another battalion was performing a similar requirement starting from LZ Ross until it met the 1/6 Infantry platoon on the road. When the minesweep was complete, the road was considered secure for vehicular movement. (A secure line of communication in RVN implies that it is open; however, security forces are needed for vehicular or personnel movement.)

Normally, 30 to 40-vehicle convoys would deploy from LZ Baldy to LZ Ross on a daily basis. The start time of these convoys would vary and they were always escorted by security forces consisting of armored cavalry, mechanized Infantry elements or both. Despite the minesweeping operations and convoy security, the enemy was successful in damaging or destroying at lease one vehicle per day as these convoys moved to LZ Ross. In addition

to vehicular damage or destruction, and the corresponding personnel casualties, the problem was compounded by the configuration of Highway 535. The road was narrow (its width accommodating only single column vehicular movement) and was characterized by several dips and turns with small villages or dense vegetation on either side. These factors enabled the enemy to emplace mines on the road after the minesweeps or deploy personnel with antitank weapons to favorable ambush locations without being observed. His successful interdiction of the road and the inability of convoy commanders to deploy their forces around damaged or destroyed vehicles because of adverse trafficability conditions on either side of the road necessitated the immediate redeployment of a maneuver company or companies to secure the convoy until tanks or tank retrievers could remove the damaged vehicles. As a result, the enemy was accomplishing three very important missions with a minimum of personnel: He was impeding the movement of convoys on Highway 535; he was demonstrating to the people in Que Son Valley that he could interdict the highway despite his recent and severe defeats in the area; and he was diverting friendly maneuver elements away from contact with the retreating 2d NVA Division.

The problem required immediate action, not only because of the enemy activity on the road, but more importantly, because of the pressing operational requirement to deploy maximum combat power forward in order to maintain contact with a large enemy force that was finding itself faced with a virtually impossible task of retreating from the Americal Division. Lt. Col. Baxley's initial decision was to deploy an entire company along the road. The decision was difficult in light of his limited combat assets. Therefore, it was necessary to eliminate the enemy force in a minimum period of time. Bravo Company, commanded by Captain Dan A. Prather, was the initial company selected for this mission. The company was directed to conduct sweeps along either side of the road during the day and ambush the road at night.

It was apparent that the enemy had deployed a covering force to support the withdrawal of his main force Viet Cong and NVA units from their objective areas. Essential to the destruction of this force was information pertaining to its strength, location, unit identification and previous operational patterns. Pending a more detailed analysis of weather, enemy and terrain in this area, it was assumed that the enemy unit was probably a local force Viet Cong platoon, since this type of unit was most capable of conducting harassing operations. Coordination with ARVN forces and their US advisory teams, and liaison visits to US maneuver battalions that had previously operated in the area revealed that the assumption was valid and in addition it was learned that this platoon dominated the activities of the local civilian population and had their loyal or coerced support.

Initially, Captain Prather was unable to make contact with the enemy. Finding the enemy during daylight was virtually impossible because of the large civilian population and the fact that the enemy knew that an open engagement with a US rifle company would be disastrous. His night operations consisted of eight to 10 ambush patrols deployed in areas of suspected enemy activity. Although his night defensive position was occasionally harassed by light mortar attacks or sniper fire, friendly initiated contact with the enemy was negligible. The enemy, on the other hand, continued to interdict Highway 535 and finding him continued to be a most difficult task.

The first break in solving this problem came partly by accident and partly from experience. Civil affairs and psychological operations teams from the Third Marine Amphibious Force and Americal Division began to conduct operations in the area. The civic action teams brought the personnel of Company B into close contact with the people, particularly children and elderly people. The volunteer informant program was also initiated and soon the soldiers of Bravo Company began to collect intelligence information. Based on his increasing knowledge of the area, Captain Prather requested that his daytime operations be confined to civic action and psychological operations and that his combat operations be characterized by a large number of moving patrols operating at night. He reasoned that aggressive night patrolling can only be accomplished by fresh troops; therefore, combat sweeps in the day would preclude effective night operations. In addition, his previous fixed night ambushes were probably compromised and always would be; not because his men did not understand and apply correct ambushing techniques or lack night discipline, but because of the hostility of the large population and an obvious enemy awareness of the fact that previous US units operating in the area habitually deployed fixed ambush patrols along Highway 535.

The success of night combat patrols in Que Son Valley was predicated on training, discipline and a detailed knowledge of terrain and the local population. Bravo Company personnel, because of their civic action and psychological operations, soon became familiar with the terrain on either side of Highway 535. They also established excellent rapport with the people in the area and obtained an unexpected wealth of intelligence information.

Because of these factors, and the high probability of contact with the enemy, Colonel Baxley approved Captain Prather's plan. A more conservative commander, given this situation, would probably have disagreed. Not only was there an increased probability of contact with the enemy, but also the risk of a small patrol being destroyed by an NVA or main force Viet Cong unit.

Captain Prather organized his company into groups of eight to 15 man patrols, with each patrol assigned a specific sector. Squad integrity, whenever possible, was maintained to encourage esprit. Each of the patrols conducted medcap operations or provided security for division civil affairs/psychological operations teams during the day. Simultaneously, they were conducting rehearsals for their night operation. Each member of the patrol knew in detail the checkpoints, rallying points, alternate routes, indirect fire reference points, and all the other patrolling control measures that are taught to every soldier prior to his arrival in RVN. In addition, they were afforded the opportunity to verify these same data in adjacent patrolling sectors to preclude friendly engagements or confusion at night. Detailed individual and group critiques were held each afternoon. These critique sessions proved to be invaluable; they enabled individual patrol members to know the strengths and weaknesses of the other men in their patrol and assignments were made accordingly. For five days the company rehearsed, and on the sixth night the plan was executed.

Since contact was anticipated, control of these patrols was shared by the company and battalion. If 50 percent of the patrols had contact and the company night defensive position was attacked, control by the company alone would be difficult. To preclude this problem, one-third of the patrols operated on the company command net, one-third on the battalion alternate command frequency under battalion control and the remaining one-third under battalion control using a frequency other than the battalion command or alternate command frequency.

Forward observers from the company's mortar platoon, the battalion heavy mortar platoon and the artillery FO team attached to the company were deployed with each patrol. Registration points were confirmed during the day at points off the planned routes to avoid compromising the patrols. Shift and fire for effect missions were SOP and armed helicopters were on call at the brigade base camp. The frequency of contact by the patrols kept the battalion tactical operations center at a high level of activity. The first night two patrols had contact, resulting in two enemy KIA and the capture of two individual weapons, six mines and several

hand grenades. During the ensuing four-week period, a total of 32 enemy personnel were killed, and 12 weapons and numerous mines and grenades were captured. An average of one friendly initiated contact occurred nightly for a 28-day period. Documents captured later during the operation revealed that the enemy local force platoon had been completely eliminated. Casualties to the 1/6 Infantry consisted of two WIA, neither requiring evacuation. More important, during the remaining six-week period that the 1/6 Infantry was in the region, not a single enemy contact took place along Highway 535. At first glance the number of enemy KIA and enemy weapons captured does not appear significant but in light of mission accomplishment and the factors pointed out earlier, the accomplishments of these patrols contributed significantly to the success of the entire division during the 1968 Tet Offensive.

One point that needs emphasizing is the patrol debriefings that were conducted each morning. Every member of the patrol participated and the intelligence furnished by a soldier with only six or eight months service was fantastic. So dedicated to success were these soldiers and so proud were they individually and collectively that they had destroyed the myth that the night belongs to Charlie that they openly participated in the debriefings. It was during one of these sessions that the term "rat" was first applied to these patrols. Although each patrol member dressed and equipped himself in accordance with FM 21-75 (Combat Training of the Individual Soldier and Patrolling) and the particular situation, there were instances when they attempted to look as much like a Viet Cong soldier as possible. Such an instance occurred in January of 1968, two months after the battalion arrived in-country. While operating west of Chu Tai, the battalion received concrete intelligence that a local VC platoon leader was going to cross Highway 1 at a specified time and place to attend a meeting in a local village. A Bravo Company platoon leader deployed a six-man patrol led by himself to intercept the VC. Camouflaging his squad, he deployed, engaged and killed three Viet Cong including the VC platoon leader. The next day, another platoon leader told him that his men looked like rats; with qualification, successful rats. In the Que Son Valley the name reappeared and Captain Prather's patrols became known as the "rat patrols."

As Colonel Baxley began to rotate companies along Highway 535, rat patrolling extended to the entire battalion. Company C had an incident which exemplifies this technique. After establishing rapport with the local population, Captain John Hurtado (later killed in action) received a report from an extremely reliable source that a local VC squad was planning a night meeting in a destroyed village along the highway. The rat patrol assigned this area approached the village at about 0200 hours on March 15, 1968. On entering the village, four Viet Cong leisurely stood up, one of them only two feet from the rat patrol leader. At this point an incident that can only take place in a combat environment occurred. The startled rat patrol leader reached for and violently took the enemy soldier's assault rifle away from him. The near simultaneous rifle firing of the other rat patrol members killed the remaining VC. During the debriefing the following morning the rat patrol leader, still visibly shaken, concluded that the Viet Cong obviously thought the rat patrol was part of the VC force.

The technique used by the rat patrols was not new; its success was based on the sound application of US Army patrolling techniques, the ingenuity and imagination of a company commander, the courage of his enlisted men, and the positive approach and leadership of a battalion commander. The success and accompanying confidence of the rat patrols was so successful that they desired to fight only at night.

Fighting on the Coastal Plains

Major General O. M. Barsanti

The end of January 1968 brought drastic changes in the tactical situation in South Vietnam. On January 31st the Communist forces launched their Tet offensive, conducting a series of attacks on cities throughout the country; one of the more determined of these was the attack upon the city of Hue. Bitter fighting in the city lasted 25 days and not only destroyed large parts of the city, but caused the death of many innocent civilians. This attack on Hue, coupled with enemy pressure around Khe Sanh, along the Demilitarized Zone, and east from the A Shau Valley, was a principal factor in the deployment of additional allied forces into Military Region 1.

The 101st Airborne Division (minus) moved to a base about five kilometers southeast of Hue, leaving its 3d Brigade in the Bien Hoa-Long Binh area. When the division closed into its new area, the newly arrived 3d Brigade, 82d Airborne Division was attached, bringing the number of maneuver brigades to three. One of the principal missions assigned the 101st Airborne Division was the external defense of Hue. But to better understand the division's mission and methods of combat used to accomplish that mission, one needs to know something about the enemy's preparations for his earlier attack and the situation and terrain around Hue.

In late October and early December 1967, the enemy began to build up his troop strength and place caches of weapons and munitions around Hue City. This buildup of enemy forces and supplies went virtually unnoticed because there were few US and ARVN forces maneuvering in the area. When the 101st Airborne Division arrived, the battle for Hue was already in its final phase but the surrounding area was still dominated by the enemy, which would allow them to mass for another attack on the city. We estimated that three enemy regiments from the 324B NVA Division — the 812th Regiment to the northwest, the 803d Regiment to the north of the Song Bo River, and the 90th Regiment south and east of the Song Bo — were in the area. These units appeared to be supported by several local force companies and hamlet militia units.

Terrain

Most of the terrain around Hue is coastal lowland plains characterized by rice paddies and marshland. Low sand dunes and sandy saltwater marshes are along the coast and the "Street Without Joy" area. Elevation in the area is usually about two feet and seldom rises above 20 feet, while the whole area is crisscrossed with numerous canals and streams to form a pattern of heavy vegetation, hedgerows, and villages that line and protrude from their banks. Fields of fire generally are good to ranges of 150 meters, but are broken throughout the area by the paddy dikes and hedgerows that vary from one-half to one-and-a-half meters high.

This area has been a major Viet Minh-VC-NVA stronghold and infiltration route for many years, and the villages along the Song Bo River and north of Hue are extremely well fortified with extensive bunker complexes and trenchlines. Some of these fortifications, in fact, extend along a few of the streams and canals, which generally are unfordable except at selected locations. This series of interlacing streams and canals with their ribbons of hedgerows and fortifications makes cross-country movement extremely difficult.

To meet the enemy, the division deployed with the 2d Brigade immediately northwest of Hue to clear the area of remaining enemy forces. The 3d Brigade, 82d Airborne Division, was deployed generally south and southeast of Hue, while the 1st Brigade, 101st Airborne Division, was to the southwest along Highway 547-547A. One of the missions of these two brigades was to stop additional enemy forces from infiltrating into the Hue area.

A major problem we encountered during most of this war has been working the enemy into a position where he must stay and fight, thereby allowing us to mass our superior combat power to deal an enemy force a blow that can destroy him. Typical of this was an action that occurred on April 10th, one that was conducted by the 2d Battalion, 501st Infantry, a part of the division's 2d Brigade.

Operating on hard intelligence, the 2d Battalion planned an attack on the village of Thon Phuoc Dien, some 12 to 13 kilometers southeast of Quang Tri and three to four kilometers southeast of the battalion's firebase. Early in the morning on April 10th, Companies A and D moved out to conduct the operation. Company A moved overland from the fire support base toward the southeast while Company D conducted a heliborne assault from the same direction. The two companies linked up while an extensive artillery preparation fixed the enemy's position. A CS concentration and a final bombardment were laid on the village, and at 1300 both companies began a coordinated attack.

They immediately received sporadic small arms fire, but both units pressed the attack to maintain contact and fix the enemy. The battle grew in intensity until by 1630 it was apparent that there was a sizable enemy force in excellent positions within the village. Company B was immediately heli-lifted to a landing zone southwest of the contact secured by elements of Company D. As the company landed, the other two companies began a cordon operation, and Company B hastened to complete the encirclement.

Encirclement

Although the encirclement was large, the excellent fields of fire made it possible for two or three-man positions every 20 to 30 meters to cover the area adequately. The 90mm recoilless rifles and 81mm mortars, along with some CS dispensers, were flown in with Company B to increase the ground firepower. The 2d Battalion continued operations throughout the night, using constant illumination and large amounts of artillery fire, and the great pressure it exerted against the enemy positions during the hours of darkness was evidenced by the numerous efforts of the enemy to exfiltrate from the cordon. No less than 20 NVA soldiers were killed during the night.

The next morning, after an extensive preparation by tactical air and artillery, Company D attacked, moving into the village from the northeast. The unit employed all available weapons to great advantage as it progressed into the village, and the enemy's bunkers and trench systems were easily overcome using the CS dispensers. The sweep met only moderate resistance and by mid-afternoon was completed.

From the 13 detainees, the enemy unit was identified as the 6th Battalion (minus) of the 812th NVA Regiment. Sixty-six enemy bodies were counted and 26 weapons were captured, while the 2d Battalion (Airborne), 501st Infantry counted seven men killed and 35 wounded.

Power

Each time we found the enemy, combat power was rapidly applied to destroy him, and our ability to continually place pressure exactly where needed, for as long as required, brought significant results. This was well illustrated late in April during a four-day battle that took place when we trapped an enemy unit on a peninsula, surrounded on three sides by the Song Bo River. The area of contact contained two small villages — Thon Duong Son and Thon Phuoc Yen — in which there was heavy vegetation, but the surrounding area was paddy land, flat and free of restricting vegetation. This allowed excellent fields of fire both into and in defense of the two villages.

The action started on April 28th at about 1400 in the afternoon, some 2,000 meters north of the Phuoc Yen village complex when two of our rifle companies made contact and drove the enemy south into Phuoc Yen. Our intelligence people had given us indications of an enemy buildup in the area and when contact was made immediate action was taken to seal off the area.

The Black Panther Company of the 1st ARVN Division moved into a blocking position that sealed the land routes out of the area, and between 1700 and 1800 hours we heli-lifted two more companies — Company A, 1st Battalion, 501st Infantry, and Company A, 1st Battalion, 502d Infantry — into the area, and sent Company B, 2d Battalion, 501st Infantry by foot toward the village complex. By 1830, the village had been further sealed off as three Popular Force platoons also moved into blocking positions. Light fire teams from the division's 101st Aviation Battalion maintained constant surveillance of the village to cut off any enemy trying to escape before the encirclement could be completed.

Continuous illumination during the night prevented any large movement by the enemy forces trapped in the village, although several times during the night enemy soldiers did make efforts to escape our tight grip. Most of these attempts were in the Black Panther Company sector.

On the following day, the 29th, contact was maintained and the Black Panther Company conducted an attack toward the south. It met stiff resistance as the enemy fought with small arms and automatic weapons, and only small gains were registered. The company then withdrew to its original blocking position to allow room for light fire teams from the 308th Aviation Battalion, tactical aircraft, and the division's artillery battalions to pound the encircled enemy the rest of the day.

Intelligence reports now indicated that an NVA battalion had been caught in the cordon, so at 1800 hours we put Company D, 2d Battalion, 501st Infantry under the operational control of the 1/501 Infantry to be airlifted into the area to reinforce the cordon.

The company (minus) was placed behind the Black Panther Company, while Company A, 1/502 Infantry, reinforced by one platoon, moved to join forces with the three Popular Force platoons. The 90mm and 106mm recoilless rifles were also brought in to give the units additional firepower, and these were immediately put to use.

Throughout the night, pressure was maintained and on the morning of the 30th, elements of Company A, 1/502 Infantry and the Black Panther Company began an attack to penetrate the village from the north. Fierce fighting erupted as the enemy fought from well dug-in fortified positions, and even though small gains were made, the two units withdrew to their blocking positions. The Black Panther Company was then relieved by Company B, 1/501 Infantry, and returned to 1st ARVN Division control. As darkness fell, the allied forces continued the pressure with illumination and artillery fire.

Mortars

At about 0440 hours the following morning, Company A, 1/502 Infantry, received a mortar attack of about 50 rounds. Immediately following, its left flank was attacked by a platoon-size enemy force. Illumination was shifted to aid Company A as the fighting intensified. At about the same time, the Popular Force platoons became engaged with other enemy elements who were trying to escape. Savage fighting ensued as the enemy was driven back into the village area, and at 0800 hours a Psywar Operations Team began broadcasting in the area. An hour later our artillery began to pound the enemy positions, a bombardment that was continued until 1100 hours when another surrender appeal was made. We also announced that a one-hour lull in our firing would take place to allow any enemy soldier to surrender in safety. During that 60-minute period, 16 enemy soldiers did surrender, and at 1200 hours we resumed the bombardment.

At 1300 hours, artillery fire was lifted as a CS grenade drop was executed over the enemy positions, this followed immediately by an artillery time-on-target (TOT) mission. Elements from Company B, 1/502 Infantry then assaulted the enemy positions, making considerable gains and inflicting heavy losses. The effects of the battle began to show on the enemy force, for by evening a total of 95 NVA soldiers had surrendered. Approximately 600 meters were gained and the cordon was tightened around the enemy. During the night the enemy again made repeated attempts to escape but to no avail, as the effective use of illumination and organic weapons thwarted each effort. On May 2d, a final sweep of the cordon was made with only minor resistance.

The results of this operation speak for themselves: 314 enemy dead were credited to elements of the division, another 115 to ARVN forces. The division captured 107 NVA soldiers and 103 weapons, while the ARVN forces accounted for another 13 weapons. Our interrogations were able to identify the encircled unit as the 8th Battalion of the 90th NVA Regiment.

La Chu

Not every situation develops as well as the set of circumstances that formed around the Phuoc Yen battle, and the time comes when the situation dictates a different solution. This is borne out by the battle of La Chu, a two-day contact which ended with an exceptionally well-executed night attack. Certainly the value of night operations was exemplified by this combined arms night attack.

On May 5th, 1968, Vietnamese sources reported to us that elements of a North Vietnamese Army battalion had moved into the village of La Chu. Based on this intelligence, Company D, 1/501 Infantry was rapidly deployed north of the village and immediately made contact with the enemy. With the information verified and the enemy located, combat power was swiftly massed as Company A, 1/501 Infantry and Companies A and C, 2/501 Infantry were heli-lifted during darkness into positions encircling the village. The tight cordon was maintained throughout the night and artillery, light fire teams, and tactical airstrikes pounded the heavily bunkered village. There was contact throughout the night as small groups of the enemy attempted to break out of the encirclement; all were beaten back.

Realizing that the fortifications inside the village would require more firepower than was present, the 2d Squadron, 17th Cavalry, with a tank platoon from Company C, 2d Battalion, 34th Armor,

was ordered to join Company D, 1/501 Infantry in an assault on the following day. This attack began at about 1130 on the morning of the 6th, meeting stubborn resistance that intensified as the men moved deeper into the village; but by 1800 the northern third of the village had been cleared and all units were in heavy contact. So as not to lose momentum, the attack was continued throughout the night until the village was cleared, and the cordon was widened to allow more maneuver room and better fire support control by the attacking forces.

Illumination

As darkness fell, illumination was placed over the enemy's positions by USAF, USMC, and Army fireships, by Army artillery, and by naval gunfire illumination. As the attack continued, the intense firepower and shock effect of the combined arms team began to take effect. With the added maneuver room allowed by the widening of the cordon, and the constant illumination, the armor elements were able to work on the enemy's flank and the latter's resistance began to crumble. This pressure was maintained until 0100 on the morning of the 7th when all enemy resistance stopped and the sweep through the village was completed. Results were 55 enemy dead, 5 detainees, and 30 weapons captured. We lost one man killed and 18 wounded.

The actions just described are only three of numerous similar operations conducted during the division's fighting on the coastal plains. They were successful because we used the following techniques:

• Multiple Actions. Using the rifle company as a basic maneuver element and maintaining an average of 30 companies on the move in the division's area of operations at any one time, day and night, a continuous flow of action throughout the area was maintained. This kept the enemy off-balance and had the effect of the division being everywhere at once, to see and be seen, and to have its presence felt.

• Continuous Attack. Once contact with the enemy was established, it was not broken. All resources of the division were made available to maintain pressure on the enemy until he was either destroyed or captured.

• No Reserve. This is not meant to say that the division was without the ability to reinforce or support its units in contact. But the situation did dictate a total effort in locating the enemy around-the-clock, so that every unit not in contact was in reserve, ready to be picked up and committed any time and anywhere it was needed. This allowed us to do all that we could to find the enemy, at the same time that it gave us the capability to react to any situation with the needed flexibility.

• Night Fighting. The ability to deny or limit the enemy's activities at night was recognized as an essential element in any battle of this war. Extensive night ambushes were used, and we averaged over 65 per night to cover all likely avenues of movement. Almost 60 percent of the division's fighting was done at night. The purpose was simply to deny the enemy the use of darkness, as well as daylight, for operations, and to maintain an around-the-clock pressure which would allow him no breathing spell. The success of the division's operations at night was evidenced by the fact that of the 7,128 enemy killed by the division between January and June, 28.8 percent were made at night. In Operation Carentan around Hue, however, which started on April 1st, two brigades claimed 1,260 enemy killed during the day and 836 at night, a ratio of 1.5 to 1, or 40 percent. These statistics pointed out to us the value of continuing operations during the hours of darkness, particularly on the coastal plains, which lend themselves to night operations.

• Mass Rapidly on Lucrative Targets. When the opportunity presented itself, elements of the division massed rapidly and used any and all available means to do so — foot marches, vehicles, helicopters. Once a company made contact, it quickly attempted to fix the enemy by fire and to encircle him. Since the enemy knew the fortified base areas and all escape routes quite well, other companies, together with ARVN and RF/PF forces, were brought to the contact area as rapidly as possible to place a cordon to prevent the enemy's escape.

  • Close Coordination with ARVN Units. Close coordination was maintained with ARVN units and local forces, especially with the district chiefs who provided a source of intelligence that was instrumental to the success of our operations. This close cooperation also provided a source of combat power that was eager to participate in combined operations on extremely short notices. In fact, our battalion headquarters were habitually collocated with the district chief.

  • Maximum Fire Support. Operating under the theory "expend shells not men," artillery, tactical air power, naval gunfire, aerial rocket artillery, and helicopter gunships were used extensively.

Once contact was established, it was maintained by the unit until all available firepower could be massed. At that time, the unit pulled back to allow the supporting fire to be massed on the target area. The use of several sources of fire on a target afforded us the opportunity to bring to bear continuous fires for long periods of time while our ground forces could be massed in enough quantity to be effective. This had two primary effects: it fixed the enemy and destroyed his fortifications, and it had a tremendous psychological impact on the individual enemy soldier.

• Special Equipment. We used several special items of equipment and techniques to exploit the enemy's weaknesses and to neutralize his strengths. The 106mm recoilless rifle and CS riot control agents were used quite effectively. The recoilless rifle, extremely difficult to carry, was placed in the fire support base area and airlifted to units when heavy bunker systems or fortified hedgerows were met. The riot control agent proved extremely effective, particularly against the well-fortified villages and bunker systems we found along the stream banks and in the hedgerows. By laying a concentration of CS using the E8 dispenser or air-delivered grenades followed by an artillery TOT, we overcame many fortified positions and took only a few casualties in the process. The use of constant illumination during our night contacts was also effective, particularly during those cordon operations that had to be continued during the hours of darkness. We also found that an extensive psychological warfare effort would bring surprisingly good results when it was reinforced by tactical air, riot control agents and artillery fires.

Since the 101st Airborne Division's arrival in the Hue area, the enemy has again tried to mass forces for another attack on Hue.

Each attempt has been thwarted by actions similar to the three described. The successful application of our methods of combat has kept the enemy off-balance and has preempted his ability to conduct another major attack on the city of Hue.

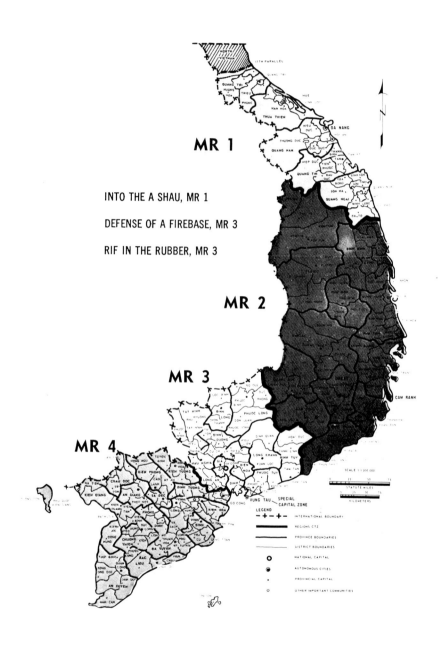

MR 1

INTO THE A SHAU, MR 1

DEFENSE OF A FIREBASE, MR 3

RIF IN THE RUBBER, MR 3

MR 2

MR 3

MR 4

Chapter 5

Allies on the Offensive

Into the A Shau

Major Emmett Kelly

The A Shau Valley, once a haven for enemy forces who commanded some of the most difficult terrain in the Republic of Vietnam, was invaded by combined elements of the 101st Airborne Division (Airmobile) and the Republic of Vietnam's 1st Infantry Division in August 1968. The combined Allied effort, named Somerset Plain, ended the enemy's long-term grip on this important communications artery into Military Region 1.

The A Shau Valley floor is relatively flat with thick vegetation consisting of secondary jungle growth and elephant grass that presents a serious obstacle to the cross-country mobility of foot troops. Travel by wheeled vehicles is limited to Highway 548 and unmarked trails. The Roa Loa River flows through the valley to the village of Ta Bat, then turns sharply to the west and continues into Laos. Mountains reaching to almost 5,000 feet flank each side of the valley. They are covered with double or triple canopy and a dense undergrowth spreads over most of the slopes. In some mountainous areas the terrain is open and the summits of the highest mountains are craggy peaks protruding above all vegetation. All of the slopes are extremely steep, limiting rapid foot movement to trails near ridgelines and stream beds.

An intelligence study of the area published in July estimated two North Vietnamese Army Regiments, one separate Infantry battalion, an artillery battalion, various support units, and possibly an armored battalion were located in or near the valley. It also was estimated that ammunition and equipment had been cached throughout the valley.

The forces to be employed in the operation were the 1st Brigade, 101st Airborne Division (Airmobile); two battalions of the 1st Regiment and the Black Panther Company, 1st ARVN Division; Troop B, 1st Squadron, 9th Cavalry, 1st Cavalry Division (Airmobile); and supporting artillery, aviation, engineer, and signal units.

Before the operation could begin, a means to reduce flight times had to be developed to make maximum use of aviation units, and additional firebases had to be constructed to ensure that maneuver units operated within the range of at least one artillery battery.

Firebase Birmingham, located approximately 20 miles east of the valley, was expanded to serve as a forward supply point. The base included two Class V helipads and four refuel points for CH47 helicopters, a refuel/rearm point for 15 gunships, a pickup zone for 50 UH1 troopships and a refuel point which could accommodate 18 aircraft, a staging area for two Infantry battalions, and a five-day stockpile of all classes of supply, except Class III, for which a two-day supply was maintained. These supplies were moved to Birmingham by truck from stocks at Camp Eagle, Hue and Phu Bai.

The resultant reduction in flight time was nine minutes for each CH47 sortie, and 10 minutes for each UH1 sortie. Supplies were flown to forward firebases by CH47s, and then to units in the valley by UH1s. Five battalions of Infantry and the Black Panther Company conducted combat assaults into and were extracted from the valley by UH1s. The attached air cavalry troop provided four days of armed reconnaissance before the combat assaults.

Prior to D-day, August 4th, Infantry, artillery, engineer and signal commanders reconnoitered sites for additional firebases. Considering the best location to support the requirements of each activity and the forces required to defend them, they selected four new firebases and named them Son, Eagle's Nest, Georgia, and Berchtesgaden.

The 1st Battalion (Airborne), 327th Infantry, was given the mission of providing security for the construction of the additional firebases. One company attacked west along the Rac Nho River and then south to the site of Firebase Son. The company met light and sporadic resistance enroute, and captured three 85mm field guns. The paratroopers cut a landing zone large enough to permit a UH1H helicopter to land engineer troops with chain saws and demolitions. By July 20th the engineers had enlarged the landing zone so that a CH47 helicopter could lift in a Minidozer. On July 22d the area was large enough for a CH54 helicopter to deliver a D5A bulldozer.

Battery A, 2d Battalion (Airborne), 320th Artillery was lifted to Firebase Son on the 23d. It then was able to support the combat assault of Company B and the Reconnaissance Platoon, 1/327 Infantry, onto Eagle's Nest, which had been used by the 1st Cavalry Division (Airmobile) during Operation Delaware in April and May 1968. Two-thousand-pound fuse extension bombs were dropped on the firebase prior to the combat assault to neutralize mines and boobytraps.

The altitude of Eagle's Nest was too great to airlift a D5A bulldozer, so a T6 bulldozer, which is lighter, was borrowed from a naval construction regiment to aid in leveling the position.

On July 28th, Infantry security elements and a squad of engineers attacked from Eagle's Nest down the southeast ridge to the site of Firebase Georgia. The decision to attack overland was made because this was the quickest way to get into the area and start construction. Positions for two 105mm batteries and three 155mm howitzers at Georgia were completed by the engineers on August 1st.

Other Infantry elements continued the attack past Georgia to the location of Firebase Berchtesgaden. Some trails had been used from Eagle's Nest to Georgia, but from there to Berchtesgaden, the paratroopers had to cut their way through the jungle. Nevertheless, they arrived at the site in one day and immediately started to clear the area of mines and boobytraps. Engineers from Company A, 326th Engineer Battalion (Airborne), completed construction of this firebase on August 2d.

At all firebases, in addition to artillery positions, the necessary bunkers for command posts, fire direction centers, communications equipment, and ammunition were built. Each firebase had a passenger and a cargo helipad. The density of personnel, weapons and equipment was great and the problems of leveling areas for the various installations were monumental. That the engineers accomplished their mission in a hostile environment, and on terrain so steep that men had to secure handholds to pull themselves up the slopes, is a testimonial of their determination to support the Infantry.

During the firebase construction period, many other preparations for the operation were undertaken. A chemical supply point for persistent and non-persistent CS, SFG2 fog oil and 10 and 30-pound smoke pots was established at Birmingham. A forward supply point for non-persistent CS and a filling and recharging point for portable flamethrowers were located at Firebase Veghel. Five defoliation missions were flown in the vicinity of Son and Veghel, to supplement similar missions flown from May to July by the USAF.

Forward air controllers of the USAF conducted reconnaissance missions, and directed airstrikes against gun positions, fortifications and troops. The air cavalry troop, attached from the 1st Cavalry Division, provided valuable assistance through armed reconnaissance. The troop averaged seven sightings or engagements daily beginning on August 1st. They located numerous trails and bunker complexes, and confirmed proposed landing zones for the assault forces. The XXIV Corps provided aircraft for a daily minimum of 10 hours for visual reconnaissance of the valley on the days preceding the operation. Complete aerial photo coverage of the valley was provided by the USAF. The 101st Military Intelligence Detachment disseminated information gained from read-outs of these photographs, and assembled mosaics for distribution down to battalion level.

Eight batteries of artillery were displaced to the new firebases prior to D-day. Each 105mm battery stocked 3,000 rounds on position and each 155mm battery 2,000 rounds. Two batteries of 175 mm guns, located at Firebase Bastogne, supported the operation without displacing.

Concurrent with these activities, two companies of the 1/327 Infantry attacked astride Highway 547A to destroy enemy personnel and equipment along this artery. The companies encountered only sporadic contact, and on August 4th, they occupied the high ground along the highway overlooking the A Shau Valley.

Infantry units located at Birmingham were waiting and ready on D-day for their combat assault onto landing zones in the vicinity of Ta Bat and A Luoi respectively. Fifty troopships were

used in the combat assault. They flew in flights of five, heavy left, and landed in a staggered trail. The flights were spaced 30 seconds apart. After the artillery and air preparations, gunships fired a three-minute preparation immediately preceding the first lift, and orbited in the vicinity of the landing zones for subsequent lifts. The 2/502 Infantry landed unopposed, but the 2/327 Infantry encountered heavy ground fire from a position 500 meters west of their landing zone. Gunships immediately suppressed the enemy fire. No troopships were lost, but near A Luoi one gunship was forced down, and another made a precautionary landing before proceeding back to Birmingham. In the vicinity of Ta Bat, two gunships were shot down and destroyed.

On the 5th, the 2/327 Infantry secured the landing zone at Ta Bat for the combat assault of two ARVN battalions. The ARVN battalions conducted reconnaissance-in-force operations to the south, while the US battalions conducted like missions to the west. Later in the operation the 1/327 Infantry conducted eagle flights to search out the valley floor. In general, enemy contact was light and sporadic. Apparently the enemy decided to fight a delaying action to enable the majority of his forces to withdraw into Laos. The last of the maneuver elements was withdrawn from the valley on August 19th.

During the two weeks of combat action in A Shau Valley, 181 North Vietnamese soldiers were killed and four taken prisoner, 45 individual and 13 crew-served weapons were captured, along with eleven 122mm rockets, 18 cases of 12.7mm ammunition, 32 cases of small arms ammunition, 54 mines, 12 tons of rice, and miscellaneous signal and medical equipment. Seven 2-ton trucks were destroyed. Friendly aircraft losses included one F4 fighter-bomber, four UH1 gunships and one light observation helicopter. Friendly personnel losses were light.

The success of Operation Somerset Plain demonstrates the ability of maneuver battalions to engage the enemy in any part of the country, in almost any kind of terrain, while receiving continuous artillery support. There were several factors that contributed greatly to the rapid deployment of fire support units during this operation that may be of use in future actions of this nature.

One key to the rapid completion of firebases was the early introduction of D5A or T6 bulldozers. In these firebase clearing operations, it also was found that two-man chain saws are more effective in felling large trees than the one-man variety. The former should be used when speed in clearing an area takes precedence over the weight of the equipment. Also, heavier chain saws are more durable, thus reducing downtime, and saws with carbide tips cut through hardwood trees more rapidly.

It was found that firebases must be evacuated with the same

care and precision that is taken when they are constructed and occupied. The first step is the retrograde of heavy equipment. All supplies except the minimum requirements of Class I and V should be moved to permanent base areas. At the same time phasing out of signal equipment should be started. In the next step artillery units fire all remaining ammunition, followed immediately by the extraction of all artillery pieces, and the remainder of communications equipment. The Infantry command post followed by security elements should be extracted last. The final step is the contamination of the area with persistent CS to inhibit enemy attempts to emplace mines and boobytraps.

In many cases fire support for the evacuation can be provided by other firebases or by tactical aircraft and gunships. By starting with the evacuation of firebases most distant from permanent base areas, it should be possible to provide artillery support for the evacuation of all of them.

During Operation Somerset Plain close coordination between aviation and artillery planners resulted in the designation of flight routes which prevented the disruption of artillery fires. Preparatory fires for combat assaults were shifted rather than terminated when gunships approached for their preparation of landing zones.

After the shift, every fifth round fired from one tube in each battery was white phosphorus. This enabled gunship pilots to identify and avoid impact areas. Pilots of CH47 helicopters contacted aircraft control at Eagle's Nest on takeoff and were directed to fly either the north or south route depending on artillery fire missions. Since the artillery units usually fired in one general direction, helipads were constructed to the rear of gun positions as an additional means of preventing the discontinuance of supporting fires.

The establishment of the forward supply point at Birmingham proved valuable. Unit field trains operated from Camp Eagle and Birmingham, and combat trains were located at Berchtesgaden and Son. Each Infantry battalion normally had two UH1 helicopters for the daily resupply of units in the valley.

In the field of signal operations, three valuable lessons were learned. The AN/TPS-25 radar can be damaged by shock waves created by the firing of howitzers. This equipment should be located a minimum of 200 meters from any artillery piece to preclude damage. The new FM radio, AN/PRC-77, was used for the first time by the 101st during this operation to provide secure voice communications down to company level.

Perhaps the most significant aspect of Operation Somerset Plain was the denial of the A Shau Valley to the enemy for an extended period of time by a comparatively small force. This is especially noteworthy because the valley has been one of the main infiltration routes into South Vietnam, and the enemy has expended considerable effort in establishing caches and maintaining roads there. It was proven that with imagination, aggressiveness and determination, the enemy's use of this main artery can be thwarted.

Defense of a Firebase

Major General Ellis W. Williamson

Division intelligence had been predicting an attack on the city of Tay Ninh since late July. To counter this possibility, the brigade commander deployed his forces beyond the city in strong points developed around several artillery fire support bases.

From these positions, each of which sat astride or adjacent to a main avenue of approach to Tay Ninh, spoiling operations were mounted to intercept the main enemy elements as they moved on the city and to preempt a coordinated assault on the province capital. If the enemy wanted to get into Tay Ninh in force, he would find it necessary to fight his way past one of these strategically located blocking forces.

A fire support base was established in early August six kilometers north of Tay Ninh. This strong point had been relocated three times to avoid a fixed pattern of operation. No serious attempt was made, however, to disguise or mask the presence or strength of the position. It now sat directly astride the main arterial road leading into the city from the north.

Two artillery batteries flanked the road. The firebase was secured by two Infantry companies and housed a battalion field command post. From here, around-the-clock operations were staged to counter any enemy activity in the flat and relatively open terrain that stretches to the north of Tay Ninh.

The position of the installation literally invited attack — a certainty should the enemy choose to move on Tay Ninh from the north.

To meet this possibility, extensive defensive preparations were made. A triple concertina wire barrier was placed around the entire circumference of the firebase. Beyond this obstacle, brush, bamboo thickets and anthills were cleared away to provide unobstructed fields of fire. The area in front of the wire was generously seeded with tripflares and immediately outside the wire numerous command-detonated claymore mines were emplaced.

Tripflares were also woven into the wire barrier to warn of an enemy attempt to cut or blow a path through the obstacle. Safe lanes through the wire were placed on the south and north sides of the perimeter where the road ran through the base.

Immediately inside the wire, a defensive bunkerline was constructed, using four to five-man fighting positions with overhead cover. The bunkerline responsibility was split, with one company in a defensive sector on the east side of the perimeter and one on the west with the bisecting road as the dividing point.

The defensive fire plan called for interlocking fields of fire for all positions. The Infantry company 81mm mortars and the battalion 4.2-inch mortars were registered to cover "dead spots." M79 grenade launchers located throughout each company sector would also serve to cover defilade locations.

To round out the Infantry portion of the fire plan, 90mm recoilless rifles were positioned to gain maximum use of the weapon's area killing capability using cannister ammunition. The company sectors themselves were closely tied together by interlocking machinegun and small arms fire.

The firepower of the Infantry weapons on the bunkerline was supplemented by planned artillery and air support. The two artillery batteries within the firebase had plotted close, self-supporting fires using the "killer junior" and "beehive" programs. Killer junior was designed around the air burst of high explosive rounds at a minimum distance of 100 meters beyond the wire barrier. The beehive used the canister round to be fired at minimum elevation and point blank range into closing enemy formations.

Each of the 11 guns in the base, six 105mm and five 155mm howitzers, were set up for independent operation. Complete firing data charts for both killer junior and beehive were computed and posted on each piece. A live fire rehearsal of killer junior had been practiced by each gun crew to insure the accuracy and effectiveness of the fire. The result provided 360 degree air burst coverage beyond the wire.

To supplement the organic artillery, defensive concentrations (defcons) were registered around the firebase, to be fired by supporting artillery batteries at Tay Ninh and a fire support base approximately 11 kilometers to the southeast.

To complete the defensive fire plan for the base, night airborne fire support was needed. Each bunker along the perimeter was equipped with several hand flares to be used on order to mark the exact outline of the base perimeter for overhead aircraft.

For personnel throughout the firebase, "hardness" requirements were strict. Each artillery weapon was revetted and the self-propelled 155mm howitzers were further protected by a six-foot-high chain-link fence to assist in the defense against rocket-propelled grenades (RPG).

Mortar firing positions were equally well bunkered and all personnel were required to have ready access to overhead cover. The battalion commander's desire to have all of his people underground in a matter of seconds, should the situation require it, was the guidance upon which the base was constructed and continuously improved.

The night defensive procedures for the fire support base also included a system of platoon ambush patrols and two-man listening posts. The ambush patrols were randomly located adjacent to foot trails and other avenues of approach to the base at distances ranging from 1,000 to 1,500 meters. The listening posts were placed 100 to 200 meters beyond the wire barrier, again using a random pattern of employment.

Enemy activity to the north of Tay Ninh had been light for some time. Despite aggressive reconnaissance-in-force missions, heliborne combat assaults and "eagle flights" against suspected enemy positions, major contact with the elusive enemy could not be established. Daily aerial reconnaissance and nightly ambush patrols achieved little success.

Operations around Tay Ninh in early August involved frequent exchanges of Infantry companies to provide night security for the fire support base. In the early evening of August 17th, an Infantry company, a mechanized Infantry company and a tank platoon moved into the firebase as the security force.

The mechanized company was deployed with two platoons on the perimeter's eastern sector. On the west, two platoons of the Infantry company occupied the bunkerline. Each company estab-

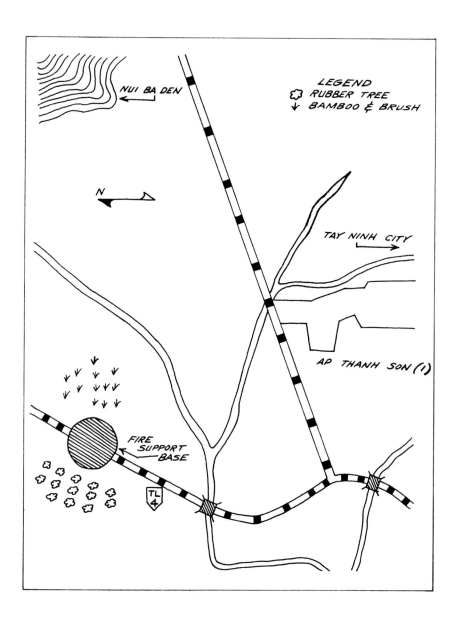

lished a platoon-size ambush patrol to the front of its sector along a principal foot trail and located listening posts immediately beyond the tripflares outside the wire.

The five tanks were deployed in the northern sector and three armored personnel carriers with their mounted .50 caliber machineguns were attached to the Infantry company on the west to augment their firepower.

At his evening briefing to coordinate the defensive activities of his subordinate elements, the battalion commander reminded all present that intelligence reports continued to predict an all-out enemy effort against Tay Ninh. Local "intel" spot reports received during the day strongly implied that tonight might be the night for the attack. Accordingly, all elements were directed to recheck their defensive preparations, test fire their weapons and be particularly alert during the night. All positions were to maintain 50 percent alert status.

At approximately 1930 hours the ambush patrols and listening posts moved through the firebase safe lanes and into their respective positions. As a steady rain fell on the darkened firebase, approximately 550 men settled down for the night's watch.

As the evening progressed, the battalion commander was advised that an ambush patrol from another battalion had detected and engaged a large enemy force to the northeast of Tay Ninh — approximately eight kilometers southeast of the firebase's position. This word was quickly relayed through the base with the battalion commander's order that a "red alert" was now in effect.

A short time later, the darkness to the south of the base was abruptly broken by the glare of a popped tripflare. The 4.2-mortar platoon immediately illuminated the area and the bunkerline positions facing the active zone used M79 grenades in a reconnaissance-by-fire mission. The battalion commander was shortly advised that no movement was detected to the south and the order was given to cease fire.

At 0045 hours the artillery batteries received a call to be prepared to fire a DARMA (defense against rocket and mortar attack) program in support of the Tay Ninh base camp. Thirty minutes later the message was flashed that the base camp was under mortar and rocket attack and a fire mission was given. The guns immediately opened up with their defensive concentrations around the big base camp.

Another 15 minutes had passed when suddenly the concussion of the firing pieces was joined by other blasts. On the northern and southern extremities of the firebase perimeter, red flashes from impacting enemy 107mm rockets lighted up the sky. As personnel scrambled for cover the entire base rocked from the impact of indirect fire. Twelve 107mm rockets and 100 rounds of 82mm mortar fire slammed into the ground within a few minutes.

145

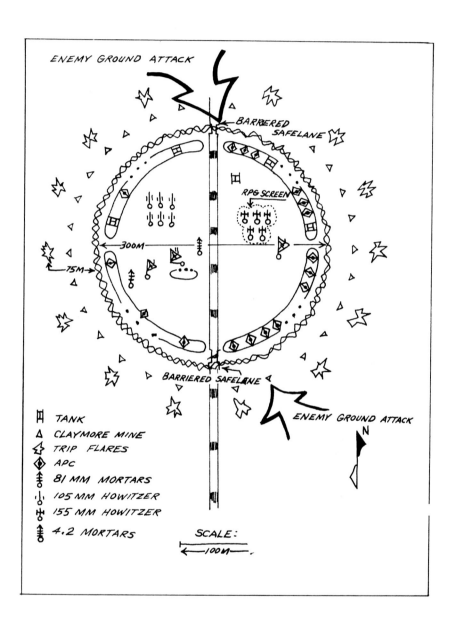

ENEMY GROUND ATTACK

BARRIERED SAFELANE

RPG SCREEN

300M

75M

BARRIERED SAFELANE

ENEMY GROUND ATTACK

N

⊞ TANK
△ CLAYMORE MINE
✧ TRIP FLARES
◈ APC
⚏ 81 MM MORTARS
⋔ 105 MM HOWITZER
⚏ 155 MM HOWITZER
⚏ 4.2 MORTARS

SCALE:
←—100M—.

The heavy fire quickly ceased but was closely followed by a steadily mounting volume of small arms, automatic weapons and RPG fire from both the north and south.

Simultaneously, a radio message came in from the leader of the ambush patrol to the west. It was engaging enemy forces near its position. This patrol and the one to the east of the fire-base remained in position throughout the night. Their greatest problem was protecting themselves from fire coming from their own firebase, some of which was impacting around them.

Within the base camp, the bunkerline quickly recovered from the initial efect of the rocket and mortar barrage and was beginning to lay down heavy protective fires. Targets were visible at 100 meters as illumination rounds from the 4.2-mortars and a 105mm howitzer lighted the surrounding area. On the north and south, enemy forces were moving forward, advancing by bounds and firing from what little cover could be found.

Adjusting from the DARMA fire mission, the artillery batteries immediately began their killer junior program. Each gun crew independently laid its weapon on its appointed azimuth. Most of the crews immediately fired charge one rounds for air bursts 100 meters beyond the wire.

As the situation quickly developed, the battery commanders moved from gun to gun adjusting fire from unengaged sectors to those in which the enemy was concentrating his attacks. All guns fired killer junior throughout the attack with the exception of one piece that was firing the illumination mission.

The artillery operated with little interference from incoming enemy fire. At one point an RPG fired at a self-propelled 155mm howitzer but its round was stopped by the weapon's protective fence. The shrapnel splash from the explosion wounded several crew members. The crew quickly recovered, however, and within minutes had resumed firing.

An unknown type enemy round struck a POL point in the 155mm battery area and started a large fire. Non-firing crew personnel from the battery controlled the fire as the guns continued their mission.

Until the enemy broke contact and all firing had ceased, the two artillery batteries fired 739 rounds of high explosive ammunition, 32 white phosphorus rounds, 194 rounds of illumination and seven rounds of "firecracker." From another firebase to the southeast, 477 rounds of high explosive ordnance, three rounds of white phosphorus and 17 rounds of illumination were fired in support. Tay Ninh base camp, firing its own self-support missions, did not engage in the fight.

Shortly after the ground attack commenced, two Cobra gunships were orbiting the firebase requesting instructions and an artillery checkfire. By this time, the battalion commander was sufficiently abreast of the situation to make the decision to split

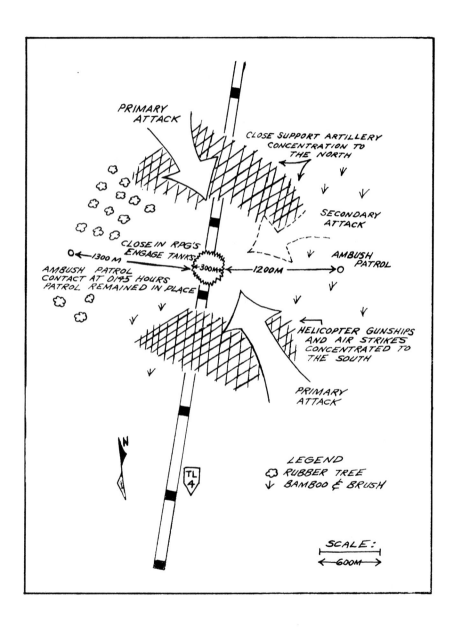

his support fires. All artillery fires were directed to concentrate to the north. The battalion commander then concentrated his aerial fires to the south. Throughout the night split supporting fires were used.

The initial helicopter gunship team rolled in for repeated rocket and machinegun runs on the enemy attempting to approach the wire. When they had expended their ordnance, a forward air controller was standing by with Air Force fighter-bombers on station, ready to assume the aerial fire support mission.

The fighters moved in with napalm strikes and bombs as the helicopters moved off station. A short time later a second helicopter gunship team was waiting to relieve the fighter bombers at the proper time and maintain the pressure on the enemy. An Air Force AC47 ("Spooky") aircraft with rapid-firing Gatling guns and area illumination capability was also used in the aerial fire-power effort.

During the course of the battle, several medical evacuation helicopters and resupply aircraft were able to land within the firebase to remove wounded personnel and replenish the ammunition supply.

Along the bunkerline the situation had been stable from the outset. Little if any difficulty was encountered keeping the enemy away from the wire. In many sectors the command-detonated claymores went unused as the enemy never closed with sufficient strength to warrant the use of the mines. A search of the area immediately beyond the barrier the following morning revealed that few enemy bodies were located within 10 meters of the wire.

The most serious threat to the bunkerline during the night occurred along the northwest sector, where several enemy, firing RPG rounds, crawled into a position from where they could deliver highly effective fire.

Primary target for this RPG fire was a tank located in the area. The tank received a round which wounded several of the crew members. The platoon leader ordered the tank to withdraw to the vicinity of the 105mm howitzer battery and then moved his command tank into the vacated position.

Minutes later, the command tank took an RPG round in the turret, setting the tank aflame and forcing the crew to abandon the vehicle. The tank platoon commander then moved to the previously damaged tank, organized a crew, and moved the tank back into the threatened bunkerline position. The .50 caliber machinegun fire and canister shot from this tank neutralized the enemy RPG positions and stabilized the situation on that part of the perimeter.

The largest single problem encountered along the bunkerline as the battle progressed was ammunition resupply. In laying down a heavy base of fire, the bunkerline positions quickly expended the basic loads initially available and the calls for more echoed frequently along the line. The company commanders and platoon leaders pressed all administrative personnel into service and drew personnel from the reserve reconnaissance platoon to move continuous relays of ammunition resupply along the line. In one location on the north, a jeep had been loaded with ammunition and moved up and down the line depositing ammunition as it moved past the fighting positions.

The lack of communications down to the individual bunkerline positions also posed problems throughout the night. Communications between the battalion CP and companies was available throughout the battle, and the companies and their platoons were in radio contact. But communications between platoon CPs and the individual bunkers had to be accomplished by shouting and moving from position to position.

By 0530 hours the enemy fire had ceased with the exception of sporadic small arms outbursts. At daybreak, the battalion commander ordered his Infantrymen to sweep the area immediately around the perimeter.

The Infantrymen located 104 enemy bodies and eight wounded personnel. Also littering the field were 15 AK47 rifles, two RPG7 launchers, 10 RPG2 launchers, one .30 caliber machinegun, one M16 rifle, three RPD light machineguns, one field radio and two pounds of medical supplies. Documents found were evacuated for intelligence exploitation.

Taken from the battlefield for destruction were 4,000 small arms rounds, 117 RPG rounds, 263 hand grenades, 21 recoilless rifle rounds, 25 bangalore torpedoes and nine 82mm mortar rounds.

By comparison, US losses within the fire support base were one killed and 26 wounded. Two tanks and one self-propelled 155mm howitzer were damaged but remained operational.

LESSONS LEARNED

How does it happen that such lopsided battle statistics can be compiled? A review of the action makes the answer simple. The defense was well organized, well prepared and well executed. There were many good things and a few flaws in the defense of the base.

• The defense of this fire support base was almost a classic example of how to do the job. From the use of tripflares far beyond the wire barrier to the killer junior firing data posted at each artillery piece, the fire support base was ready for the attack. Obstacles and anti-intrusion devices were well placed, fields of fire were cleared and interlocking fire plans, which included coverage of dead spaces by indirect fire and hand grenades, were effective. Close in, self-supporting artillery programs were computed and registered to insure adequacy and accuracy. Defensive concentrations of artillery from distant fire support bases were also plotted and fired. Protective cover for both bunkerline personnel and those within the perimeter was readily available — 550 men within a relatively small area do not take a heavy volume of indirect and direct fire and escape so lightly without doing quite a job of digging in. When the attack came, each Infantryman and artilleryman knew exactly what was expected of him and did it almost automatically. In short, they were ready, and the enemy learned it the hard way.

• Many times the commander is plagued by the problem of coordinating his massive support fires to extract their maximum value. When to checkfire artillery to allow helicopter gunships to roll in for their rocket and machinegun runs? When to clear the helicopters out of the area to make room for the fighter-bombers? What to do about the FAC complaining that his orbiting aircraft are running low on fuel and will have to go off station if they aren't soon given clearance to go to work? The situations are legion. In this situation the commander managed his support fires in such a way as to have both artillery and aerial firepower working for him at the same time. When it can be done — and there is little reason why it can't be done more often — the effects are devastating. Certainly, the matter requires close coordination and judgment on the part of the commander. But, fortunately, we have the people to do it.

• Fire discipline is a big point. The area killing power of the claymore is well known. The claymores were in place but not used (and correctly so in this case) because the targets were not there. The killer junior, the aerial firepower and the bunkerline fires were keeping the enemy at bay. The few that were able to crawl to within 10 meters of the wire had done so within the cover of dead spaces and were properly engaged and eliminated with grenades and indirect fire. The claymores would not have stopped them and if the mines had been blown, it would have been a useless expenditure. The soldiers used good judgment in the application of their firepower. Had the situation somehow deteriorated, the claymores were still ready for use against the targets they are best suited to engage. In the use of firepower, always think in terms of proper fire discipline. Economy of firepower is a valid concept.

• The situation arose in which the resupply of ammunition to the bunkerline became a problem. It was necessary for a considerable number of people to be mustered, travel some distance in an exposed manner, and distribute ammunition. It need not have happened. In the preparation of a defensive position, the location of reserve ammunition at points where it can be conveniently distributed with minimum effort and minimum exposure of personnel is critical. In planning and constructing bunkerlines, include frequent and easily accessible ammunition bunkers. Also have the cooks, clerks and other administrative personnel assigned in advance to such positions, to move the ammunition when and where it's needed. Work good ammunition resupply procedures into the defense plan.

• At one point in the battle, an artillery commander wanted to use beehive to clear out an RPG position that was endangering the line. The mission was never fired. The personnel on the bunkerline did not take cover after the proper red star cluster signal had been given and would have been cut down had the round been fired. What went wrong? It was determined later that the troops had disregarded the signal because numerous red star clusters had been fired earlier for one reason or another. An established procedure had broken down in battle. When pyrotechnic signal plans are set up, they must be followed to the letter. The arbitrary firing of pyrotechnics must be stopped. The confusion of battle offers no excuse. Had the defensive situation deteriorated to a point where beehive became mandatory, the commander would have had a problem on his hands. Make sure fire discipline training includes the proper use of pyrotechnics. Capitalize on this lesson.

• Combat communications down to the individual position is a goal toward which each unit should constantly strive. In this action, communication to the bunkerline left something to be desired. Voice commands and physical movement from point to point had to be used. This is not acceptable in a relatively permanent installation. Field telephones and wire are available and should be used. Use every asset that is available — and good communication equipment is available.

The successful defense of a fire support base depends upon a commander's ability to plan in great detail and then insure that the plan is followed. To learn by making mistakes in combat is a costly proposition. To learn from other's mistakes — and successes — is the mark of a good leader.

Rif in the Rubber

Major William W. Witt
Captain William W. Hansen

In November 1968, after the 1st Cavalry Division (Airmobile) moved from Miltary Region 1 to 3, it immediately began operations in the rubber plantations in the Quan Loi—An Loc—Loc Ninh area. The 2d Battalion, 12th Cavalry received opcon of B and later C Troop, 1st Squadron, 11th Armored Cavalry Regiment for these operations. 2/12th CO, Lieutenant Colonel James W. Dingeman, decided to form the cavalry troops and an airmobile Infantry company into a task force and employ it in RIF (reconnaissance-in-force) operations. The mission was to develop intelligence on enemy locations and activities in the rubber plantation area. Instead of operating separately on parallel routes, these two forces were integrated as a single force, to take advantage of the cav troop's mobility and firepower and the airmobile company's security and close combat capability. This task force had great success in locating and destroying enemy units because of its ability to adapt equally well to the area of operations and the enemy.

Rubber Plantation Area Analysis

Military Region 3 contains some 1,000 square kilometers of rubber plantations. The location of these plantations within MR 3, together with their proximity to the Cambodian border, combine to give these plantations tactical and strategic importance. Names like Michelin, Filhol, Xuan Loc and An Loc—Loc Ninh are reminders of many important engagements that have occurred in these rubber plantations.

The nature of these plantations and their strategic location provide the enemy with both infiltration routes and avenues of approach for major units moving from Cambodia to the Saigon area. Because they were cut from the jungle, the plantations are bounded by thick vegetation on all sides, affording the enemy a nearby safe area should he need to break contact and hide while moving through plantations. The plantations themselves provide overhead concealment and hinder the employment of friendly air suppport.

In a rubber plantation the trees are contour-planted in rows five to six feet apart. By the time they reach maturity in seven years, they have been thinned to rows 10 to 15 feet apart. As long as an armored force moves with the contour in mature rubber, there is not too much restriction on mobility. However, trying to run against the grain offers severe control and mobility problems. The density of trees and the amount of vegetation close to the ground makes areas of young rubber impassable for mounted operations. The Infantry of a combined arms force has no difficulty moving through this terrain.

In some areas the rubber is no longer being worked and a secondary growth of underbrush has grown up on what is normally a well-manicured plantation floor. This overgrowth impedes tracked movement to a degree and affords excellent camouflage to enemy forces operating in these areas. Most plantations contain several small villages strung throughout the rubber. These population centers provide the enemy with food, information and liaison personnel necessary for continuing infiltration. These same villages can, if the friendly force utilizes the intelligence potential inherent there, provide current information on enemy dispositions in the area.

The plantation usually has good drainage, with irrigation and antierosion ditches running with the contour between the rows of rubber. These ditches become minor obstacles to mounted movement and are readily converted into bunkers by the NVA and VC forces that operate in these areas. The road network in the plantations includes good all-weather dirt roads. If the plantation is in a productive stage and being worked, enemy mines will not usually be found in the road network. In abandoned or unworked plantations, extreme caution must be used in moving on or crossing roads and they should be mine-swept prior to use.

Trafficability in the dry season is excellent but during the wet season, movement is hindered by small roots and the gummy clay base of the plantation soil which tends to build up on the suspension systems of armored vehicles, especially tanks. The weather has no other adverse effect on equipment, but does require additional emphasis on personal hygiene.

With the exception of the local VC liaison and reconnaissance elements native to the area, the enemy is NVA. The proximity of these plantations to the infiltration routes allows the enemy to move his units intact through the rubber. In a matter of a few hours, NVA units can walk from the sanctuaries of Cambodia into the covered areas of the plantation. In another few hours battalion and regimental-size base camps can be constructed within the rubber, using the natural materials provided by the rubber trees. While working out of these base camps, enemy units will usually ambush targets of opportunity and harass local district or province capitals. Seldom is an NVA force employed in less than company strength, and it is not at all uncommon to encounter battalion-size maneuver units. Because of short supply lines, the enemy is relatively fresh and has ample quantities of food, ammunition and demolitions.

The enemy has the capability of conducting sustained operations. He first attempts to fix US maneuver units through the use of firepower and then maneuvers against the flanks or rear. If tactical success is not achieved, the enemy delays, to provide sufficient time for the bulk of his force to evacuate the area.

Tactics and Maneuver

The wedge formation used by the 2/12 Task Force is designed for maximum firepower to the front without sacrificing security to the flanks or rear. The ACAVs are aligned perpendicular to the direction of movement, with four or five vehicles echeloned or flared at the flanks. Troop headquarters, including the CO, FO, and medic vehicles, is located 25 to 50 meters behind the front line. This position puts the troop commander in the best possible location from which to control the front line. He has positive control of the FO and medics and is afforded free lateral movement. If tanks or Sheridans are available, they are best used at the front line corners to add firepower across the front as well as to the flanks. Additional tanks are interspersed along the front line. Vehicles such as VTRs and AVLBs are located behind the troop commander where they are easily protected and readily available.

The Infantry is spread around 360 degrees inside the line of ACAVs with the preponderance of strength to the flanks and rear of the formation. The Infantry company's weapons platoon is best used along the front, a few paces behind the ACAVs. This platoon adds to frontal firepower with small arms grazing fire and hand grenades. When the force passes over an occupied bunker area, it is always necessary to check out the bunkers individually and destroy the enemy troops remaining in the area. If not eliminated, these enemy troops wait until the ACAVs have passed over the top and then attempt to hit them with RPG and small arms fire from the rear. Infantry troops are an absolute necessity for eliminating this threat if the momentum of the attack is to be maintained. With this pattern of teamwork, the force can continue to move through a strongly defended area without stopping and without leaving the job half done. The force accordingly overruns the enemy positions and conducts mopping-up operations simultaneously.

Infantry rifle platoons are positioned on each flank and to the rear of the formation. If enemy contact is initiated from either of the flanks or rear of the formation it is a relatively easy task to shift the ACAV firepower to meet it; the enemy can be fixed by the Infantry troops already engaged. The flank and rear Infantry platoons are responsible for elimination of enemy snipers in trees in and around the formation. The entire rear security platoon walks backwards, always keeping the observation and firepower oriented to the rear. The Infantry CO and his headquarters are located somewhere inside the formation, depending upon where his personal presence is necessary. The combined arms force so organized and distributed makes maximum use of the inherent advantages of both armor and Infantry units. It has outstanding firepower and security. Properly maneuvered, it becomes a very effective force.

The force is assigned a terrain objective based on current intelligence. Route planning is accomplished by the force commander to insure contact with the enemy. He should be allowed maximum freedom in his selection of the route to be used. Once contact is made, he needs maximum freedom of action in order to gain the tactical advantage. Movement through the rubber is necessarily slow, as the rate of movement is regulated by the slowest element within the force, the Infantry rear security platoon. Speed averages about two miles per hour.

The force is turned by pivoting the front line on one of its flanks. The Infantry platoons remain oriented on the front line in such a manner as to maintain their general relationship within the formation. This method of turning insures that firepower and security are maintained. When contact is made, the force is maneuvered and turned as necessary so that maximum firepower can be brought to bear on the strongest point of the enemy's defense. This insures decisive results and makes optimum use of the firepower differential between NVA and US units.

Road movement to and from areas of operations is accomplished with Infantry mounted so that speed is attained. The firepower of ACAVs with Infantry mounted is sufficient for self-protection. In critical areas the Infantry can dismount to provide additional security. Antiambush techniques must be predetermined and aggressively executed. Upon contact, the ACAV column stops in a herringbone formation and places maximum controlled .50 caliber and 7.62mm machinegun fire on enemy positions.

Positioning of both armor and Infantry platoons within the formation is designated prior to movement so that if contact is made while on the march, the force can slide easily into the wedge formation.

Control of the formation is accomplished principally through SOP. If the armor and Infantry commanders have discussed in detail actions to be taken under all contingencies, then control becomes elementary. Hand and arm signals are used extensively during the conduct of operations.

Because of the noise level during contact, Infantry radios become almost useless unless radio operators have headsets. Also, communications with outside stations may have to go through armor communications channels.

The advantages of using this type of task force is not limited to firepower and security considerations. To the Infantry soldier, working with the ACAVs means that he no longer has to carry a heavy pack; the ACAVs carry it for him. He can store his reserve ammunition on an ACAV where it is always readily available. Water is no longer a critical resupply problem—nor is chow. Instead of carrying individual C-ration cans in socks around their necks, the Infantrymen place their cases of C-rations on an ACAV. These small advantages to the individual soldier substantially affect the fighting efficiency of the unit. The soldier enters the battle fresher and, consequently, fights longer and harder under more adverse conditions. For the armored force there is the advantage of added security. The cavalryman no longer worries about the bunker he just ran over but didn't search—or the sniper that may be in the tree just passed. Night defensive positions have the comforting Infantry security that enables all to rest a little easier in preparation for the next day's operation. A feeling of mutual friendship and confidence develops between the Infantrymen and cavalrymen after only a few hours' work together.

Fire Support

Since the armor force must normally maintain a fixed installation as a base of operations to which it periodically returns, its organic motars are not carried while on operations. Instead, they are kept at the support base for a defense of that installation. If the maneuver force is working within range of these 4.2-inch mortars, they can be used as a good source of indirect fire support. The Infantry force carries at least one 81mm mortar. Since ACAVs are available for transportation of these weapons, more 81s can be carried. However, when working in rubber plantations, their use is limited because of overhead vegetation. They can be used when the force sets up a position on the edge of the rubber where overhead vegetation does not exist, or for self-illumination when inside the rubber.

Tube artillery is used extensively by the force for recon by fire and in support of troops in contact. The two FOs with the force can closely control and observe fire from two separate locations or call two fire missions simultaneously. Once again, communica-

tions must go through the cavalry troop during a contact, because of noise level. Because of its capacity to penetrate the vegetation, delay fuze is preferred. It is the most effective round of artillery ammunition against troops who are not dug in.

If the enemy is dug in and cannot be dislodged by artillery or fire and movement, then tac air is used. The force has an advantage over other units when employing tac air because of the relatively easy and effective method of marking its location for tactical airstrikes. The force, when in contact, has its ACAVs in a well-defined line facing the main enemy position. The cav troop commander designates a color and each ACAV pops smoke. The result is a solid, well-defined line of smoke 250 to 275 meters long, upon which the spotter aircraft orients. The tac aircraft then make their passes parallel to the line of smoke at a distance designated by the ground commander. If the smoke is not rising enough because of tree height or weather conditions, then the smoke grenade is placed on top of the ACAV with the opening facing the exhaust pipe, which blows the smoke straight up. The ACAVs provide protection for the cavalrymen inside them and the Infantrymen behind them so that indirect fire support can be brought in closer than usual. The same type of marking and controlling procedures are used when employing helicopter gunships or aerial field artillery in close support.

Logistics

The command relationship of the cavalry troop to the airmobile Infantry battalion was not purely opcon. Rather, it was a variation of opcon and attachment. The cavalry troop's headquarters maintained responsibility for personnel and administration, but the airmobile battalion inherited logistical responsibility. This was due in part to the area, type, and duration of the operation, but primarily to the fact that the cav troop's organic squadron forward support area was over 100 kilometers away. Initial logistical problems encountered by the 2/12th in support of the cav troop were overcome by close liaison and command emphasis. A request for 185,000 rounds of .50 caliber ammunition forwarded by the cav troop after an eight-hour firefight was astonishing to a unit which, until then, had only two organic .50 caliber weapons. This type of problem was diminished by collocating a small supply element under control of the troop XO, with the 2/12th service support element to assist in forecasting and handling troop requirements. An ammunition dump was established at the 2/12th fire support base for the cav troop. A complete basic load of ammunition and demolitions was stored there. An immediate request for ammunition resupply by the troop could then be honored and replenishment of the dump accomplished through normal supply means. This obviated the necessity of declaring a combat essential supply request.

The maintenance problems resulting from the extended distance of the troop from its normal direct support facility was solved by the attachment of a maintenance contact team to the troop. Engines and transmissions were replaced in forward areas and over 90 percent of the ACAVs remained operational. Major components were transported overland to the 2/12th forward support area and then delivered by air to the fire support base. The troop maintenance section and attached contact team were then able to repair downed vehicles quickly and efficiently.

Medical service available to the force was enhanced by pooling the medical facilities of both armor and Infantry forces. The focal point of medical service during contact was located at the cav troop's medic track where the senior medics of both units were located. The additional security provided by the Infantry allowed medics to work undisturbed by the enemy situation. The Infantry troops enjoyed the advantage of additional medical supplies, such as litters, dressings, splints, and plasma, heretofore carried only in limited quantities. Medical evacuation was accomplished by dispatching one or two ACAVs (carrying the wounded) and a squad of Infantry to the closest LZ. This small force possessed the necessary firepower, communications and security to conduct isolated medevac operations during contact. As a result, the commander of the force was rid of the problem of conducting medevac operations which normally would have required breaking contact.

RIF At Loc Hoa

In late November 1968, the force was operating near the Cambodian border in the Loc Ninh rubber plantation. It had moved north from An Loc, the Binh Long Province capital, to Loc Ninh, a district capital seven kilometers from the border. At Loc Ninh the 2/12th had two rifle companies and a battalion command group working from its fire support base, LZ Kelly. On November 27th, the combined force of Troop C and Company B departed LZ Kelly for another RIF in the rubber north of Loc Ninh. At approximately 0900 hours, a plantation worker being questioned indicated that an enemy force was located in the small, half-empty Montagnard village of Loc Hoa, located two kilometers northeast on the northern edge of the rubber. The task force requested that the brigade's aeroscout section fly a visual reconnaissance of this area. The scouts reported seeing 20 to 30 military-age males attempting to hide in Loc Hoa, and requested that an aerorifle platoon be inserted to check it out. Due to the possibility of a much larger force being located in the area, the task force requested and received permission to perform this task. The Infantry mounted the ACAVs and the force set out toward the village. A hasty

map recon showed a direct route into Loc Hoa approximately two kilometers to the east. A small east-west stream running across the route presented a possible obstacle, but it was felt there would be a ford or culvert at this point.

Upon arrival at the stream, the force found that the ACAVs couldn't cross because of the steepness of the banks. Meanwhile, the 2/12th CO, who was airborne, had located a road not shown on the map, about one kilometer northwest, which had a semi-intact culvert across the stream. The force quickly moved back to Highway 13 and followed the route the CO had discovered. The force closed on the stream and paused to dismount a platoon of Infantry to inspect the crossing site. While waiting for completion of this mission, the lead ACAVs detected several individuals with weapons running north toward Loc Hoa. The force quickly shot its ACAVs across the stream in pursuit. As the force engaged these individuals (who, it was later determined, were manning observation posts for the 3d Battalion, 141st NVA Regiment, 7th NVA Division) it began to receive RPG, recoilless rifle and automatic weapons fire on its east flank. The task force wedge quickly oriented to the east in order to address the preponderance of the

162

enemy's strength. The enemy occupied well-prepared camouflaged bunkers, but as a result of the feint the task force had inadvertently performed earlier, he was caught oriented to the southeast instead of to the west, the direction from which the force closed.

Because the force's initial assault into the enemy position failed to rupture his defensive line, artillery, aerial field artillery and tactical air were requested and expended on the base camp. Following a pounding with several sorties of tac air armed with 750-pound delay bombs, the force assaulted into the base camp and again encountered RPG, recoilless rifle and small arms fire. At one time the enemy attempted to flank the task force by moving an NVA company up the stream bed located on the force's southern flank. Due to the inherent security and firepower of the wedge and the gunships' strafing attacks, that maneuver proved unsuccessful. The force moved through the base camp and the leading line of ACAVs pinned the enemy in their holes. As the ACAVs passed over the bunkers, the skytroopers of 2/12th grenaded the holes, relieving the mounted Blackhorse troopers of rear security worries. Upon reaching the limits of the base camp, the force policed the battlefield. In this action the US troops had killed 58 NVA, captured several 57mm recoilless rifles, a 60mm mortar, numerous RPG rounds and launchers, 22 AK47s and five light machineguns. The force suffered 15 wounded. This action was successful in locating and destroying the lead elements of the 7th NVA Division in their attempt to infiltrate into MR 3. This contact, and subsequent engagements during the next few days of November, resulted in the decimation of the 141st NVA Regiment and thwarted the 7th NVA Division's drive toward Saigon.

A Note On Task Force Command

During all of the operations conducted by the task force, the ground commander was either the Infantry company or cav troop CO, whoever was senior. The usual method of placing the battalion S3 or XO in command was not used. The battion CO felt that the company/troop commanders, because of their familiarity with the ground situation, could effectively command the force as a whole without loss of control. The battalion was conducting concurrent operations with its other rifle companies, and to assign either the S3 or XO as a task force ground commander would have caused a shortage of command and control capability elsewhere. Further, the battalion CO felt it necessary to keep a C&C ship over the task force at all times. To place an indispensable battalion staff officer on the ground would have handicapped this capability. The result of this command relationship was to afford the company/troop commander with maximum flexibility and freedom of action in all situations.

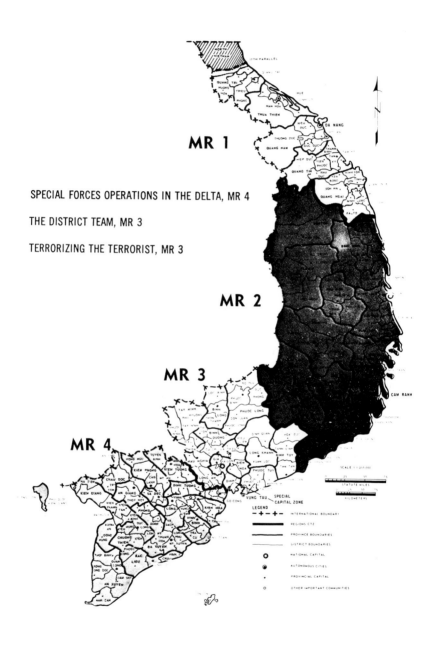

SPECIAL FORCES OPERATIONS IN THE DELTA, MR 4

THE DISTRICT TEAM, MR 3

TERRORIZING THE TERRORIST, MR 3

MR 1

MR 2

MR 3

MR 4

CAM RANH

VUNG TAU SPECIAL
CAPITAL ZONE

LEGEND

- + - + -   INTERNATIONAL BOUNDARY
━━━━━━━   REGIONS CTZ
──────   PROVINCE BOUNDARIES
─ ─ ─ ─   DISTRICT BOUNDARIES
○   NATIONAL CAPITAL
◉   AUTONOMOUS CITIES
·   PROVINCIAL CAPITAL
○   OTHER IMPORTANT COMMUNITIES

SCALE 1:1,000,000

STATUTE MILES

KILOMETERS

Chapter 6

To Build An Army

Special Forces Operations in the Delta

Major Nicholas Sellers
Captain Railey W. Macey III

One mission of Special Forces is to provide assistance to nations engaged in combating insurgency. Popular misconceptions have given a glamorous and unlikely role to Special Forces as a sort of commando or quasi-CIA organization. The fact is that for most Special Forces units the task is a simple Infantry mission; engaging in small unit operations by leading or advising indigenous troops. The only real difference between a line company commander and a Special Forces A Team commander is that the latter has Vietnamese rather than American soldiers, a battalion of troops instead of a company, and usually has much less air, artillery and other support. But for both, the mission is to find and destroy the enemy.

The Delta terrain is almost uniformly a low, flat, fertile plain, respresenting the centuries' accumulation of silt from the estuaries of the Mekong River. At Can Tho, the capital and geographical center of Military Region 4, the elevation is seven feet above sea level. To the northwest is a vast, marshy Viet Cong refuge known as the Plains of Reeds; to the west, a similar area, the Tram, extends along the Cambodian border; and in the Ca Mau Peninsula in the south, a third great swamp, the U-Minh Forest, also provides sanctuaries for the guerrillas. Along the border, too, are the only mountains in MR 4: the Seven Mountains region — these are precipitous land masses which were once islands in the China Sea and, now, rising incongruously from the flat rice fields, still have the aspect of scattered islands in a sea of mud. These mountains are heavily wooded and riddled with caves, providing strongholds for the Viet Cong.

The headquarters and forward supply point of Company D, 5th Special Forces Group, was at Can Tho, the MR 4 capital. The subordinate A detachments were in remote and scattered camps, in unpacified critical areas, primarily in three border provinces — Kien Phong, Kien Tuong, and Dinh Tuong — along the Cambodian border and near the "Parrot's Beak." One camp was in the Seven Mountains region, and two more in the Tram to the south of it.

Special Forces camps in the Delta were physically very different from the installations in the northern areas of Vietnam. The high water table obliged virtually all construction to be above ground, and the difficulties in supply and transportation severely limited the amount of actual construction, much of which was done locally without engineer support. In some instances, the camps were little better than mud forts vulnerable to both heavy enemy fire and the seasonal effects of rains and rising waters. One camp, A433 at My Da, achieved distinction as the "floating camp" of Vietnam: Every building was mounted on 55-gallon drums to prepare the installation for another inundation such as they had in 1966 when the entire northern Delta was flooded and camps were submerged under as much as 15 feet of water. VC mortar fire, however, riddled the drums before their floating role could be put to the test.

The Vietnamese troops which were used by Special Forces, under the name of Civilian Irregular Defense Groups (CIDG), were in two categories: Camp Strike Forces (CSF) and Mobile Strike Forces (MSF). The former were the soldiers who manned the Special Forces camps, and the latter were those of the mobile element, better known as the "Mike Force." Each A camp had roughly a battalion of CSF troops, three to five companies with a TOE strength of 132 men each. Additionally, the organization included a 36-man combat reconnaissance platoon (CRP). This unit, consisting of soldiers somewhat better trained, armed and paid, was the elite force of CSF, to be utilized on reconnaissance or other independent missions, or as a point element for larger operations. These CIDG troops were largely lowland Vietnamese, and the heavily populated districts of MR 4 were used for recruiting by Special Forces. There was a substantial minority of Chinese and Cambodians, particularly in the Mike Force troops. In two camps, virtually all the troops were of the Hoa Hao religion, a peculiar sect antagonistic to the Viet Cong, but also seemingly to everyone else in Vietnam. An occasional violent dispute between these minority groups was not an unusual feature of Special Forces experience. While their families were not permitted to live in camp, they were generally close by in a "dependent village," sometimes constructed entirely by American aid, but more usually hastily put together with nipa palm and pilfered materials into a sort of trashy slum development. In a remote situation, this new Vietnamese village might exist virtually apart from the normal life in the area; in other regions, it became a focal point for local inhabitants seeking a place to live in safety.

The Camp Strike Force had limited capabilities and it was remarkable that their actual performance was well in excess of that which might have been anticipated. The CIDG, originally established as quasi-mercenaries recruited and paid by American

Special Forces, were subsequently accorded a military status by the Vietnamese government. The pay was slightly better than ARVN, and this was a strong consideration to induce them to enlist with Special Forces. Most were very young, 18 or less, of limited or no education, and without experience other than being born and raised in a country always at war. Some received a basic training course at the training center on Phu Quoc Island conducted by Special Forces; others received some slight instruc-

tion at their own camps, and many were trained wholly in the field by receiving their instruction from "real" training aids who fired back, often with better weapons. These CIDGs were soldiers who would cut up their canteen covers to make green fur collars for their uniforms; who could struggle all day through thigh-deep mud, carrying half their own weight on their backs without complaint, other than an occasional "Number ten!"; who would bang two B40 rockets together like indian clubs to see if they would explode (yes, they do); who might run under fire; or who might ignore it to carry a wounded American to safety.

The mission of the Camp Strike Forces was generally border surveillance and interdiction: preventing the enemy from moving into Vietnam from the safe haven they enjoyed in Cambodia, and engaging them in ambushes or in combat when the opportunity was presented. The success of some camps was testified to by the enemy's shifting his routes of infiltration or by his reduced level of activity in the area. In other regions, particularly in that southern portion of Dinh Tuong and Kien Phong provinces known as "The Pocket," the Special Forces camp might be in a state of virtual siege, faced with enemy in superior strength or able to mass it in a short time, and capable of repeatedly harassing the camp or even attempting occasional ground attacks. Air and artillery support might outweigh the enemy's numerical superiority, but these were not ready assets.

The actual conduct of operations varied widely from camp to camp, depending on the particular organization of the individual camp as well as on the enemy situation. In the Special Forces camp, the Vietnamese Special Forces (VNSF) Detachment CO was the titular commander, while the commander of the US Special Forces (USASF) detachment was his advisor. The camp, however, was constructed entirely from materials procured from US Special Forces, and all supplies came through these channels. The troops were paid, clothed and armed by the American advisor. The Vietnamese commander had no direct authority over the physical property, and could call nothing his own except the bare authority to give orders to the troops. The American advisor, controlling every asset, could and did exercise a considerable measure of control. In some instances, the American commander functioned purely as an advisor allocating resources and monitoring their expenditure, while the VNSF ran the camp, commanded the troops, and conducted operations with US advice and coordination. One camp, Vinh Gia, was turned over at an early date to the sole control of the VNSF, although supplies and pay were still furnished through USASF channels. Vinh Gia had an outstanding operational record and was a model camp, a feat attributable to the efforts of a singularly able Vietnamese commander, Captain Nam. In other camps, the US commander was in virtually complete control, planning, conducting and leading the operations. Very often, the character of the individual USASF or VNSF commanders was the single factor which determined the nature of the command relationship.

Most camps followed a very similar pattern in the conduct of operations. The primary mission was to engage the enemy and, secondarily, to drive him out or deny him access to the area of operations. The customary scheme of maneuver involved saturation patrols of platoon or company-size, covering the area of operations as fully as possible. Emphasis was placed on night operations, and small ambushes, four or five in number, were positioned in different locations each night. It was policy that 50 percent of the operations should be at night, and while this doctrine was adhered to in spirit by the establishment of night ambushes, these were rarely little more than listening posts, and actual engagements with the enemy were uncommon.

Company-size operations rarely exceeded a week's time in duration, and short search and clear patrols of two or three days were frequent. Until the middle of 1969, it was very rare that a CIDG operation could have the luxury of airmobility, or any support outside of its own resources. These patrols, moving no more rapidly than the slowest man, afforded the enemy ample warning of their approach and the VC/NVA would generally avoid engagement unless conditions were favorable to them. The generally open character of the terrain did not favor surprise for either side, but remarkably large enemy forces could conceal themselves in the tree line along a canal or in the reeds and low palms of the marshes, constructing emplacements and shelters which could not be distinguished from the air. Control of a CIDG operation always presented problems. While the US personnel quickly learned simple commands in Vietnamese, reliance on interpreters was necessary for most instructions, coordination with the local RF/PF, and communication with ARVN units. The slight delay caused by translation, and the inevitable misunderstandings, were constant hazards to be faced. The primary weakness of the CIDG was a lack of subordinate leadership — squad and platoon leaders for practical purposes did not exist — so that the force inevitably would draw together into a single mass under the immediate control of the one or two responsible CIDG leaders and the USASF/VNSF commander, or string out in a long single file incapable of control. Without an effective chain of command, orders were poorly transmitted to the troops, and might not be carried out effectively except by those soldiers within the sight and voice of the operation commander. Sending out small patrols or establishing observation and listening posts often resulted in very limited or even totally ineffective action by these smaller elements when they were not accompanied by USASF or VNSF leaders. The only effective way of operating was to have one American with each platoon or, at the very minimum, an American with each company.

The major fault of the individual CIDG was his limited or complete lack of training, and poor fire discipline was the immediate and most serious result. A standard VC action on the approach of a CIDG patrol was for a trail-watcher to fire a couple of shots. The entire element would come to a halt while attempts were made to locate and engage the sniper, and the larger VC force would have ample time to effect its escape or reposition itself for subsequent engagements. A CIDG patrol might exhaust its entire basic load in the first small firefight and, in the absence of any means to bring in a resupply, would have to return to camp. As the M16 rifle did not begin to become available to CIDG until 1969-70, the troops had carbines which were no match for the superior AK47, and there was some justification for a heavy volume of fire from the CIDG troops to counter the more effective weapons of their opponents. Because the CIDG did not have the M60 machinegun, the old, too heavy, .30 caliber A6 was still used, and a critical shortage of M79 ammunition following the Tet Offensive and for a year thereafter were further limits to an operation's firepower.

The primary heavy fire support on which a patrol could rely was from its own camp, and it would rarely move outside the fan of this fire. All camps had the 4.2-inch and 81mm mortars; a few had the 105mm howitzer, possibly that of a collocated ARVN unit. To permit a wider operating range, a small firebase with one or two 81mm mortars could be set up to cover particular operations. The 60 mortar was still standard to the Vietnamese and their operations had the benefit of this fine weapon, although the unreliability of the World War II ammunition was a constant hazard. Some camps set up permanent forward operating bases (FOBs) in their area, usually to secure critical terrain, and these could also provide support. Such FOBs were usually manned by a company of CIDG, and a camp with its own defenses and one or more FOBs to support might find it difficult to mount an operation with more than a single reinforced company. Except for the camps which participated in operations of the 9th US Division, Special Forces detachments could expect to receive air support, gunships or other assistance only when they came under attack or when they got into trouble beyond their own capability to handle. The responsiveness of the assistance would depend entirely on its availability at that particular moment — on its not being committed elsewhere — and an inherent risk of Special Forces operations in the "bad" areas — on the northern border and in the Plain of Reeds — was that the operation would be overwhelmed before relief arrived. One camp in this situation took 200 percent USASF casualties in a single month. Medevacs operated with the same restrictions, two to 12 hours time at best for the more distant camps — while policy prohibited altogether the sending of helicopters to Phu Quoc Island. Such slow or unaviliable medevacs were reflected in the troops' unwillingness to risk casualties.

A final aspect of CSF operations to be mentioned was the training center run by one detachment for Special Forces in MR 4; this camp was located first on Phu Quoc Island, and later at To Chau (Kien Giang Province) on the mainland. The team conducted an eight-week basic training course, and occasional special refresher courses of one or two weeks duration. Each basic training cycle concluded with a graduation FTX conducted along the Cambodian border, where it was certain that genuine aggressors would participate. This brought the CIDG recruit from civilian life to combat in less than two months, so further training and field experience at his own camp was needed to make him an effective combatant. Moreover, the To Chau Training Center had difficulty accommodating more than two trainee companies at a time, and this limited capacity required the individual camps to continue to conduct their own training for new recruits.

The most effective tactical effort of Special Forces was accomplished by the Mobile Strike Force. While the average CSF troops were perhaps not very different from the RF/PF militia, the Mike Force soldiers were conspicuously more aggressive troops and could be equated to the ARVN Rangers. The Mike Force was an airborne unit and, although the limited facilities at the Dong Ba Thin jump school restricted this qualification to a minority of the MSF in the Delta, the airborne spirit was in evidence, and gave them qualities of an elite unit. They enjoyed a higher rate of pay as a reward for the hazardous nature of their operations. A large number of the MSF came from ethnic minorities — the Nungs or Cambods — and this tended to set them apart. New troops were trained at the MSF headquarters at Don Phuc, although later some companies were sent to the training center at To Chau. The quality of the Mike Force leadership was noticeably superior to that of the CSF; some of their company commanders were veterans of many years experience whose command abilities and quick discipline were very evident. The overall command of the Mike Force was American, and this was a direct command authority, not in an advisory capacity.

The organization of the Mike Force was generally similar to that of the Camp Strike Forces. Three companies (TOE: 150 men each) of MSF troops were under the command of an American Special Forces A detachment, headed by a captain or a lieutenant.

The individual Mike Force companies were each under the command of a particular USASF noncommissioned officer, and their leadership was the backbone of the Mike Force effort.

The mission of the Mobile Strike Force was to act as a quick reaction force to any camp under attack or to support an operation which was in trouble. It also acted as a mobile element to be utilized throughout MR 4 wherever the enemy and opportunity presented themselves. The emergency relief mission was infrequently demanded, so that the MSF could generally be engaged in operations of its own.

One of the most successful of these operations was its employment in conjunction with air cavalry units of the 7/1 Air Cavalry Squadron. A helicopter reconnaissance element would conduct search patrols until the enemy was sighted or hostile fire was received. While the helicopters were expending their ordnance on the enemy positions, an MSF company which had been standing by would be airlifted and inserted into the area. If the enemy massed strength, additional MSF units would be deployed. These "Black Hawk" missions, depending upon mobility, quick reaction and close fire support from the helicopters, resulted in numerous successful engagements and the discovery of substantial caches.

Another effective operation, conducted primarily during the spring and summer of 1968, was the concept of a "mobile camp." The Mike Force would be given an AO in a region where there were no Special Forces or other elements. A force of two companies, or one reinforced company, would be inserted in this area to conduct operations on a continuing basis. Every 30 days a company would be replaced by a fresh unit. The operations would interdict suspected infiltration routes, search for caches and conduct other similar small unit operations. The enemy, who had learned to avoid the AOs of the fixed camps, now found such "mobile camps" in areas where he had long been unchallenged. Supporting these operations was much less expensive in terms of overall cost than maintaining a fixed SF camp. However, since all support, both fire and logistical, had to be made by air, these mobile operations made a heavy and constant demand on the slender air assets of MR 4, resulting in their eventual discontinuance after several months in spite of excellent results during the brief period that these were undertaken.

For virtually a full year, 1968 to 1969, the entire Mobile Strike Force was committed to the reduction of a single VC stronghold in the Seven Mountains region—Nui Coto. A huge rocky mass, penetrated with caves, and close to the Cambodian border, this mountain was held by a VC force of one to two battalions, and it had long been regarded locally with fear and superstition. In 1967, a single company of Mike Force troops led by Captain John Griffith had climbed to the top one night, and held the peak for nearly two weeks against a force triple its size. When air support could no longer be furnished, the company fought its way to the base, where it linked up with a relief element. The myth of Nui Coto's impregnability had been destroyed but the mountain was back in the hands of the VC. Other attempts to secure the hill were soon to follow.

Equipped and organized for a mobile quick reaction role, and without organic heavy weapons and support, the MSF was not designed to be utilized in an assault against a strongly held fixed position. In excess of 600 American and Vietnamese casualties were taken by the Mike Force in securing the hill, and the VC were never completely dislodged. The MSF assault even included

a parachute jump of selected Mike Force troops on the hill. Tons of bombs stripped the vegetation from the slopes — one portion of the mountain earned the name of "The Rockpile" — but American power was simply incapable of knocking over a mountain and the enemy sheltered in the deep caverns seemed to be untouched. After some of the caves had been cleared, the mountain was considered secured by March 1969. But in May an

NVA unit executed a surprise attack across the border, reached the summit undetected, and wiped out the Mike Force element which had been left to hold the hill. Nui Coto was retaken immediately by friendly forces, but the NVA ultimately brought in three regiments, and Nui Coto and most of the Seven Mountains area once again became VC territory.

In 1969 the MSF organized a detachment, A405, whose purpose was to train and develop small reconnaissance units, similar in concept to our long range patrols (LRPs). While this detachment was rarely used for actual long range patrols as such, it was employed in reconnaissance and intelligence gathering missions. Operating in remote villages and hamlets, particularly in the Seven Mountains region, this unit was able to gain valuable intelligence from the inhabitants. Civic action missions were often conducted simultaneously to gain the confidence of the peo-

ple. At this time, surveillance and intelligence were improved by the use of sensor devices, by both MSF and CSF, and their employment in the Delta was the first instance of training the Vietnamese in those devices.

The increased availability of air assets during 1969-70 permitted the support of airmobile operations for both the MSF and CSF. At the same time, the MSF was enabled to reactivate the "mobile camp" tactic, particularly in the Tram. This technique was modified by inserting two bases, one at each end of the temporary AO, conducting patrols from these for a three to 10 day period, and then moving the force to a new area. Black Hawk operations were carried on once again, and the MSF also participated in joint operations with ARVN Rangers in the Seven Mountains region. Perhaps the last Mike Force operation of significance was the commitment of 1,500 MSF soldiers in the Cambodian incursion during the summer of 1970.

Thereafter, Special Forces was increasingly engaged in the close-out and turn-over of its camps, in contemplation of its entire withdrawal from the Delta by the end of the year. Company D had earlier, in 1969, lost much of its independence of action when it was placed under the operational control of the 44th Special Tactical Zone. The Mike Force was reduced to a single A detachment, with three companies of troops. Whether the Regional Forces, supplemented and strengthened by the former CIDG soldiers, could meet the challenges from within and from across the border, is a question for the future to determine.

The overall value of the Special Forces effort in the Delta may be found in an evaluation of its results, significant in light of the minimal cost of the program. While the system suffered from certain inherent difficulties — chiefly limitations in support assets and the problems caused by the division of command between Americans and Vietnamese — combat operations and area pacification were both conducted with success. Areas which had been insecure to the very edge of the camp's mud berm became pacified to an extent which permitted the resumption of normal trade and traffic, and induced the former inhabitants to return to their abandoned homes. The cost of equipping and maintaining a CIDG soldier was a bare fraction of the cost for an American Infantryman. Most significantly, the Special Forces effort was a successful implementation of the Vietnamization process, long before this term became popular. This process was very much more than mere advice and support to existing units. The Special Forces program brought into being a Vietnamese counterinsurgency force by recruiting, training, and employing CIDG troops in combat, thereby developing not only a force of combatants, but also an experienced cadre capable of continuing the nation's resistance to Communist aggression.

The District Team

Lieutenant Colonel Karl V. Hurdle

The tranquility of early dawn was shattered abruptly by the crack of rifle fire. Immediately, machineguns from the district compound bunker line returned the fire, followed by a steadily mounting volume of small arms fire from soldiers scurrying to their positions. Ten minutes later a platoon-size force began aggressively advancing from the compound, engaging the enemy forces as it maneuvered. Another 15 minutes and the calm was restored. Net result — three enemy captured, two killed and a probability of other casualties among the fleeing enemy force.

Three months earlier, a similar situation would have resulted in a chaotic response. The difference reflected the result of the cumulative efforts of both Vietnamese and Americans working together in a Vietnamese district towards a common goal. The story of the district has been told many times, each version being as unique and unusual as the 240 different districts in Vietnam. The stories all contain their own problems and solutions, but in the final analysis, the basis for effectiveness or ineffectiveness is directly related to competence, professionalism, and interaction between the district chief and the district senior advisor. In this regard, one more chapter of the story may be appropriate.

The District

The district of Xuan Loc is located northeast of Saigon in a rich, undeveloped and underpopulated (81,000 inhabitants) area of approximately 144,000 hectares. The majority of these inhabitants are settled in 10 villages and 61 hamlets. The area is typical of the surrounding region: an economy based on rubber and assorted crops, but deficient in the basic staple of rice, producing barely one-third of its needs. Religion is a strong unifier in the area with about 60 percent of the population Catholic, 20 percent Buddhist, and the remaining 20 percent primarily Confucian ancestor worshippers.

Within this environment a district chief, a handful of Americans, 36 Popular Force platoons, and six Regional Force companies fought a unique, challenging and very little publicized type of warfare. The enormity of the tasks and responsibilities in the district were, and still are, somewhat bewildering and perhaps only fully understood by someone who has served on a district advisory team. Nearly all of the policies and programs of government in the Vietnamese society are implemented on a daily basis in the Vietnamese district and, in addition, the district advisory team receives numerous policies and directives from higher echelons of the Military Assistance Command for implementation. Initially, instituting these tasks and policies in Xuan Loc District was a slow methodical process, marked by periodic setbacks. However, with patience, persistence, understanding, and the coordinated efforts of the district team and the district chief, appreciable progress was eventually attained.

The District Chief

The pulse rate of the district is regulated by the district chief — what he accomplishes, what he fails to accomplish and his methods of operation. He is the administrative chief as well as the military leader of the district. His job encompasses a myriad of tasks, duties and responsibilities, often compared to that of a mayor of a small city in the United States. To assist in implementing policies and to monitor progress in the district, the district chief theoretically had 10 elected village chiefs, 61 elected hamlet chiefs, and a number of minor village and hamlet officials. In reality, however, several hamlet chief positions were vacant because of Viet Cong assassinations. Incompetence, lack of concern and corruption made others ineffective; in at least two villages, the dominant authority was not the village chief or even the district chief, but the Catholic priest residing in the area.

On the military side of the ledger, several of the RF companies were understrength, and leadership, morale and training left a lot to be desired. Frequently, operations were conducted repetitiously in the same areas, which normally resulted in a walk through the jungle with little, if any, enemy contact. The RF platoons were confined to outposts for the most part, offering little protection for the hamlets. Though sporadic progress was being made, the general feeling appeared to be one of lethargy and satisfaction with the status quo.

The turning point came during the latter part of July 1968, with the appointment of a new district chief, a diminutive major with experience as a lawyer, teacher and commander of a Vietnamese Ranger unit. His first act as district chief was to conduct a meeting with his key staff personnel, leaders and the district senior advisor. In this meeting he outlined what he expected from all. He presented a well-thought-out plan for improvement in the

district, indicating where areas of responsibilities lay, what goals were to be achieved and what progress was expected.

The district had received a shot in the arm. During the next three months, progress in the district moved ahead rapidly. The major dedicated himself to his job 24 hours a day. He was competent, honest, enthusiastic, fearless, genuinely concerned about the people of the district and, probably most important, he listened and reacted positively to advice and assistance rendered him by the district team. As a result, the small number of personnel on the district team were required to work excessive hours, many times barely having enough time to sleep. However, each man felt he was making a significant contribution to a common effort in the district, which was evident each day as tangible aspects of success began to materialize.

The results at the end of three months were significant. Incompetent company commanders, platoon leaders and village officials were replaced. Military operations in the district doubled; 21 battalion-size operations, 101 company-size operations, 50 platoon-size operations, and 2400 squad-size operations took place. During this period, 60 to 70 Viet Cong were killed, many were captured, 80 members of the Viet Cong infrastructure were apprehended, and 25 Hoi Chanhs were returned to the Government of Vietnam.

These figures were not impressive when compared to the results of large US or Vietnamese units, but in the district it was a sure measure of progress. These operations resulted in increased security, accelerated pacification and a decrease in Viet Cong activity. At the end of three months, over 60,000 of the district's population was considered to be in secure areas, both day and night. Once a semblance of security was established, elections were held for village and hamlet chiefs and other previously unoccupied government positions. This was followed by additional emphasis on self-help projects, civic action, new life development, organization of self-defense groups, and other improvements in the general category of pacification.

The District Team

The mission of the district team is to extend the governmental effectiveness of the Republic of Vietnam by advising and assisting the district chief and his staff in the overall effort against Communist aggression and in the conduct of military operations within the district. A special relationship exists between the district team and the Vietnamese people. The advisory team lives and works with the Vietnamese. Shortly after assignment, each member of the team becomes immersed in the Vietnamese culture where he lives and functions. His relationship with the people is genuine; he shares a part of their lives, their good fortune and happiness, and their disappointments and grievances.

The district senior advisor becomes an integral part of the Vietnamese community. He represents and is a spokesman for the United States. Within the Military Assistance Command he is considered to be the grass-roots expert on everything which happens in the district. The wide range of his involvement varies from the conduct of military operations to the current price of each of the three grades of rice being sold on the local market. He becomes cognizant of the district's organization, administration, logistics, agriculture, and military effectiveness.

Operating within these parameters, the district team is involved daily with military operations, psychological operations, security, intelligence, Regional and Popular Forces (training, logistics, administration, and morale), rural development cadre, self-defense groups, the Chieu Hoi program, civic action, self-help projects, refugees, medical assistance, and the general economic and military posture of the district. Every day is different and more often than not the district team is performing three of four different functions in as many different locations at the same time. A typical day might start out with an early morning cordon and search

operation in a Viet Cong-controlled hamlet, with an airmobile operation being conducted concurrently in a different location, in hopes of locating a Viet Cong base camp. The district medic might be involved in a medcap outside the district headquarters, other personnel from the team might be involved in moving food, arms and personnel to a remote district outpost, others supervising the construction of dependent housing for the Popular Force soldiers and others monitoring the progress of the district self-help or civic

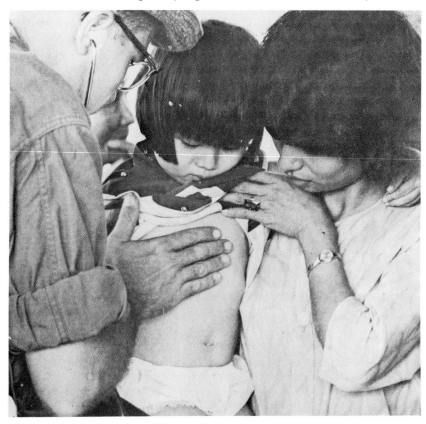

action projects. As the day progresses, there might be a joint meeting at provice, district, or village, an inspection of RF/PF units, coordination with US units, dedication of a school, attendance at a funeral, briefings for visiting US or Vietnamese officials, construction or improvement of local defenses, or investigation of an accident involving US and Vietnamese personnel. Evenings involve additional preparation for the nightly ambush patrols conducted throughout the district, monitoring Viet Cong activity in the area and preparing a reaction force to be dispatched if necessary.

In Xuan Loc District, the senior advisor made it a point to accompany the district chief wherever he went. His schedule was that of the district chief whenever possible. This accomplished a two-fold purpose; it helped develop rapport with the district chief and helped the senior advisor to understand the various functions of the district. He had to be aware of the forces at the district chief's disposal, what additional support was available from US and Vietnamese units, and the reaction time required for this support. Consideration was also given to the formation of a district reaction force to assist the PF/RF units when needed, plans for evacuation of casualties, and plans to coordinate actions of the RF/PF, RD cadre, and a reaction force which might all be engaged with the enemy in the same area.

Although the primary mission of the district senior advisor was to advise, the DSA had an equal responsibility in commanding his team. Numerous additional duties and responsibilities had to be assigned in conjunction with maintaining the unity and manageability of the team. To be effective, the team had to work together in close harmony, and consisted of the district senior advisor, assistant district advisor, intelligence officer, intelligence operations NCO, medic, and two radio-telephone operators.

Long Haul

The district advisor in Vietnam is directly involved in the United States' most pressing political and military problems; the intricacies of dealing with Vietnamese who desire our support while possibly resenting any hint of interference; the grass-roots administration of our aid to Vietnam and the confrontation of Communist guerrilla warfare. His responsibility is unique in that he is required to focus the policies and priorities of the United States on the realities of Vietnamese life. Considering the magnitude of the advisor's work, it is understandable that he is considered the backbone of the advisory program. Owing to the demands and challenges of this type duty, the selection and preparation of the district advisor should be a matter of utmost importance. The preparation of district advisors in 1968 was somewhat lacking with regard to training. Many did not attend any training course and consequently received no out-of-country preparation prior to assignment. The district advisor who had received training often found that the training was inadequate preparation for the type of duty and responsibilities he eventually assumed.

The job of advising is difficult and depends a great deal on the ability of the advisor to influence his counterpart effectively. The circumstances surrounding the various districts in Vietnam are as different as the individuality of their district chiefs. To advise a man you must understand him. How this is done depends on the district senior advisor, the district chief, and experience. However, some of the following guidelines proved useful in Xuan Loc District and might be applicable elsewhere:

* Make every effort to understand the district chief, his culture, philosophy, personality, background, goals, and methods of operation.

* Look at the problems in the district from the point of view of the district chief.

* Be willing to compromise on issues that are not vital to your interests.

* Never put yourself or the district chief in a position from which you cannot retreat without losing face and from which you cannot advance without serious consequences.

* Develop a ground for mutual understanding, be willing to accept advice as well as give it.

The fundamental mission of the advisor is to advise, but his advice is of little consequence if it doesn't receive the consent of the district chief. The advisor must influence, not force, the actions of the district chief in such a way as to promote constructive ideas and policies without adversely affecting the ideas, opinions and authority of the district chief. In sum, the district senior advisor is a full-time soldier-statesman in the Vietnamese countryside, helping to develop an effective governmental system with accompanying military progress.

Terrorizing the Terrorist

Captain Kenneth R. Mineau

From August through November of 1968, a small group of South Vietnamese accompanied by two American advisors conducted a series of operations designed to alleviate pressure from local Viet Cong actions taking place in Gia Kiem Subsector, Military Region 3. Although the body count and the actual number of forces involved was small, the psychological effect of these operations proved to be extensive.

Main Force Viet Cong and North Vietnamese units had been relatively successful in this area during the 1968 Tet Offensive, although the enemy had taken heavy casualties. As a result, local Viet Cong morale was high and their operations were becoming increasingly bolder, while local Vietnamese forces were experiencing difficulties in mounting friendly operations.

The terrain consisted mainly of rubber plantations, rice paddies and villages located adjacent to Highway 20, all surrounded by primary jungle.

Approximately three reinforced platoons of Viet Cong were conducting classic guerrilla warfare operations in this subsector. Three Regional Force (RF) companies and numerous Popular Force (PF) platoons were needed to counter them.

The local VC were not strong enough to do more than conduct mortar attacks on outposts, ambush military units and withdraw when reaction forces arrived, but they had managed to gain a definite psychological advantage. South Vietnamese were subjected to frequent bombing within the villages. Taxation points were frequently set up by the VC along Highway 20, and a major propaganda campaign was launched by the VC in the Bien Loc area. An RF company had been ambushed and routed east of Bien Hoa Village and these forces were subsequently reluctant to operate in that area, allowing the VC full use of it.

In August 1968, two American officers decided to attempt to use the local element of the Province Reconnaissance Unit (PRU) in harassment operations against these VC. One officer was the local intelligence advisor and worked closely with the PRUs, while the other was an Infantry advisor to a local RF company.

The PRUs were interested in the operations, but were never able to field more than 15 men at one time, and frequently operated with five men plus two advisors. This limited firepower was augmented by the use of an M60 machinegun usually mounted on a 1/4-ton truck. Trucks were utilized to react quickly to fresh intelligence and get troops into a contact area.

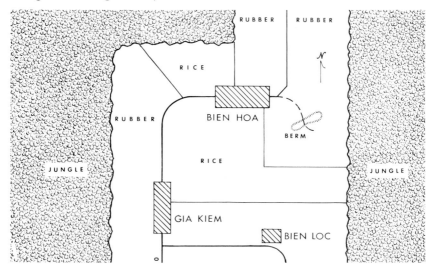

The use of such small forces in motorized operations with a limited number of vehicles made them vulnerable to ambush and this vulnerability was countered by two methods. First, stringent security was ensured by conducting operations as soon as possible after receiving intelligence information. Reaction time varied from one to four hours and depended upon immediate receipt of reliable local intelligence.

Secondly, routes into an area were varied randomly as much as possible and all operations were designed to indicate that the RF units were operating as the point element of a larger force. As

a result the VC almost invariably tried to break contact with them although the RFs rarely held numerical superiority.

The first operation was conducted when it was learned that the VC had set up a tax point approximately three kilometers north of Bien Hoa Village along Highway 20. Fifteen PRUs were loaded into a 1/4-ton and a 3/4-ton truck and moved into the rubber plantation west of the tax point, where they made contact with the VC. The VC immediately scattered, leaving behind some equipment but taking no known casualties. Further patrols conducted in this area· resulted in one VC killed and one AK47 captured. More significantly, after the initial contact in August, no more tax points were set up in this subsector until March.

The second operation occurred after Bien Loc Village was attacked by an estimated VC battalion. The attack was beaten off, but local defenders were reluctant to venture into the surrounding rubber plantation. The VC planted their flag in the area and subjected rubber workers to propaganda every time they went out to work.

A 1/4-ton truck was loaded with PRUs and moved into the area with no definite objective in mind except to look for VC. Almost immediately they surprised four VC who had rounded up a group of rubber workers and were holding a propaganda meeting. The M60 machinegun fired an initial burst at them, but suddenly jammed. Before the PRUs could engage the VC with small arms fire, the enemy fled, placing the workers between themselves and the PRUs. The PRUs were forced to hold their fire and the VC escaped. After this action, the VC ceased to hold propaganda meetings in this area and the local PF forces again operated freely around the village.

Another operation was planned, this time against the VC platoon which had ambushed an RF company east of Bien Hoa Village in early August. This platoon had become extremely aggressive and controlled virtually the entire area from the eastern edge of the village to the jungle. Once they grenaded a two-man outpost and on another occasion they opened fire on a group of soldiers drinking beer in the market place. In both cases the VC took no casualties.

It was obvious to the PRUs and their advisors that it would not be possible to operate directly against this platoon with the small number of personnel available, but indications were that the VC platoon's security forces — the trail watchers — were vulnerable. It was decided to try and destroy the morale of these important trial watchers. Without the security they provided, the VC platoon would have to change its tactics.

Both RF and VC operations had fallen into a definite pattern in this area. The RF almost invariably utilized a small road to

move into the area from their outpost and the VC kept two trail watchers next to an old village berm which ran into the trail. Although the location of these trail watchers was known, observation was such that no one could surprise them and any force moving into the area was immediately fired upon. The VC platoon was then alerted and it generally attacked or attempted to ambush the approaching force. Vietnamese local forces carefully avoided operating in this area.

Early one morning, a group of eight PRUs and one American advisor moved into the area on foot and set up three ambush positions east of the trail watchers and, hopefully, west of the VC platoon.

Once the PRUs were in position, a second element composed only of Americans in a 1/4-ton truck with a mounted M60 machinegun, made its move. Units of the 11th Armored Cavalry Regiment had operated in this area during the Tet Offensive, and this element was attempting to appear as though it was the lead vehicle of an armored column. To enhance this impression, the advisors wore flak jackets and steel helmets, not usual practice for advisors in this area.

The vehicle moved rapidly down the trail until it came in sight of an old village berm. At this point, the vehicle halted and begun to turn around. The M60 fired in the general direction of the berm and one advisor talked frantically on the radio. The idea was to make the VC think they had been spotted and reinforcements were being called for.

A few moments later, one of the ambush positions reported that it had sighted two VC running across an open field near the berm and had fired at them. The trail watchers had fled, fearing they would be engaged by a much larger force than the PRUs. For the first time, the enemy's confidence in his relative immunity from local force action had been severely shaken. As a result of continued operations of this type, the VC platoon moved its trail watchers back into the jungle and was forced to sharply curtail its operations in the village area.

These three operations were followed by many more of the same nature. The basic concept was to rapidly deploy small and aggressive Infantry units against small VC units based upon timely local intelligence. The overall effect on both the VC and the local Vietnamese was impressive. Viet Cong daylight operations virtually ceased. No more tax points were set up north of Bien Hoa Village, the propaganda campaign in the Bien Loc area was halted, and local Vietnamese units began to patrol freely around both Bien Loc and Bien Hoa Village. A unit rarely numbering more than a squad had broken the enemy's long-time hold on the area and had permanently taken the tactical initiative from him.

1969

A YEAR OF TRANSITION

The new year got off on a hopeful note with the release of three American soldiers captured by the Viet Cong in 1968 and the escape the day before of Special Forces Major James Rowe, a VC captive since 1963. Peace talks were continuing in Paris and Richard M. Nixon was inaugurated as President of the United States.

The year was marked as one in which the ARVN played a much larger role in the war effort and American redeployment began. ARVN and American soldiers jointly conducted Operations Russell Beach, Vernon Lake II and Nevada Eagle in early 1969. The enemy suffered serious setbacks in all three encounters.

Defying Allied warnings that continued attacks could only end in defeat, Communist gunners stepped up the shelling of cities and military bases with rocket and mortar fire as their spring offensive got underway. The attacks continued through March, April and May. Enemy losses were heavy as U.S. and ARVN soldiers successfully defended military bases and positions, while continuing to receive minimum casualties.

In early June, Presidents Nixon and Thieu met at Midway Island and announced a 25,000-man redeployment of American troops. It was then that President Nixon promised further announcements would be made when the time was right for additional replacement of American troops with Republic of Vietnam soldiers.

Plans were made to redeploy the 9th Infantry Division back to the States. During September and October of 1969 the 1st and 2nd Brigades were inactivated and the 3rd Brigade remained at its base camp in Tan An, where it stayed until its redeployment and inactivation in October 1970.

As summer ended, elements of the 1st, 9th and 25th Infantry Divisions, along with units of the 199th Light Infantry Brigade; 3rd Brigade, 82d Airborne Division; and the 1st Cavalry Division (Airmobile); plus ARVN and other free world forces, concluded the third phase of Operation Toan Thang throughout Military Region III. The operation yielded numerous captured enemy caches and inflicted heavy losses on the North Vietnamese and VC forces.

The country gained a new posture of pride as each day better trained and better equipped South Vietnamese forces flexed their strength against enemy soldiers. Each day this new strength enhanced the possibility of future withdrawals of American units.

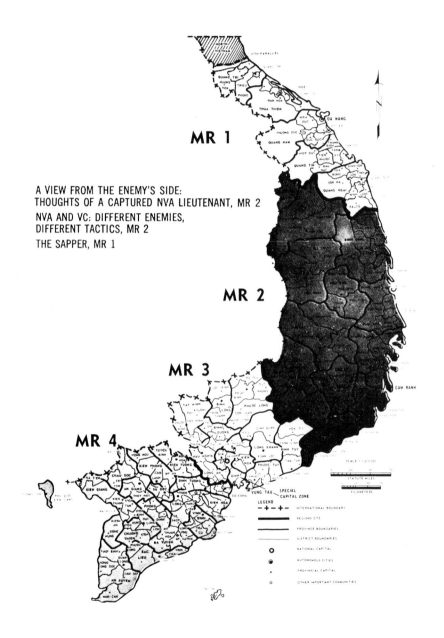

A VIEW FROM THE ENEMY'S SIDE:
THOUGHTS OF A CAPTURED NVA LIEUTENANT, MR 2

NVA AND VC: DIFFERENT ENEMIES,
DIFFERENT TACTICS, MR 2

THE SAPPER, MR 1

Chapter 7

To Know The Enemy

A View from the Enemy's Side:
Thoughts of a Captured NVA Lieutenant

Major Malcolm A. Danner
Major Billy J. Biberstein

My parents were rice farmers and owned 50 hectares of rice fields in North Vietnam, but when I was born, my father was dead and my mother was renting most of the land to neighbors. When I was six to 10-years-old I had to move from Nam Ha to Ngol Cao village in Hoa Lu District of Ninh Binh Province because of the fighting between the French and the Viet Minh.

I am not pleased to be under the Communist regime or yoke. Before it was established, my mother was able to sell our farm products to the people but after they came, she had to sell her products to the cooperative. There is very little profit now.

The North Vietnamese people don't like it under the Communist party but they dare not express their feeling for fear of punishment. If they speak out against the government they are arrested and sent to a reform center for one to four months. If it is a more serious offense they are sent to prison for six months or more. I don't believe anyone is executed unless they commit a serious crime such as murder.

The people of North Vietnam do not like to see their men drafted into the NVA but the government says they must go. This makes the government unpopular and the people do not like the Communist party. The families of the drafted youth do not like to see their sons infiltrated into South Vietnam, but this is an order from the party and it must be executed. As very few men ever return to North Vietnam, the people know there is little hope of one's return. They believe the soldiers are a sacrifice and will die. The only soldiers that get back to North Vietnam, other than the wounded, are the cadre of infiltration units that bring the replacements down. They return to train more soldiers, then bring them down.

I know I'm sick and tired of the army, being in it for the duration; however, there are very few men who reject the military draft. I don't know the punishment for those who do, but you never see them again. The time of departure from North Vietnam to South Vietnam is the most critical time. There are a lot of volunteers in the NVA but they are the hot-bloods. The age group is from 16 to 21-years-old. These are the young and hot-blooded elements and they want to fight. They haven't seen the brutality of the war.

NVA Basic Training

There are very few of the age group 17 to 35-years-old left in the hamlets and villages in North Vietnam. In the hamlet, where I was living when drafted, there were 120 families and a total population of 4,000 to 5,000 people. There were only three or four men of the 17 to 35 age group left and they were not in good health. They were either sick, deformed or paralyzed. There will always be a constant supply of manpower for the army, however. It will be furnished by the school children as they grow up. The problem is that the youths will lack combat experience and all our experienced soldiers are getting killed.

I was drafted in early 1965 and was assigned to a reconnaissance unit from the start. I initially took a few tests but most of the tests were given later and were on recon subjects such as map reading. The drafted personnel go into different branches depending on their civilian trade and schooling. After a period of basic training the cadre normally selects personnel for certain branches. The basic training varies from a minimum of one

month for an Infantryman before he goes to the battlefield, to a minimum of one-and-one-half years for a recon man. Our reconnaissance units are considered to be the elite organizations. In order to become a member of one, a soldier must be selected and trained specifically for reconnaissance. Our higher headquarters normally furnishes the replacements we need and we will not accept soldiers from subordinate elements as replacements. One-and-one-half years is the minimum training period for a recon soldier and the maximum is four years.

The recon soldier is treated best and has good quarters and food, but the training is very difficult and the hours are long and tiring. The recon units are issued and carry two sets of fatigues plus two sets of camouflaged fatigues. The regular soldier is issued only two sets of jungle fatigues. Our uniforms are manufactured in North Vietnam. We also get the new type AK weapon manufactured in 1957. We were issued steel helmets in North Vietnam and wore them initially in South Vietnam but after several incidents in which local and main force VC units shot and killed our soldiers, the regimental CO ordered us to discard the helmets. We then went bareheaded.

The sappers are the second most elite units. They are selected by the cadre and are not volunteers. They have a required six-months minimum training period and a maximum of one-and-a-half years. They train on the use of demolitions only and many get killed because they lack training in tactics.

We had many weapons in the army while in North Vietnam; more weapons than personnel. I personally like my K54 pistol the best (Chicom automatic) and I also like the AK47, which is better than the M16. Although I never fired the M16, the AK47 is more practical, as it is smaller, easier to handle and clean and the round does more damage.

There are Russian advisors with all our army units such as the artillery, Infantry and armor, but I do not know about the Air Force. We have many tanks in North Vietnam, a whole army corps of tanks, but I have never seen them in South Vietnam. During my movement through North Vietnam to the south, I saw a regimental-size force of Chinese soldiers in Thai Nguyen Province. This was in a mountainous forest area.

Travels South

We left North Vietnam in February 1968 and went into Laos. We were on a military road through forests and jungles. I do not know much about Laos as we never really met the people. I don't really know whose side Laos is on.

I didn't get to know the Cambodian people either. In theory and practice, Cambodia is neutral. I don't know why we get to use it; I expect it's like a chess game. The NVA made the right move and uses Cambodia; I suppose the South Vietnamese could also use it if they knew how to.

In South Vietnam I never passed through villages or hamlets and only talked with South Vietnamese laborers controlled by the NVA. They were sociable.

A Typical Day

During the day when I am not on an operation my life with the NVA is very easy. I wake up at 0600 hours daily, brush my teeth and bathe. I eat breakfast with my fellow officers at 0700 hours. The enlisted soldiers eat together in another area. After breakfast I join the men of my company and talk to them until about 1100 hours. We talk about personal matters like families, home and, of course, sex. At 1100 hours I eat lunch and take a

siesta until 1400 hours. Our food is usually rice and canned meat. The food is from China and is prepared for us by the two cooks of my company. As executive officer of the Company I am responsible for the preparation of the food. The canned meat is usually pork and we get tired of eating it so often. Sometimes the Vietnamese people provide us food. In Darlac, Kontum and Pleiku, the people were sympathetic to us and gave us rice.

In the afternoon I go fishing with one or two members of my company. We do not go more than two kilometers from our base camp. We are very careful with members of our unit who appear to be worried or if their morale is low. We watch them closely and accompany them continuously. There is nothing to do during the day except go fishing.

At 1800 I eat supper and then at 1900 the entire company assembles for a meeting at which the political officer is in charge. At this daily meeting the political officer praises NVA heroes and slanders the South Vietnamese government. He also talks about the great victories we are achieving against the ARVN and US units. I do not think the political officer is effective; the soldiers do not listen attentively and become bored very quickly with his speech. One reason he is ineffective is because he never accompanies us on our combat operations and he never sees us take casualties. The soldiers know this and do not believe his stories. Sometimes I get together with my men after the political meeting and we sing and tell jokes to try and cheer each other up. At 2100 we go to bed. If we are located away from the enemy we sleep in hammocks; if we are close to the enemy we sleep in trenches and foxholes.

When we are in the mountains avoiding contact and on a rest period our most vulnerable elements are the patrols we send out, and some of the companies that we have guarding our outer perimeter. The food we normally have in advance, and the rest area will always be around some source of water.

It is easy to distinguish our officers during the battle as they attack with the headquarters element. The headquarters element consists of the CO, XO, radioman, and runner. The officers don't wear pistols or insignia of rank during the battle and are dressed the same as each soldier.

When moving large units in South Vietnam our forces do not use the existing trails. These trails do not necessarily speed your movement up because of the security requirements and fear of detection; the personnel weave on and off the trails. While moving, we have a squad linking battalions to each other. When we arrive at a perpendicular trail, we break branches to show the direction. In thick vegetation we cut bamboo stalks and place them about waist-high in the foliage with the pointed tip showing the direction. There is no set distance for spacing these stalks.

Prior to an attack we prepare a plan. Normally the recon unit has seen the area and can diagram it in detail. This normally is given to the sapper units who will go in first or maybe with the attacking Infantry.

All units must go by this plan and a soldier must execute an order even if many get killed. They must launch the attack at all costs. The plan always shows how to get into the objective area, where key points to be destroyed are located and how best to exfiltrate. Artillery support is fired prior to the attack to confuse and pin down the enemy. During the battle sometimes artillery continues firing and kills our own men, but this is normally done only where there is a lack of communications. If the enemy gets our attacking forces pinned down, artillery is employed in order for them to withdraw. Artillery is also used when we want to break contact or exfiltrate.

There are several reasons why our artillery is inaccurate and not too effective. One is that we don't get to choose the terrain all the time. Another reason is because of the tactics involved and the last reason is the enemy.

After the battle if we have many dead, we rest and bury the dead. It is NVA discipline that you always try to recover a friend's body. We have no religious service for the dead, we just bury them. His personal effects are kept by his friends. If a unit has suffered lots of casualties their morale is low and replacements are needed. That unit is rarely used to attack the same objective.

We used a control technique to help weak soldiers by organizing into three-man cells. The selection is not made by friendship, but by picking two skillful men and one weak one.

I never saw a self-criticism session and don't know if they are effective or not. The men in my unit made written statements of self-criticism but I just filed them in their records.

My reconnaissance unit is usually briefed on our mission at least one day prior to moving out. Our regimental commander or the executive officer briefs us on our mission. After we received our mission we stay together in the unit area. We never use guides when we are conducting our movement because they are not reliable. Guides are used by larger units only for long distance moves or marches. For our movement, we use maps and compasses to navigate. The maps we use are 1:100,000 or 1:50,000 scale and are French-made with Vietnamese writing. Our division supply element can provide these maps for any area very soon after request. Normally there are not enough compasses for every man, so every third man is issued a compass.

During the day when my unit is on an operation, we start the day at 0430 or 0530. The necessary rations and equipment are obtained and prepared the day before the operation begins. The special equipment we usually carry consists of radios, maps, compasses, binoculars, notebooks and a knife. I inspect every man to include the condition of his weapon, ammunition (90 rounds per man), two grenades and equipment prior to departure. We move out at 0600 hours. During movement to the reconnaissance objective, we usually travel about three kilometers per hour, taking a 10 to 15 minute break every hour. We rarely travel more than a day and a half without sleeping. During movement we keep our weapons on safety because we have had accidents with triggers catching on bushes, etc. We do not sleep at mid-day during movement.

At 1500 hours we find a place to make camp for the night. When we arrive at the reconnaissance objective, we usually establish an OP approximately one or two hours distance from the objective. Next we dispatch small teams (two or three men) to move in as close to the objective as possible. If we possibly can, we try to penetrate and enter the objective area to determine the exact enemy strength and location. We try to locate and count the number of heavy weapons such as 105mm howitzers and 81mm mortars. If we are successful and are not detected we withdraw using the same route.

We are never assigned a straight combat mission to engage the enemy. We are only told to observe and report what we have seen. Near Chu Do, in the western highlands of Kontum, one of my reconnaissance squads saw a US reconnaissance team on three different occasions. Each time I ordered my men to hold their fire and not engage US troops unless we were discovered. If we were discovered, we would return fire immediately and attempt to disengage and withdraw. US reconnaissance teams always fire into suspected positions and this is not effective as they disclose their own location. We know where they are after they fire and all we have to do is bypass them. Often we are able to determine the reconnaissance objective of the US team because of these mistakes. As reconnaissance personnel we do not fight in battles. During the attack we usually remain at a secure area with the regimental staff until the main body has returned.

In our reconnaissance of cities we are normally met by local force liaison people at a prearranged location within or close to the city. The liaison people escort us to the exact positions or locations to be attacked. If there are several ARVN soldiers in the area, we usually disguise ourselves as ARVN. But in cities where there are only a few ARVN soldiers, we wear civilian clothes. Normally we use challenge and passwords to recognize the liaison people. Before we reach the city, usually at our secret base, the code words are issued by the local force underground organizations (VCI) along with ID cards.

When we complete our reconnaissance mission, we return to our unit as soon as possible. We never rely on civilians or others to relay our information. After an attack, we normally take two or three weeks off and rest and treat the wounded and conduct "lessons learned" meetings. My reconnaissance unit did not train unless we had more than six weeks between missions and I never experienced a lull longer than three to four weeks.

When you do a good job in the army you are awarded by being promoted and given a certicate of commendation. I was happy when promoted as I knew my leaders recognized my good performance. Recently in South Vietnam, the NVA has started giving the Medal of Victory. I did not get one and none of my men earned one. There are no monetary awards given.

We are taught and given training on sand tables about American defensive perimeters in general. We have much training on how to disarm mines. The claymore is the easiest. We have received lots of training on disarming four or five particular mines. One is the small plastic antipersonnel stepmine. The second is the claymore and the third the ground and tripflares. We also were trained in the one that has either the push or pull firing device in the safety pin hole. I have never seen one of my men blown up while disarming a mine and have only seen two of my men step on mines and neither of those mines exploded.

All the US defensive positions are very easy to get through. I can say that I have never encountered a tough one in my experience. We just crawl slowly through the wire, cutting the bottom strands. In case we are detected while inside the camp and must make a hasty withdrawal, we use wood planks or ladders if available and go over the top of the wire. In training we have a man lie on the wire and run over him but we never do this in combat operations. You had lots of wire around Polei Kleng but it was easy to get through. I just don't think you have a defensive barrier that is effective against us.

We have one doctor and one medical specialist who work at the regimental dispensary. We also have two medics in the company. Physical examinations are not routine in the NVA and are given only when you're ill. The doctors in the NVA are very good. If a man loses a leg he is sent back to North Vietnam after receiving proper medical treatment. I never saw a wounded soldier in North Vietnam. When they go back the government keeps them in medical centers as they don't want the people to see them.

When we have cuts or infections we take anti-infection pills to cure the infection. We do not take any type of medication prior to going into battle and only the doctor has morphine.

Although we take the malaria pill, most of us have malaria. The pill is used only to prevent malaria, but due to the poor physical conditions of our personnel, we often contract it. I believe all 70 men in my unit had contracted malaria at one time or another and it was in various degrees of seriousness.

We also take B1 vitamins daily. Three men in my unit had paralysis and couldn't feel pain or anything. We didn't know what this was and just sent them to the hospital. I never saw them after they went to the hospital.

The only women in the NVA were the nurses who worked in the hospitals and they didn't go with the combat units into the battles. We didn't have much sex life in the NVA unit. However, sometimes during infiltration we met girls at the communications and liaison stations in North Vietnam, Laos and Cambodia. The girls in North Vietnam and Laos were Vietnamese or Laotian, the ones in Cambodia were Vietnamese. The girls seemed to like us and we were nice to them, sometimes giving them North Vietnamese money and gifts.

The Day I Was Captured

I will never forget the day I was captured. We had finished our recon and were returning to the base camp area when my unit of eight men became surrounded by an American Infantry company. Artillery was fired on us and I received a serious wound in the stomach and another in the left thigh. I felt mad that my unit was leaving me but I knew they must or they would all become wounded or captured. I gave my friend my pistol, machinegun, watch, ring and a map. I kept only my compass and placed two grenades under me. I expected to die and today I can hardly believe I'm still alive. I was going to use the grenades on my captors if possible and kill them if they hit me or if it appeared they were going to kill me. Leaving the grenades with the wounded is not a policy; I just thought maybe I could kill some of you.

Instead of being mistreated, as soon as I was found, a medic came up and started giving me medical treatment. I could have killed the medic — a US captain — and two other men with the grenades as they never searched me, but after getting the medical help I gave them the grenades.

I am glad to get good treatment as a PW and the doctors and people have been very kind to me but I would rather be with my unit so I could move freely. I want to feel free. If I could I would accept South Vietnam.

If there was a PW exchange I would be happy. Then I could go back to my unit, maybe another unit, or be released and be a civilian. I would not be watched as the exchange would be official.

The political officer tells us that if captured by you, we will be tortured and killed. When I was wounded and captured, I expected to be killed. Of course now I have changed my mind. An ARVN major showed me a South Vietnam brochure on treatment of PWs and I realized then I would not be killed.

I don't know how you could make the NVA soldier believe you don't kill PWs; one way might be to let some PWs return after you have given them proper medical treatment. However, if I was released and went back to my unit I would be watched very closely at all times.

We are told to try and capture American soldiers if at all possible because they are very valuable to our propaganda effort. I have never seen an American or South Vietnam prisoner. While in training we were told not to hit any PW we captured and to give them good treatment. I have never heard of any PW being mistreated by the NVA.

The only soldiers who enjoy the army are the young hot-blooded ones. Most of us are draftees who don't enjoy it. We don't care about not getting paid as we couldn't spend it anyway but there are many hardships. Many times there is a shortage of food and equipment in the NVA while in South Vietnam and this really affects the morale of the troops.

American Units Are Weak

The North Vietnam soldier is better than the South Vietnam soldier but the ARVN have artillery. The American soldier is stronger and more intelligent but he is not familiar with the terrain so the North Vietnam soldier has an advantage. The US soldier is very poor when moving through the terrain. The American Infantry units are weak, their firepower is poor and their equipment is poor. An example of this is that an American unit cannot take or destroy a machinegun position in a properly prepared bunker except by calling for air or artillery; however, the NVA can destroy any American bunker with its B40 or B41 rocket.

The ARVN forces are weak because their equipment is poor; more than poor. The RF/PF and CIDG are also poor. There is some collaboration among RF/PF units done by the local force VC units and then the arrangements are passed on to the NVA. I feel there are many Communist agents and sympathizers in South Vietnam units and agencies. I know that on the B52 strikes we normally had advance warning as to where and when they would occur. The warning usually came by a message from division to the regiment and it normally arrived two hours prior to the strike. As I remember, the most time we ever had was four hours. In one instance, warning arrived just minutes before the airstrike and we just made it out of the area when it was hit and demolished. I think that 70 to 80 percent of all NVA casualties are caused by artillery or air.

The quality of our officers is good to bad. Some are knowledgeable about military matters and some are not. This depends on the unit. The officer-EM relationship in the NVA is very good. During off-duty hours we talk with each other, and have a mutual understanding as we all have the same problems and troubles.

Without the local force units in South Vietnam the NVA is useless. The LF are the link between the NVA and the South Vietnam battlefield areas. The NVA soldiers feel very sorry for the LF units, even pity them, as they lack weapons, food and equipment. The VC units are very poor—they are weak both politically and militarily. We all have an understanding though and the VC and NVA are close and united.

I have heard of the Chieu Hoi program but I don't know what it is. I have heard a little about it from an airplane but we really didn't pay much attention as it was very poor propaganda and the voice did not sound sincere.

I have seen lots of the psyops leaflets but they are very poor and we laugh at them; they make no impression on the soldier of the NVA. I saw them in Kontum and Darlac provinces as we moved toward our objectives. The quality of the writing is very poor and not good Vietnamese. The Americans should let the Vietnamese compose them, as they know how to put the story or what you want said into poetry. The Vietnamese are a very poetic people.

All the men in my unit could read and write and they had

to have a minimum of a second class education. In the Infantry units, the education minimum is lower but most can read or write to some degree.

We have radios to listen to and when we can get batteries, we listen to music. We are not allowed to listen to the South Vietnam radio station and I do not like to listen to the news because it is usually propaganda and political.

I have heard about free elections in South Vietnam. It is quite normal for South Vietnam to have free elections but we do not know if the elections are a political trick or if they are real.

Many soldiers worry about their loved ones. I thought of my mother many times but there was no mail. When we first entered South Vietnam eight months ago, our superiors assembled the unit and instructed us to write a letter home to our relatives and tell them we were happy and in good health. I had a letter box number and so did my men. Our leaders told us it would require four months for letters to arrive in North Vietnam and five months to return. I have never received a letter from North Vietnam and none of my men have either.

The people in North Vietnam are like the deaf and blind, they do not know what goes on, just what the Communists tell them. When North Vietnam denies having the NVA in South Vietnam, our leaders are speaking incorrectly. They are lying. I think it is silly and ridiculous. If we don't fight, our families will be harassed by the government. This kind of propaganda is for you to pick up, it is not broadcast to the North Vietnamese people or our military units. This really doesn't affect the morale of our troops as they are not made aware of it.

The North Vietnamese people have no opinion of the allied forces assisting South Vietnam as they are too far from the front. Among the NVA forces in South Vietnam this kind of talk is not carried on because of the political officer's presence. I am not surprised at the presence of the Free World Forces in South Vietnam as they have a right to request aid the same as the North Vietnamese government.

I really don't know about the bombing halt as I've been in South Vietnam since February. At first the people in North Vietnam were very scared of the bombs but now they consider it a rule of the war. The people just complain that they don't know why you bomb them; the people don't really know the political situation. I hear they were pleased and happy when you stopped bombing them. They had guessed you would stop the bombing before you did. They feel that you stopped the bombing because you wanted peace.

I have heard a little about the peace talks on the radio from Hanoi but I have no opinion on them. I think the only answer is a North Vietnam and a South Vietnam. There are just too many differences on each side. Once divided, the country should be controlled by an International Commission at the DMZ. The UN cannot control it as they have the problem of Communism versus the free world. Most of the people want a united Vietnam because they want an end to the war. They want a unification of both sides.

I compare the war to a Chinese chess game. The Americans and the South Vietnamese are compared to the horse (a knight of our chess game). They are strong but don't know the moves. The NVA is a weaker horse, but knows the moves.

We know we cannot defeat Americans as it is almost impossible to defeat you, but the military operations just occur to back the political aspects. We will win the war politically, not militarily.

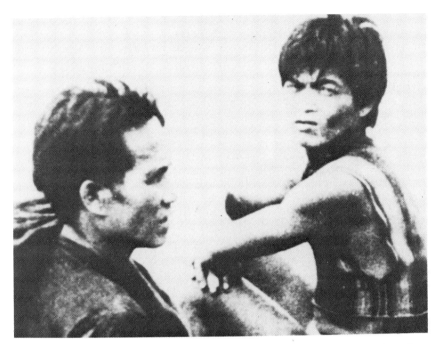

NVA and VC: Different Enemies, Different Tactics

Captain Anthony V. Neglia

When a soldier is sent to the Republic of Vietnam, he finds that his unit has adopted tactics for fighting the enemy in its area of operations (AO). The individual soldier soon learns these tactics and becomes effective against the enemy, whether it is the North Vietnamese Army (NVA) or the Viet Cong.

However, numerous problems arise in a sudden transition from one enemy to the other. Successful habits which have been carefully cultivated are hard to break, and a state of mind that has been developed for a specific kind of fighting is hard to change. One Infantry battalion found itself facing these problems when it was shifted from An Khe to Landing Zone Uplift in Phu My District.

From early 1968 to March 1969, the 1st Battalion, 50th Infantry (Mechanized) operated around An Khe. Its primary mission was security of Highway 19 (QL 19) from the An Khe Pass to the Mang Yang Pass. The 4th and 5th Battalions of the 95B Regiment were the main North Vietnamese Army units operating in the area. It was known that 95B was targeted against QL 19, the convoys using it and the fuel line which paralleled it. It was of vital importance that the logistics which flowed on QL 19 and through the pipeline not be disrupted. QL 19 was the lifeline for the 4th US Infantry Division at Pleiku.

Although there were some VC in the vicinity of An Khe, they were not a factor. For all practical purposes, the enemy was entirely NVA. The 95B Regiment was a typical NVA regiment, with its battalions varying in strength from 180 to 250 men. They had the normal complement of AKs, RPG2s and RPG7s, mortars, and recoilless rifles. An organic engineer unit was often employed in attempts to blow up sections of the highway.

The 95B utilized hit-and-run attacks on convoys, stand-off mortar and recoilless rifle attacks on pump stations and fire support bases, and nighttime sabotage of the pipeline and highway.

The enemy was an expert in camouflage. He remained dispersed and avoided contact until he was ready to fight. During a firefight, he was highly adept at breaking contact by use of a small delaying force. Other than that, he had no special talents in combat. He didn't employ boobytraps, and although he used mines, the results were usually ineffective.

He was susceptible to our intelligence gathering systems and artillery, gunships and jets could then be employed against his positions. In a firefight he displayed little aggressiveness and his tactics lacked imagination. This was the 95B NVA Regiment.

The morale of the 1st Battalion, 50th Infantry (Mechanized) was extremely high. The battalion had devastating firepower — the armored personnel carriers had two mounted M60 machineguns and one .50 caliber machinegun. However, good platoon leaders insured that the troops didn't stay glued to their APCs. They were aggressive and readily made dismounted sweeps when required.

Although daylight actions were usually initiated by the NVA, the 1/50th's quick reaction and firepower gave it the upper hand. The troops quickly learned the advantage of pressing the attack once fire superiority had been achieved. After months of unsuccessful attacks on convoys and regular combat units, 95B's troops limited themselves to halfhearted ambushes and stand-off attacks.

With the exception of some minor sabotage, the enemy's night operations were also failures. He had to come to the highway to do his dirty work, and the Americans were already there. Additionally, the battalion knew every approach to the highway and every culvert that could be blown, as well as the enemy's favorite assembly areas. The US troops had spent almost an entire year in that area, while the NVA were usually more than 20 kilometers away and had to travel discreetly in order to reach their targets. This lack of familiarity with the terrain forced the NVA to guide continually on the same ridge or stream bed, even after some of its units had been successfully ambushed on these same approaches.

The battalion had several highly successful ambushes, including one that took place before dark. The last convoy normally passed through the AO at 1730, with the road security force pulled out shortly thereafter. Since the NVA were not familiar with the area, it was thought that they might try to move in before dark, just after the security elements had withdrawn.

At 1500, a lieutenant went to Strongpoint (SP) 10, ostensibly to relieve the personnel there. An ambush party was concealed within the APC while a normal SP contingent was riding on top of the carrier. Just before the APC returned to the company base at 1745, the ambush party secretly off-loaded from the carrier and moved into position. About a half-hour before dark, eight NVA were observed crossing the highway. Although not in the killing zone of the ambush, they were engaged and four of them were killed. Results such as these were normally achieved when intelligence dictated concentrated efforts in specific areas.

As might be expected, quick reaction to enemy-initiated contact also provided good results. APCs were strategically located at SPs along the highway and provided complete observation of the road for its entire route through the battalion's AO. The moment enemy activity was observed, reaction forces were directed to the area to engage the enemy or assist units in contact. As a result of this type of action, 95B's hit and run tactics degenerated into more run and less hit.

When the battalion left the An Khe area, it also left a beaten and demoralized NVA regiment. The 4th and 5th Battalions of that regiment were no longer combat effective. The 4th Battalion suffered further humiliation when it was later converted into a transportation unit. Heeding the exhortation of their battalion commander, the US troops had "leaned on Chuck."

In March 1969, the battalion moved to the coastal region in Military Region 7. It was to perform pacification missions south of Bong Son while operating out of LZ Uplift. The intelligence reports were sketchy at best, and the S2 knew only of a 30-man VC force operating east of Highway One. This was the first difference noted between the NVA and VC. The VC were much less susceptible to sophisticated intelligence gathering machinery. Hard work was now required to produce every little scrap of information.

Another lost advantage was that the VC were not targeted against any single location, as the NVA had been. The VC between QL 1 and the South China Sea were seemingly satisfied with just being able to exist. They felt that their mere presence exerted influence over the villagers. Their primary goal was, in fact, the control of the populace, which made the villagers the crux of the situation.

Initially, daylight operations in the coastal area were not so much a matter of searching for the VC as for boobytraps. Trails had to be avoided. On patrols, the troops walked in the footsteps of the man in front. Haste became anathema. Despite all of the precautions taken, boobytraps were triggered and casualties were taken. Nothing is more frustrating or wasteful than the loss of a soldier to a boobytrap.

The VC employed boobytraps, mines and an occasional night attack on perimeters. The traps and mines had a psychological impact on US personnel, while the night attacks were conducted halfheartedly, appearing to be more for the benefit of the villagers than anything else. Long periods of inactivity also occurred. It

was strange fighting an enemy that seemingly ignored you at times, while you couldn't afford to ignore him.

The tactics used to cope with this situation were developed as much from reflex action as from conscious effort. Since mechanical and electrical intelligence devices didn't produce the results they had obtained against the NVA, the villagers became the primary source of information. Deriving intelligence from the people proved to be a tedious job, but it was the only method that produced results.

An investigation might produce the name of a village where the VC would sometimes stay, but careful interrogation and search might produce no results at all. In such situations, an interpreter was indispensable. One platoon which had an assigned interpreter captured two hard-core members of the VC infrastructure.

Friendliness towards children, an instinctive American trait, produced some of the battalion's best intelligence. One young boy helped identify a VC living in his village, while others brought in several hundred dud artillery rounds, each a potential mine against our APCs. For such information, the children were given monetary rewards under the Volunteer Informant Program (VIP).

Other children showed us where satchel charges had been set around the perimeter of the fire support base. These explosives were to be hurled into the area by propelling charges. The propelling charges were electrically detonated, while the payload employed a pull-delay fuze. Three such charges were fired at LZ Uplift one night, two of them detonating within the wire while the third went all the way over the base. All three exploded in the air. What the system lacked in accuracy was made up for in range — nearly 200 meters.

Children also solved the interpreter problem. Platoons that didn't have an interpreter assigned adopted boys between the ages of nine and 14 after they had been cleared by the National Police in Bong Son. The youngsters proved to be outstanding in obtaining information from other children.

However, it was soon learned that children can be a two-edged sword. Children wandering in the rice paddies just outside the perimeter were not carefully scrutinized until two boys were caught collecting spring-action devices from the smoke grenades used to guide in helicopters. The boys stated that the VC had told them that they wanted these devices. It was times like these that brought home the difference between the NVA and the VC. The VC would use anyone, including women and children, to operate against US forces.

Although some VC stayed in the mountains with their NVA advisors, most of them lived in villages situated away from US bases. The VC who lived in these villages were first-priority targets for US tactical operations.

We learned from friendly villagers that the VC hid in tunnels or holes when Americans came into the hamlets to conduct searches. The tunnels or holes had wooden covers or straw mats placed on top after the VC were inside. They were then covered with soil or sand, to blend with the surrounding area. Patrols were instructed to carry long poles with which they could probe the ground. They were also told to be alert for any sand seeping into the ground.

It was the telltale sign of sand seeping into the ground that ended the fighting days of two VC. While on a village search and clear mission, a sharp-eyed squad leader spotted the slowly disappearing sand. The sand and a cover of logs had been cleared away when a VC's head popped into the opening. He appeared to be coming out when his head was suddenly replaced by a claymore mine. Before the mine could be detonated, all personnel were clear of the area with one good running leap. After several hand grenades were tossed into the hole, activity in the area slowed considerably. A PFC, armed with a .45 caliber pistol, went into the hole to check it out. He killed a second VC who was in the act of throwing a grenade.

While aggressiveness and quick reaction were prerequisites for success against the NVA, against the VC the essential qualities were patience and thoroughness. For example, a young platoon sergeant who believed in thoroughness not only checked a Vietnamese family's bunker, but the walls as well. He found a removable panel and two very startled VC.

The night ambush which, at An Khe, had been one of the most successful tactics against the NVA, was initially a total failure against the VC. The standard procedures of having the ambushes move out after dark, or of employing stay-behind ambushes, did not produce results.

At An Khe the NVA had to move long distances to reach the highway for an operation, but in the coastal villages the VC were already in the area in which they were going to operate. In some cases, they did not even have to leave their own village. Thus, their vulnerability to an ambush was greatly diminished.

At An Khe, when it was felt that the NVA were coming up to the highway before our ambushes got into position, stay-behind ambushes were successfully employed. The fact that the NVA did not have knowledge of our exact strength, even if they did keep us under observation, made the success of the stay-behind ambush possible. The VC, on the other hand, not only knew our exact strength, but probably conducted a headcount as US units returned to base camp each evening. Stay-behind ambushes under such circumstances did not deceive the VC.

A technique which improved the results of night operations was saturation ambushing. When using this technique, companies operated with two rifle platoons, while the third platoon worked independently. The mortar platoon, which was down to nine men at times, added little flexibility. When battalion operations permitted both platoons to operate together, one platoon was used

solely for night ambushes. Four to five ambushes were sent out nightly, depending on the unit strength and radio availability at the time.

Ambushes were usually set up around villages. If the VC were aware of these ambushes, they would at least be denied access to the saturated area. Also, if basic precautions were used, the VC would have no way of knowing that multiple ambushes were out. After a few days, several ambushes picked up unarmed men outside villages and, in time, the VC were hampered severely.

Here again, another difference arose between fighting VC and NVA. At An Khe no civilians lived in the areas where field operations were conducted and anything that came into the kill zone could be fired on. However, in the coastal area, with ambushes laid near villages and, in some cases, inside of the villages, discipline and self-control by the troops was imperative. Indiscriminate firing was outlawed. The ambush leader had the added problem of distinguishing between armed and unarmed personnel. In the case of unarmed personnel, he had to decide whether to apprehend or continue to observe.

In reviewing the problems which were encountered in the transition from NVA to VC, there were differences both in the nature of the enemy himself and in the way he fought. The NVA were often emaciated and racked with sickness. Plastic packages filled with narcotics were found on the soldiers of the 95B Regiment. A lack of motivation could be assumed, if the pot was used as an artificial means to stimulate the NVA desire to fight. The general lack of ferocity in 95B's attacks tended to corroborate this assumption.

On the other hand, the VC were well-fed and healthy. In all cases, the VC were found to be highly motivated and dope was never found. The VC could be quite aggressive and daring when they saw an advantage. One or two VC would not hesitate to sneak up on a US platoon or company perimeter, or wait beside a trail with a claymore mine for an unwary US patrol.

The troops were quick to notice the difference in quality between the NVA and the VC. The difficulty in capturing or killing a single VC gave Charlie a certain mystical air, and praise for successful operations became more important than ever before. The confidence and morale of the troops went up immensely when a VC was reported captured or killed, regardless of which platoon got credit.

Against the VC, the rifle companies had to produce most of the intelligence. The individual soldier had to be made aware that he would have to gather intelligence and had to be instructed in all facets of VC operations. Coupled with this knowledge, along with alertness for any deviation from the norm, riflemen were able to provide accurate and timely intelligence about the areas they worked.

One soldier noticed an unusually large amount of rice stored in a village. Questioning of the village chief revealed that the VC were obtaining rice from the villagers through coercion. The village was then kept under observation and added pressure was brought to bear upon the VC.

The intelligence gathering program received added impetus when the troops learned that the VC didn't intend to fight them head-on, but would have to be ferreted out. Against such an enemy, fire superiority was meaningless. Little effort was required to overcome a VC force in combat. The rub was to find it in the first place.

Much has been said of the advantages possessed by the VC. However, the VC had the distinct disadvantage of remaining in their home area, no matter how badly things were going for them. Once they had to leave the area where they had probably spent their entire lives, they were like fish out of water.

If a unit should face the transition from NVA to VC, it should not be assumed that the necessary operational changes will be obvious to the troops. They should be informed of what to expect from the enemy and what is expected of them. They must be aware that the results they achieve will largely be dependent upon the intelligence they themselves gather. To capture or kill one VC takes much effort, but the sense of accomplishment in having met and defeated a tough foe in his own territory is great.

The Sapper

Staff Sergeant Frederick P. Peterkin, USMC

Following the Tet Offensive of 1968, neither the Viet Cong nor the North Vietnamese Army were able to overrun or hold any position manned by Free World Forces in the Republic of Vietnam. Instead, the main force VC and NVA units resorted to raids employing sapper units. This tactic has been used frequently and should be understood so that its effectiveness can be thwarted.

215

The sapper battalion does not have a specific table of organization and equipment, but each unit has the following basic organization:

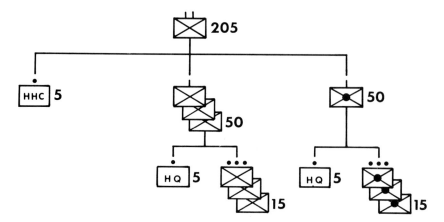

Weapons include AK47 rifles, rocket-propelled grenade launchers (RPGs), and 82mm and 60mm mortars.

The sapper is a tough, well-trained and highly motivated soldier. He is a veteran who has volunteered to receive extensive specialized training. His primary mission is the destruction of Free World Forces' weapons, installations, equipment, and personnel through the use of demolitions.

The training a sapper receives is rugged and thorough. During his first month he concentrates on hand-to-hand combat and infiltration tactics — the art of approaching an objective undetected. The next two weeks he learns how to detect anti-intrusion devices and breach defensive obstacles. Once the fledgling sapper has mastered that phase, he then spends a week studying mines and boobytraps, including their detection and disarming. It is believed that live ordnance is used for this training. After he studies tactics — how the sapper unit attacks outposts, fire support bases, and built-up areas — he receives his final classes in the use of sophisticated and field expedient explosives.

When the sapper completes this specialized training and the concurrent political indoctrination, he has complete confidence in his ability to successfully execute any task assigned.

The sapper company commander normally receives orders for an attack four to 10 days in advance. While he and the platoon leaders are concerned with the tactical aspects of the mission, unit political officers are doubling their efforts to instill the highest possible esprit in the men.

Like any leader, the sapper company commander begins planning the attack by making a detailed reconnaissance of the objective. All aspects of the surrounding terrain and the objective's defenses are analyzed. Key terrain features, routes of approach and withdrawal, location of listening posts, patrol patterns, and automatic weapons positions are carefully noted. A sequence of events timetable is developed to cover all phases of the attack.

Finally, the plan of attack is formalized and a detailed map of the objective that depicts the exact location of each bunker, magazine, crew-served weapon, command post, artillery piece, and re-supply point is prepared. The strength and composition of the defenders is known almost to the man.

A minimum of three days is spent rehearsing the attack. Sketches and sandtable models of the objective are used to help explain to each individual exactly what to do and how to do it. The routes of approach, assault, and withdrawal are given time and again to each squad. The timetable and special signals are memorized and the entire operation is developed with utmost precision and efficiency.

The assault slowly builds up to the short, violent climax that is finally experienced by the defenders. Sometimes as much as an entire day is spent by the sapper working his way to within a few hundred meters of the objective. The hours between sunset and the actual assault are consumed by the sapper's painstaking advance through the defensive obstacles and avoidance of the listening posts and anti-intrusion devices. His approach is completely

silent. Any noise made while breaching an obstacle is timed to coincide with artillery fire missions and vehicle movements.

The sapper's route of approach normally will be through the most difficult areas where observation by the defenders is most unlikely. When breaching a wire obstacle, the sapper uses bamboo poles to raise it, mats to crawl over it, or wire cutters to go through it. If the final defensive wire cannot be breached by one of these methods, it may be blown apart with bangalore torpedos or small charges of plastic explosive.

The first indication of a sapper attack usually is a preparatory attack by mortars and RPGs. To increase the noise effect of these fires, the sapper will throw small explosive charges, hoping to delude the defenders as to the true nature of the attack. By using mortars and small charges, the sapper achieves the first goal of the attack — forcing the defenders to take cover. Once this has happened, the sappers move rapidly to their assigned objectives virtually unopposed.

Few of the sappers are armed with rifles, but those that are do not fire until the perimeter has been breached. Use of rifles prior to the actual breaching would disclose the impending ground assault. Once inside the perimeter, the riflemen deploy to engage the defenders as they emerge from their bunkers. They also help cover the withdrawal of the sappers.

The withdrawal is executed upon a prearranged signal and the sappers attempt to take as many of their dead and wounded with them as possible. As they leave the area, they continue to throw charges into positions that have not been previously silenced or destroyed.

A typical example of a sapper attack occurred at a Marine position on the southern approach to Liberty Bridge, Vietnam, in March 1969. At 0200 hours the defenders began receiving RPG fire from the northern side of their position. It was considered a stand-off attack until 0230 hours when the southern side of the perimeter began receiving intensive mortar, RPG, and rifle grenade fire. By this time the sappers had penetrated the perimeter in seven places on the eastern and western sides and were engaging the defenders with flamethrowers, explosives, and small arms fire.

Prior to 0230, the sappers had infiltrated past five listening posts and through the defensive wire around the perimeter. During the approach, the sappers did not set off any tripflares or anti-intrusion devices, even though more than 300 of them were deployed. The sappers were camouflaged and their movement was masked by the defender's artillery fires and the initial stand-off attack.

The success of a sapper attack depends upon surprise, achieved primarily through stealth, and the reaction by the defenders to the initial preparatory fires. Without these two elements, the sapper is unable to exploit his special ability.

The sapper often takes six or seven hours to cover the last 200 meters to the objective. An effective early warning system should detect and stop him during this phase of an attack. Patrol routes, ambush sites, and listening post locations should be varied as much as possible to avoid becoming predictable. Short, rapid sweeps of likely avenues of approach should be conducted just prior to sunset and constant shifting of anti-intrusion and detection devices should be done without establishing a pattern. Whenever feasible, persistent CS crystals should be used to deny the sapper easy use of selected areas or routes of approach.

Harassing and interdiction (H&I) fires are a normal part of the night defense but are often executed haphazardly. An effective H&I program employing M79 and 81mm mortars for close-in fires can disclose the sapper's attack prematurely.

Since the sapper uses darkness to help conceal his presence, extensive use of night vision devices is in order. Once a stand-off attack is initiated, use of mortar and artillery illumination can expose the sapper. While immediate counterbattery fires are important, special provisions should be made to provide the needed illumination until flare aircraft can arrive on station.

The sapper is not a "hopped up" individual charging blindly into a position to toss satchel charges. He is an elite, professional soldier who is well trained and dedicated to his mission. Nevertheless, he can be defeated by effectively planned and executed defensive measures.

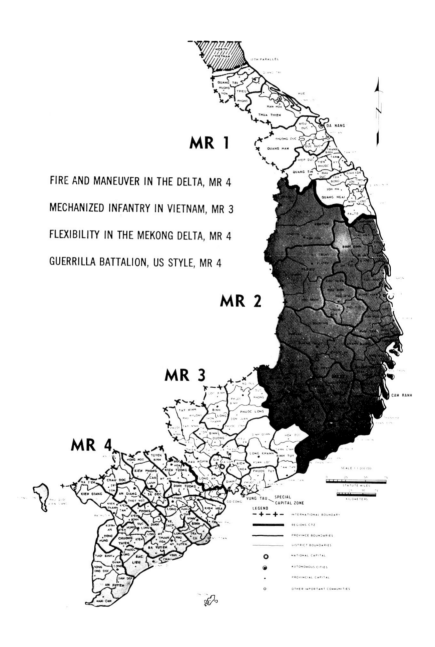

MR 1

MR 2

MR 3

MR 4

FIRE AND MANEUVER IN THE DELTA, MR 4

MECHANIZED INFANTRY IN VIETNAM, MR 3

FLEXIBILITY IN THE MEKONG DELTA, MR 4

GUERRILLA BATTALION, US STYLE, MR 4

Chapter 8

Changing Tactics

Fire and Maneuver in the Delta

Lieutenant Colonel William L. Hauser

The Mekong Delta campaign was a brigade commander's war. It was also a productive testing ground for techniques of fire support. Never before has the Infantry soldier been backed by such a preponderance of firepower. Seldom, however, has the application of firepower been so difficult to coordinate and bring to bear effectively on an elusive enemy.

The Delta is a pool table-flat expanse of rice paddies and marshlands, with widely spaced wooded streamlines and canals. More than one combat-seasoned commander has described it as "one big LZ." Wide fields of fire are plentiful, and observation, although restricted by treelines, is excellent into open areas. Cover is poor, unless a defender has ample time to dig into paddy dikes or into the earthen mounds created by drainage ditching in orchards. and coconut groves.

The Tactical Problem

Given such terrain, along with overwhelming firepower and airmobility, the advantage would seem to lie completely with the offense. To assume this, however, is to forget the political nature of Delta warfare. The typical Delta battle was not an engagement between two forces intent on battle, nor was it assault and defense of a position. The relationship between forces was rather that of hunter and hunted.

This tactical situation is basic to counterinsurgency in populated areas. The mission of the insurgent main force unit is to dominate the countryside, keeping rural troops shut up in their outposts. The government's mobile reserves are tied to cities and towns, for population centers are highly vulnerable to attack by guerrillas. With the countryside thus dominated by main force units, rural guerrillas are free to put muscle behind the tax-collecting and recruiting functions of the insurgent infrastructure.

If government mobile units venture into the countryside to break the main force-rural guerrilla-infrastructure chain, main force units simply evade contact, and guerrillas and infrastructure melt into a rural population terrorized into silence. Concurrently, urban terrorists step up activity calculated to bring the mobile reserves back to the towns.

The countryside is once again dominated by main force units, and government rural troops withdraw to the vicinity of their outposts. There is, however, a weakness in the insurgent cycle — the need for the main force unit to come together for purposes of control, discipline, training, and esprit. If friendly mobile forces can catch the insurgent unit when it is concentrated in platoon or company formation, the cycle can be broken.

This is a difficult thing to do, as any veteran of the Delta will attest. The main force unit concentrates only intermittently, and then only for periods of a few hours to a few days. Assembly is usually in wooded areas, along streams or canals which provide concealment and routes of evasion. If the unit is discovered by a superior force, prearranged signals are given to disperse to hiding places or nearby populated areas, the rural populace itself being a hiding place.

The insurgent soldier is more suitably armed, trained and organized for evasion than is the American for pursuit. Also, while US commanders traditionally demonstrate high regard for the welfare of individual soldiers, the insurgent leader has a tactical advantage in not having to account minute-by-minute for each and every man in his unit. When the company commander receives the order to evade, he tells his platoons to head for their respective rally points; the platoons give similar orders to their squads. The entire battalion to a man knows where to go when evasion becomes necessary. Of course, a dispersed insurgent battalion is not easy to put together again — a minor inconvenience compared to destruction.

Jitterbug

The problem for friendly forces is the traditional one of finding, fixing and fighting the enemy. The insurgent is anything but traditional in his ability to avoid being found and to evade being fixed. To counter his elusiveness, jitterbug tactics were developed and refined in the Delta by the 9th Infantry Division in 1968-69.

The insurgent is so skilled at hiding that he must be surprised into revealing his location. This can be accomplished when US forces move on the enemy as quickly as possible without prior reconnaissance, taking advantage of airmobility and open terrain. The enemy commander may engage by fire, thinking himself discovered and in danger of being cut off from his escape routes. Perhaps his company "eight ball" (they have them too) may panic and run, or fire a shot. The result is that the enemy is found.

The Pile-on

The brigade commander must make an early decision on whether or not to encircle the enemy. He does this by estimating the size and disposition of insurgent forces, which requires a keen sense of terrain and an understanding of enemy tactics, organization, equipment, and friendly capabilities. Once the decision is made, friendly firepower becomes a basic element in tactical planning. The process is largely intuitive, but if analyzed would look something like this:

> The encirclement must be sufficiently large to allow firepower to be placed therein. A circle with a diameter of about 500 meters, and therefore a circumference of about 1,600 meters, generally works best. An Infantry company can cover about 200 meters of Delta terrain to prevent enemy soldiers from escaping. Thus a typical encirclement will require at least eight Infantry companies, or two battalions. Assume a typical situation. The nearest friendly battalion is 20 kilometers from the insurgent position, with another battalion 40 kilometers away. Two assault helicopter companies are available to bring troops to the area to be encircled, and assault support helicopters (Chinooks) can bring the farther battalion to within 10 kilometers of the area. Assault helicopter turn-around time is about 20 minutes for 20 kilometers and about 12 minutes for 10 kilometers, and Chinook turn-around time is about 40 minutes. In this situation, a two-battalion encirclement can be made in a minimum of about four hours.

What fixes the insurgent while he is being encircled? Three means are available — artillery fire on concealed escape routes, helicopter gunship surveillance on relatively open areas and early piecemeal encirclement by airmobile assault. The first of these is relatively ineffective, because artillery fragmentation effects are limited in heavy woods, and the second depends on the enemy to be either foolhardy or stupid. In truth, he is neither.

Only the third means, Infantrymen on the ground in an apparently random but actually well-calculated pattern, will deceive the insurgent. By the time he discovers where the gaps are, it will be too late — the door will slam shut.

While the Infantry is piling on, coordination of fire and maneuver is very important and immensely difficult. Artillery, air cavalry, gunships, airstrikes, assault helicopter insertions, command-and-control ships, and dustoffs all compete for airspace over the battlefield. A good solution is for the brigade commander to turn over coordination of elements with relatively fixed trajectories — mortars, artillery and airstrikes — to the direct support artillery commander, while retaining full control of helicopter fire and movement.

Overall coordination is performed by the brigade commander, through the artillery liaison officer. The liaison officer is the key to really successful coordination, and he must therefore be an expert artilleryman, a seasoned soldier and a diplomat of the first order.

A major factor is the psychological impact upon the insurgent of continuous and constantly changing firepower and airmobile assault. The result is confusing even to the brigade commander who is controlling it. Hopefully, it is utterly baffling to the enemy.

The Doughnut

After the encirclement is completed, fire support coordination is simplified but still difficult. The technique called "shooting the hole in the doughnut" is hazardous, especially if the encirclement is small. All the skills of the artilleryman must be summoned to place killing fires throughout the encircled area. The enemy is presumably dug in, even if he was surprised in a position he had occupied for only a few hours. If not, he will adopt hugging tactics, to escape fire and seek an exit.

The encircling forces are probably not well dug in, because of time, the convenience of paddy dikes and the American soldier's disinclination to dig. To avoid endangering friendly troops, the bulk of fire is concentrated at the center, where the enemy probably is no longer located or, at least, is well protected. Thousands of artillery rounds and dozens of airstrikes plow the ground, making up in volume what they lack in precision.

There are ways to increase the precision of this fire, however. Infantry units that are well trained, well led and experienced know that fire support in this situation has to be placed close to friendly troops to be effective. These troops make maximum use of available cover and leaders note carefully the location of all friendly elements. Then the artillery forward observers become the craftsmen of the battlefield, walking the fire in as closely as possible.

Coordination of fires is still highly centralized by the direct support artillery battalion commander, who usually also acts as an aerial observer. Forward observers, liaison officers and firing units are all on his radio net, tightly controlled to permit a maximum number of fire missions simultaneously. With skillful attention to dispersion patterns and bursting radii, the doughnut becomes a lethal bowl, with the inside scoured right up to the brim.

Wasteful and crude as it is, no substitute for this technique has been devised. In sparsely populated areas, it might work better to find the enemy, chase him and kill him as he runs. In heavily populated areas, however, where the heart of counterinsurgency lies, the enemy must be fixed before he can be fought. Hence the doughnut remains an indispensable technique.

An Unresolved Problem

Fire support coordination during the doughnut phase has been well publicized, and many units in Vietnam became highly skilled in the technique. In the opinion of most artillerymen, however, much of this massive application of shot and shell is wasted. It is not after the circle is closed, but rather during the encirclement process that the enemy sustains most of his casualties.

No circle is completely airtight — a well-trained insurgent unit can always find a hole in the net, and usually does. During the pile-on, however, while the insurgent is still confused and still frantically seeking a way out, he is most vulnerable.

As noted previously, coordination of airspace is most difficult during the pile-on, and the brigade commander must establish priorities. Airmobile assaults rightly take first priority, gunships must have flexible flight paths or their effectiveness is much reduced, dustoffs and C&Cs have high priority for different but

225

equally compelling reasons, and airstrikes can't wait. The natural tendency is for the maneuver commander, in hopes of reducing confusion, to shut off the artillery. Tactically, nothing could be more unsound. Enemy confusion is an asset, not a liability.

Undiplomatic as it sounds, some Infantrymen do not have a good understanding of coordination of artillery and air fire support and maneuver. Not understanding it, they tend to fear it. At times the Infantryman demonstrates the ultimate in physical courage when he leads his men into battle without all the fire support they can and should have. The commander fears for the safety of his men from the awesome destructiveness of friendly fire support. To protect them, he tends to piecemeal that fire support, which seriously diminishes his chances of success in destroying the enemy.

These tactics are not for every situation, nor for every commander. The situation requires relatively open terrain, a lightly armed enemy, and the necessity to encircle quickly, lest the enemy melt into the nearby population. It is a rare brigade commander who can handle these tactics successfully, and even he needs skilled and gutsy subordinates to carry it off. He especially needs a truly expert fire support coordinator, one who possesses and deserves the commander's complete confidence.

A Proposed Solution

Brigade commanders of the 9th Infantry Division made good use of these tactics in the Mekong Delta. The greatest weakness was in fire support coordination, in the tendency to piecemeal fire support during the encirclement process. This is understandable to anyone who has participated in such complex operations, but not excusable. In fact, it was usually not at the brigade commander's initiative that fire was curtailed, but at the request of junior commanders or aviation elements who did not have the overall perspective and multiple radio nets necessary to see the entire situation.

Somewhere, the training system has fallen down on the job of teaching fire support coordination. The weaknesses noted above were not peculiar to the 9th Infantry Division; many artillerymen have returned from Vietnam with the same story. To remedy this situation, the maneuver arms schools should concentrate far more heavily on fire support and fire support coordination techniques. Leavenworth should do the same, as part of brigade-level tactics instruction.

Every Infantry and armor officer should become so proficient at fire support coordination that artillerymen will have to become twice as good just to stay ahead. The result will be mutual confidence between maneuver and fire support that will enhance the battle skills of both. This can be one of the greatest "lessons learned" to come out of Vietnam.

Mechanized Infantry in Vietnam
Lieutenant Colonel William E. Klein

In the late spring of 1969, my battalion received word from our brigade commander that the new field force commander would visit us (1st Battalion, 5th Infantry, Mechanized) and had requested a briefing on our operations for the past six months. The brigade commander, Colonel H. S. Long, Jr., stressed that both Major General Ellis W. Williamson, the division commander, and he wanted the briefing to emphasize the capabilities of mechanized Infantry.

Many thoughts ran through my mind as I prepared my notes. I had then commanded the battalion for over six months and was to keep it for almost eight. I discovered, as a novice to mechanized forces, that a mech battalion is first and foremost Infantry. But it is unique Infantry with great mobility, increased firepower, and above all, it is Infantry that can sustain itself on the field of battle.

To give you a general idea of the effectiveness of mech Infantry, the battalion had killed over 700 North Vietnamese and Viet Cong soldiers during that six months and had captured almost 400 enemy weapons. Our units had also found their fair share of caches and had even captured a local VC tax collector laden with a considerable sum of money in piasters.

The record, however, isn't as important as how we went about it. The 25th Infantry Division used an excellent system of area responsibility, with battalions being assigned primarily to a district, even though the actual area of operations might extend a considerable distance beyond the district boundary. For instance, our area of operations was the Cu Chi District, but also included the Hobo Woods, which was outside the district. The Hobo, as

227

we called it, was a large, thickly wooded area adjacent to the Saigon River and we operated there frequently, since it was a major refuge area and infiltration route for the Viet Cong.

The reason for the district principle was to allow close coordination between the battalion commander and the district chief, with whom we had excellent rapport. This coordination ran the gamut from exchange of intelligence to civil affairs. It included combined operations, coordination of tactical operations and security efforts, and assistance in the Vietnamization program where applicable. A battalion liaison officer and a combined reconnaissance and intelligence platoon (CRIP) of US and Vietnamese soldiers were stationed at the district headquarters as a rapid reaction force, to take advantage of spot intelligence involving small Viet Cong groups.

Most of the battalion's effort was geared toward making our area secure and establishing a protective umbrella under which the district chief and his regional and popular forces (RF/PFs) could work on the local VC without fear of running into NVA and VC main force units. We had a variety of missions from brigade which we could expect on a recurring basis. These were escort for convoys, road-clearing and security, and protection for land-clearing teams (Rome plows) as they worked at cutting down the hedgerows and jungle areas which the VC used for refuge. In addition, there were always reconnaissance-in-force missions, in which our principal task was to find, fix and destroy the enemy.

The recon-in-force missions, usually based on hard intelligence, proved to be the best source of contact. The land-clearing security missions also produced contact, primarily because the local VC, and sometimes regular NVA units, would either harass us or attempt more violent action to block our efforts to destroy their refuge areas. Finally, we achieved contact by investigating suspicious areas when actually on another mission.

One day in February 1969, when Company A was being sent to Cu Chi base camp for a 24-hour stand-down, I decided to have them check out an area located along the main supply route (MSR) on their way in. We hadn't been in that area for a week or two and it was within rocket and machinegun range of the convoys. So Alfa Company stuck their nose in, upset an enemy ambush and got themselves entangled in a four-hour fight that resulted in 14 enemy killed, 1 captured and 7 individual and crew-served weapons destroyed. The results aren't as important as the fact that an obvious ambush on the MSR was spoiled and the action saved both US lives and materiel. That company commander took great pride in reminding me time to time that his unit could start out for R&R, whip the enemy on the way in and still meet its stand-down schedule.

Another example of investigating suspicious places produced one of the most efficient small unit battles I have ever seen. The battalion, minus one company, moved to the Hobo Woods for a combined operation with a Vietnamese battalion. The combined task force consisted of two of our mechanized companies and an ARVN Infantry battalion, and I was designated the commander. The plan was to operate in separate areas while moving to the Hobo Woods, laager in different locations the first night, then join forces for a combined laager the second night and a combined sweep the third day.

As the US elements were nearing the position chosen for the night encampment, we directed one company to set up a night defensive position and the other to patrol circularly around the position.

As the S3 and I flew over the area we noticed one square hedgerow, out by itself, that showed signs of recent use. We threw smoke grenades from the command and control helicopter to designate the spot and had the patrolling company move over to investigate. The lead elements drew fire from a range of 200 meters. We immediately requested helicopter gunship support and the artillery LNO started bringing artillery fire into the hedgerow complex.

I gave the company commander an opportunity to see the area from the air and we discussed his plan of attack. Fortunately for us, the hedgerow was almost isolated in the center of a large open area. This is most unusual, as hedgerows abound in this part of Vietnam and are usually planted in a series around individual homes and farm plots in villages. From the ground, they often look thick enough to resemble jungle. The Viet Cong in our area had a bad habit of using these hedgerows to set up the old Foreign Legion type of square defensive positions.

The company commander used one of his flame tracks to burn one side of the hedgerow bare and expose the enemy fighting positions. He put his other tracks on both sides of the square at an angle and used .50 caliber machinegun fire to pin down the

VC in the two sides perpendicular to the burned-out hedgerow. The back hedgerow was worked over by the helicopter gunships. Then, by squads, the Infantry moved in on the hedgerow and worked over the bunkers one at a time using fire and maneuver, emplacing shaped charges, bungalore torpedoes, and hand grenades in and around the bunkers and tunnels. When one side was cleared, the whole operation just shifted in a clockwise movement. Shortly after nightfall, the operation was completed under flares. Net result: 38 NVA soldiers killed and 38 weapons captured (including a wheel-mounted machinegun and two RPG7s), at a cost of two US soldiers slightly wounded. The epilogue to this action is that later in the evening an enemy RPG team fired at the night defensive position and the organic 81mm mortars responded in rapid fashion. The next morning we found two more bodies and an RPG7. It was obvious that this RPG team must have been the last of the platoon that had been eliminated that afternoon, since no attempt was made to take the bodies away and the VC are too proficient at policing the battlefield to have made an error like that.

I discussed these fights in my briefing for the field force commander and then went on to give some examples of engagements which required us to exercise our rapid mobility over extended distances and either engage the enemy on our own or reinforce other units.

Then I covered our considerable capabilities from the standpoint of firepower. As an example, the .50 caliber machinegun on each track will easily penetrate a rice paddy dike and hit a target on the other side. This can best be emphasized with an example. One night, in a two-company defensive position, a VC force hit us with automatic weapons and RPGs. I had just given a big lecture to the two company commanders involved because in the afternoon fighting, which preceded our move to this position, the .50 caliber machineguns had been shooting too high. The company commanders briefed their personnel and that night I will never forget both of them yelling "Shoot low, shoot low," and it paid off. The next morning there were 12 VC lying along the perimeter wire and every one had been hit by .50 caliber fire. You could see how the rounds had virtually eaten up the dike in front of the enemy's firing position before taking him out of action.

In addition to the .50 caliber on each track, there were three flamethrower tracks. This was a great weapon which not only eliminated some formidable enemy positions but also helped get us out of rough spots, such as extracting wounded from open areas or getting a track out of a hedgerow complex after it had been hit by RPG fire.

Another weapon which the mechanized units used with great effectiveness was the 81mm mortar. It was always carried on every operation, mounted in the track from which it fired and was therefore readily available. The crews were so well trained that they fired almost simultaneously with the crack of the first enemy bullet, provided, of course, that they were in a free-fire zone, as most of our engagements were. It was my experience that the majority of our firefight casualties were sustained in the initial exchange or in the first 10 minutes of contact. Thereafter the key to success was to pile on with firepower. So the 81mm mortars were extremely effective in putting out a volume of responsive indirect fire before the artillery cranked up and the gunships and tactical aircraft arrived on station. The 81s were also invaluable in company-size night defensive positions.

The 4.2-inch mortars were kept in general support at the battalion firebase and were used extensively to support the companies when they were within range. Additionally, the 81mm and 4.2-inch mortars furnished illumination for movement of the tracks during the hours of darkness, as well as illuminating the battlefield in an offensive action or for a defensive position if necessary.

During the last four months of my command, the battalion had either a platoon or company of tanks attached. Admittedly, while the wet season has a much greater limiting effect on the mobility of the M48 tank than on the M113, the tank's firepower is remarkable. The men soon found out that tanks aren't invincible, however, and when they are employed improperly or used without Infantry protection they were apt to be on the receiving end of an RPG7. The tank itself, as a weapons system, had great application in our fighting. The 90mm HE round in a bunker was far more effective than anything except a direct hit by a 750-pound bomb, and that would be a rare occurrence. The 90mm cannister round was also very effective in clearing a hedgerow or keeping the enemy pinned down in order to maneuver to a blind side or get close enough to pinpoint him.

In night defensive positions, the firepower that four or five tanks can add to a perimeter is almost unbelievable. The firepower aspect of one mech company with tanks is devastating.

I often had airmobile Infantry units operating under battalion control and many times after an hour or two of fighting the request for more ammunition came in. Invariably, our solution was to redistribute our own ammunition and have the mechanized unit fighting alongside replenish the Infantry supply. While it is understood that airmobile units can carry only so much, it was

convenient to be able to call upon the mech to provide whatever was needed.

In discussing capabilities, it would be appropriate to mention one limitation of the mech — movement of tracks at night. There is absolutely nothing wrong with moving tracks at night so long as there is adequate flank security, e.g., through an open area or along a road with clear fields of fire. But to move tracks at night through a built-up or a thickly wooded area is sheer folly. You are asking for trouble and will probably find it, especially in an environment such as Vietnam where the enemy can be anywhere, operating mostly under the cover of darkness.

This doesn't mean that tracks can't fight or move at night, or that you should put them in a firebase and leave them there when the sun goes down. But you should carefully select your mission and the terrain over which you intend to operate, and then insure that your plan provides for flank security.

The idea of running M113s up and down the MSR at night in order to prevent the VC from putting mines, dirt piles or trees on it to harass the troops on their morning road-clearing operation isn't a very sound one, to say the least. The MSR in our area was bounded by thick hedgerows in some places and many villages were located adjacent to the right of way. When we played road-runner, the VC would simply wait until after the tracks had passed to do their dirty work or take RPG potshots as we passed. The best way to stop this type of harassment is to saturate the road with foot ambushes and do everything possible to get the district chief to do the same with his RF and PF units.

These points fairly well wrap up the big picture of our operations and include the majority of the material used in the discussion with Lieutenant General Julian Ewell, then II Field Force Commander. The wrap-up phrase that best described mech operations in Vietnam for me was **staying power**, the inherent ability of a force to sustain itself on the battlefield.

As I saw the war in Vietnam, it belonged to the company commander. He was the key to success — a planner, a doer, an independent operator, and a leader of men. The battalion commander's job was to provide guidance and move unit commanders in the right direction, help them out when they got in trouble, insure they had the resources needed to do the job, buck 'em up when they made a mistake and, above all, let them know that they and their men were the toughest, finest and bravest soldiers who ever donned a uniform. The latter came easy . . . as no one believed it more sincerely than I.

Flexibility in the Mekong Delta

Captain G. O. Hillard, III

From September 1968 until its withdrawal and deactivation in July 1969, the 2d Brigade, 9th Infantry Division — the Army component of the Army-Navy Mobile Riverine Force — conducted an intensive, aggressive, varied, and flexible campaign against the Viet Cong in watery Kien Hoa Province. The terrain influenced many of the techniques used by the 2d Brigade, and free-thinking and innovation contributed to the effort.

The most significant characteristic of the province is its extensive water network. Knowledge of these waterways and the capability of moving and fighting on them enabled 2d Brigade forces to operate effectively against a mobile enemy in a hostile physical environment. The brigade conducted watermobile, airmobile and footmobile operations into nearly every part of the province, penetrating into areas which would normally have been unaccessible.

Kien Hoa Province

The province is located about 75 kilometers south of Saigon and is characterized by approximately 50 kilometers of coastline on the South China Sea and countless miles of inland waterways. The terrain is quite flat, mostly rice paddy, but also includes thick jungle areas with numerous banana dikes and coconut groves. The province is laced with waterways which serve as lines of communication; many canals and streams are concealed by thick vegetation. The enemy's intimate knowledge of these waterways meant that extensive use of them at night could be expected. Viet

Cong base camps in thick jungle had numerous water routes in and out, which assisted them in breaking contact during hours of darkness.

For the farming peasant, the waterways were the most heavily used routes to and from the cities. Viet Cong control of these waterways provided a highly effective avenue to the populace for collection of taxes, recruiting and resupply. It was apparent before the campaign began that control of the waterways would be a critical factor in the effort.

When found, the Viet Cong was generally located in heavily wooded areas. The open paddies leading to these areas did not provide an acceptable route of march, because the complete lack of cover and concealment increased the risk of sniper fire. Fortunately, the local snipers were generally poor marksmen. These same paddies, however, with dikes up to three feet high, provided good to excellent night defensive positions with 360 degree fields of fire and ample opportunity to employ friendly snipers equipped with night vision devices.

The road net in Kien Hoa connected the district centers, but at the outset of the campaign, it was quite insecure. A major bridge near Ben Tre was down and all roads were generally in a poor state of repair.

Due to the high and varying water table, underground tunnel complexes were not encountered, but strong mud bunkers were numerous, particularly along woodlines and in potential landing zones. The tides were a significant factor and varied as much as eight or 10 feet each day. A stream easily forded at one time of day could be 15 feet deep several hours later, requiring ropes, inflatable boats, or sampans to cross the time-consuming obstacle.

9th Division Operations

On July 26, 1968, the headquarters of the US 9th Infantry Division moved from Bearcat, near Saigon, to Dong Tam, on the My Tho River, about seven kilometers west of My Tho City. The division's three brigades operated generally in three important provinces around Dong Tam: Long An, Kien Hoa, and Dinh Tuong. The division's deep thrust into the Mekong Delta was characterized by flexibility and versatility. Two assault helicopter companies provided airmobile assets and support from two air cavalry troops was available, in addition to the air assets of the 9th Division's organic aviation battalion. The 1st Brigade operated in Dinh Tuong Province and used airmobile assets almost continuously. The 3d Brigade, headquartered in Tan An, Long An Province, included one mechanized Infantry battalion but frequently relied upon airmobile forces. The 2d Brigade was organized as a riverine brigade of three battalions plus a field artillery battalion, operating from ships and small craft of the US Navy.

Kien Hoa Province, with its myriad waterways, was the logical target for this force.

Designed to operate with three battalions from the converted LSTs of the Mobile Riverine Force, the 2d Brigade also used airmobile assets of the 162d Assault Helicopter Company (Vultures). When one rifle battalion (3d Battalion, 47th Infantry) was landbased in the heart of Kien Hoa, additional flexibility was obtained. The riverine capability was retained because of substantial waterways nearby. Pick-up zones near each base camp made airmobile operations easy to stage, and numerous footmobile operations were run daily. Trucks were also used to increase the range of these operations. Most significant was the fact that a well-dispersed rifle battalion and its supporting battery of 105mm howitzers had been permanently based astride a major communications-liaison route of the Viet Cong, posing a constant threat and hampering the former ease of movement and operation which the Viet Cong had enjoyed.

The Mobile Riverine Force

The Mobile Riverine Force provided the allies with a unique operational capability in a unique environment: the Mekong Delta. Its Navy component consisted of four APBs (Self-Propelled Barracks Ships), which were 328-feet-long converted LSTs. Each was equipped with a barge moored alongside, from which riverine operations were staged. These four large ships also provided mobile billeting facilities for Army and Navy personnel and operations centers manned by both staffs. In essence, they served as base camps for the troops and the smaller boats used in actual watermobile assaults. The brigade's four OH6A helicopters made their home aboard one of the converted LSTs. Each APB had a flight deck topside capable of taking one UH1 aircraft and, at least once, this small platform was used to stage an airmobile assault with the choppers coming in singly to pick up the troops. The APBs were armed with two 3-inch/.50 caliber rapid-fire single mounts, two 40mm quad mounts, and eight .50 caliber machineguns.

There were three general types of small boats used for actual watermobile assaults. The armored troop carriers (ATCs or Tango Boats) functioned as the general purpose carrier of the river assault squadrons and normally carried one rifle platoon each. The assault support patrol boats (ASPBs or Alfa Boats) were fast, highly maneuverable craft for fire support, minesweeping, patrolling, and convoy escort on inland waterways. They were armed with 20mm cannons and machineguns in varying combinations. Monitors, or heavies, were fire support boats used mainly during water movement assault landings; they were armed with 105mm howitzers, direct-fire 81mm mortars, 20mm and 40mm guns, and machine-

guns. Additionally, several of these craft were modified and mounted twin flamethrowers forward.

The term MRB was used to refer to the fleet of ships: Mobile Riverine Base. Part of the MRB's effectiveness was its ability to be near the action; it could move to anchorages in different parts of the province in a matter of hours. The ships were blacked out at night, but flight operations could be and were conducted during hours of darkness from the flight decks. As a matter of technique, the MRB shifted its anchorage several hundred yards each night to lessen the chance of enemy mortar or rocket attack during hours of darkness. Company supply shacks and other facilities were located on the barge alongside each APB; the troop carriers (Tango Boats) loaded for operations from this barge.

The Navy component of the MRF was commanded by a Navy captain. Navy staff counterparts of the brigade staff worked closely with Army staff members aboard the flagship. The Navy's cooperation and dedication added significantly to the joint efforts in Kien Hoa.

Existing Situation

The overworked phrase "long a VC stronghold" was an understatement when applied to Kien Hoa. Historically, Kien Hoa had been a stronghold for river and coastal pirates, political dissidents, and other malcontents for several hundred years. The French never established truly effective control over the province, where the inhabitants resisted or ignored governmental influence regardless of who was in power in Saigon.

Kien Hoa was the home of the Viet Cong 516th Main Force Battalion, an elite unit honored by being awarded the title of 1st Kien Hoa Battalion. This unit, in recent years, dominated Kien Hoa as it moved through the province at will, having little difficulty with Regional/Popular Forces and units of the 7th ARVN Division. The 516th took part in the Tet Offensive of 1968, entering Ben Tre and occupying the headquarters of the ARVN 10th Regiment.

Additionally, elements of the 550th Local Force Battalion and several local force companies operated in Kien Hoa, though the 550th did not appear to be a unit of the stature of the 516th. Numerous village and hamlet guerrillas, usually poorly equipped but geniuses with boobytraps, were in existence as 10-man squads near each village. All these units made extensive use of the water lines of communication throughout the province. The larger elements (companies of the 516th) moved at night, while the local guerrillas did not. These local guerrillas sniped and harassed but spent the major portion of their time setting boobytraps. This presented a significant problem to US units: the vast majority of our casualties resulted from boobytraps, ranging from Chicom and US grenades to 105mm projectiles; both tripwire and command-dotonated mines were encountered.

One of the 516th's major base camps was located in dense woods (with numerous water routes in and out), six kilometers west-northwest of Giong Trom City, well within striking distance of Ben Tre, the province capital. The strength of the 516th was as high as 700 at one time, and the unit was, at the outset of the campaign, well supplied and equipped. The 516th operated in company-size elements as a minimum and bragged of its successes during Tet 1968; it claimed to have accomplished almost all assigned missions during that offensive.

Immediately prior to the 2d Brigade's campaign, the VC political effort in Kien Hoa had been effective. The populace, dependent upon the waterways to move produce to market, could seldom travel a given waterway without encountering a Viet Cong tax collection or control point. This situation existed up to July 1968. Documents captured during the period July to December 1968 indicated how well the VC were doing: they claimed broad popular support, adequate taxes and sufficient food. It was during this period that the 3d Battalion, 47th Infantry was placed on the ground in Giong Trom District.

Objectives

The 2d Brigade's objectives in Kien Hoa were straightforward and the campaign was designed to achieve them as simply and convincingly as possible:

* Eliminate the 516th Battalion's hold on Kien Hoa, and thus relieve the pressure on Ben Tre, the province capital.

* Open routes of communication from the districts to Ben Tre in order to aid economic development and increase government officials' influence to the districts.

* Demonstrate interest in the province and raise the confidence of the people in the government's ability to protect them.

* Increase Regional/Popular Forces' proficiency through integrated and combined operations.

The Campaign

In late September 1968, the 3/47 Infantry moved into four base camps located along Highway 26 between Giong Trom and the Chet Say Canal. This complex became known as the Tiger's Lair. Alfa, Charlie and Delta Companies all had separate base camps, while Bravo and Headquarters Companies were collocated approximately in the center of the layout. Each company base camp was located within several hundred meters of an RF/PF outpost. Alfa Company's base camp was farthest from the battalion CP, about five kilometers, and received a ground attack by an estimated 40 VC the second night of occupancy. The VC were believed to be from the 516th, and were armed with B40 rockets and automatic weapons. Charlie Company's base camp was along a road leading north to a densely wooded area, which was heavily boobytrapped. Delta Company's new home was the least covered, being built from the ground up in the middle of a paddy.

Each base camp measured about 100 by 200 meters and consisted of engineer-constructed sleeping and fighting bunkers. Sandbags, timber and mud were used to complete fortifications. Existing masonry buildings on site were used during the day but were not considered safe at night due to the lack of overhead cover. The base camps were set up with emphasis on defensibility: it was not possible to clear out all wooded approaches near the camps. However, concertina wire, claymore mines, tripflares, and other devices were used around all base camps, and recoilless and automatic weapons were placed where they could be most effective. Night vision devices ranging from individual weapon sights to large, crew-served devices, were employed every night and repeatedly proved their worth.

Approximately three kilometers west of the battalion CP, along Highway 26, Charlie Battery, 3d Battalion, 34th Artillery established Fire Support Base KLAW II. The position was centrally located to support battalion operations and all base camps. KLAW II was built in the middle of a giant rice paddy; it was felt that this open position would take advantage of the battery's direct fire capability and facilitate the use of night vision devices and ground surveillance radar. A large radar set was mounted on a tower at the artillery base and acquired targets were fired upon nightly. Fields of unattended ground sensors were emplaced along known VC routes of movement with the readout station at KLAW II. Readouts of sensor activations were used in conjunction with radar sightings to vector ambush elements toward suspected VC activity. Artillery was fired on the target if ambush elements were not in range. It should be pointed out that Kien Hoa was not generally a free fire zone and clearance, except for contact fire missions, was frequently denied by ARVN and GVN officials.

Brigade Operations

The pattern of the brigade's operations in Kien Hoa emerged early, it was to be a process of wearing down the 516th, searching relentlessly and fixing the enemy in place to pound him with airstrikes, artillery and ground forces.

The province was divided into numerous areas of operation (AOs) and assignments were made by the brigade commander, who also portioned out the airmobile and watermobile assets. The brigade generally issued no formal operation orders: the brigade commander elected instead to react constantly to current intelligence. The flexibility already described facilitated this, and hot intelligence reports often resulted in airmobile assets being transferred rapidly to another battalion for exploitation.

Delta Troop, 3d Squadron, 5th Cavalry conducted daily scout and fire support operations throughout the province, taking into account the plans for the day. Many times, the Cav's early morning scouting kicked off the action. One UH1H command and control ship, two OH6A armed scouts, and two AH1G Huey Cobras made up the team, which was extremely responsive and often shuffled back and forth between battalions, depending upon the changing situation. The cav C&C ship normally carried a personnel detection device (people sniffer) and was armed with a .50 caliber machinegun for added firepower in low level operations.

The pattern, on more than one occasion when decisive contact was made, was generally as follows: One hour or more before the day's first airmobile or watermobile assault, the cav would start

to work the area. On several occasions, they spotted enemy troops with helmets, web gear and carrying crew-served weapons — which indicated something other than local guerrillas — probably the 516th. Thus we had an early indication of the day's work ahead. The cav remained on station throughout the action, often well into the hours of darkness.

The brigade also used the Ranger teams of Company E, 75th Infantry, the 9th Division's Ranger company. Six-man teams were employed on scaled-down eagle flights (insertions of opportunity), and hunter-killer operations using two teams were also mounted. Rangers were also inserted by boat, but most of their operations were airmobile.

In reacting to current intelligence, numerous "dry holes" had to be expected and were, in fact, experienced. Normally, if a company found nothing after working an area 60 to 90 minutes, it hustled back to the pick-up zone to be reinserted elsewhere. Four or five insertions per day was generally the maximum. When a company landed in a hot area it was usually apparent right away and other companies with dry holes could be picked up rapidly and inserted to influence the action.

The assault helicopter company was used extensively and freely. The 3/47th's location in Kien Hoa reduced flight times to objective areas and truly efficient use of the air assets was a reality. Typically, after insertion of three rifle companies of one battalion, the air assets would go to another battalion for similar operations in another part of the province. The assets were exchanged repeatedly and reinsertions throughout the day covered all possible intelligence targets.

Airmobile and watermobile operations with the local RF/PF units were conducted as a matter of routine. Cordon and search operations were conducted with National Police units from Ben Tre, Giong Trom and Ham Duong.

Decisive Contacts with the 516th

On the morning of January 4, 1969, Delta Troop, 3/5 Cavalry conducted a visual reconnaissance of a projected landing zone and spotted enemy troops with helmets, web gear and a tripod-mounted .50 caliber machinegun. They engaged and killed about eight VC. However, before Alfa Company, 3/47 Infantry could be inserted, the VC retrieved the machinegun. Alfa Company was inserted into a landing zone which proved to be in a major base camp of the 516th; they landed in a paddy right in front of a main line of bunkers, part of a mutually supporting complex of fighting positions. The second force to be inserted was an RF unit which did not alter the tactical situation. Alfa Company remained pretty well pinned in place. Close air support with 750-pound bombs was used on the bunkers, and air cav support was continuous. About

1450, Charlie Company, 3/47 Infantry was inserted some three kilometers south of the contact area and moved north, crossing a major stream. It immediately found itself in the midst of the living area of the 516th base camp. Numerous large motorized sampans and a sizable quantity of rice were destroyed. Charlie Company received no resistance of any consequence and linked up with Alfa Company at dark. The two companies moved to night positions about 500 meters south of the woodline, linking up with the RF company. The next morning, all three units entered the bunkered woodline without resistance. Artillery and an AC47 Spooky gunship had pounded the area most of the night, and the result of the contact was an estimated 57 VC killed.

The morning of February 20, 1969, air cav scouts of Delta Troop spotted and engaged about 10 VC wearing helmets and web gear, and received a heavy volume of automatic weapons fire from the south bank of the East Ba Lai Canal, about six kilometers east of Charlie Company's base camp. As Bravo and Alfa 3/47th and Bravo 3/60 Infantry were inserted, it became apparent that a large part of the 516th had been caught at the scene of its previous night's encampment. An RF unit was also employed and heavy support from fighter-bombers and cav gunships was continuous. Artillery support from KLAW II was also quite effective. The battle continued until 2200. The US units suffered light casualties from close range small arms and automatic weapons fire. Action continued sporadically through the night, and early on the 21st. Alfa, 3/47th, ambushed about 10 VC attempting to escape by water. The 516th lost over 100 troops in the contact.

A sizable contact of this nature was exactly what the 516th could not afford, but when detected, could not avoid. These engagements usually lasted one day, as the VC exfiltrated during the night, taking all they could with them. An exception occurred in late May 1969, near Ham Duong on the south bank of the My Tho River, not far from Dong Tam. Elements of the 3d Battalion, 60th Infantry and 4th Battalion, 47th Infantry engaged a unit of the 516th in dense woods. It was an intense fight at close range and terminated just after dark. Continuing the reconnaissance-in-force near the area of contact the next day, these units discovered the 516th was still close by and another heavy engagement ensued. As usual, tactical air support and cav gunships were used along with artillery. This rare two-day engagement cost the 516th over 100 casualties.

Engagements of this sort wore the 516th down; its seasoned veterans were becoming casualties and the 516th was beginning to feel it. It was probably during March, after several tough engagements, that the 516th dispersed into 10 to 15-man groups and avoided contact throughout the province. Whenever they

massed, the brigade's intensive search and pursuit efforts pro-
voked a decisive contact.

During a campaign in which the strategy resulted in part from
the fact that few results had been realized by large-scale daylight
operations, small unit night operations were conducted extensively.
These ambush patrols left the base camps in reinforced squad and
platoon-size elements and covered known VC routes of travel,
particularly the main communication-liaison route through central Giong Trom District. They also covered many of the small
waterways and these "aquabushes" frequently netted results. A

unit of the 3d Battalion, 60th Infantry ambushed an element of
the 516th traversing the Ma Cau Canal near Mo Cay in sampans
loaded with mortar ammunition. The result was devastating. As
the mortar ammunition exploded an estimated 21 VC were killed.

Sniper teams of two men each, armed with National Match
M14 rifles, telescopic sights and starlight scopes were employed
by each battalion in night defensive positions and on small unit
ambush/aquabush operations. The sniper teams were often flown
in by helicopter if it had been decided that a given company
would remain overnight in position. The effectiveness of the
snipers and the night vision devices used by all units was significant and increased night operations capabilities.

The large paddy surrounding Charlie Battery, 3/34 Artillery
lay along the previously mentioned communication-liaison route
used by the 516th. The route ran generally north and south and
provided couriers with access to the 516th's base camp areas south
of the Tiger's Lair. This route was a logical target for night ambush operations and the 3/47th put out several platoons each

night for that purpose. Several engagements kicked off right after dark, and on one occasion, a courier armed with a pistol and carrying documents was killed, along with several members of his party. The attempt to continue using this route in spite of the 3/47th's presence indicated the confidence of the VC in Kien Hoa at the outset of the campaign. However, traffic decreased as the VC found it increasingly hazardous.

At the outset of the campaign, the major waterways, not to mention the minor ones, were quite insecure, and aerial coverage by gunships was essential for boat convoys. After vigorous operations in the province, the situation improved considerably. All waterways of tactical importance were used by US forces at will; the firepower of the Navy ASPBs and Monitors, particularly the 105mm howitzers, 40mm guns, and flamethrowers, made it fairly hazardous business for the VC to attempt sniper or rocket fire at a column of boats at close range. Frequent use of the waterways by US forces naturally limited VC freedom of movement and curtailed their access to the people along these heavily travelled lines of communication and commerce. Vigorous patrolling and reconnaissance-in-force operations eliminated or reduced VC tax collection and other control points along waterways and the use of these waterways by the people naturally increased. A curfew from dark until 0600 along all waterways was observed, so traffic during these hours was engaged.

Innovations

Several innovations used by brigade units are worth mentioning. A major difficulty of the campaign was locating the VC, particularly the 516th, and the reasons for this have been brought out. Some of the brigade's solutions to the problem were:

Immediate Reinsertion. After working a dry hole for 60 to 90 minutes, a rifle company, for example, would be extracted. After a brief orbit away from the cold area, the unit would be reinserted in the same area or very close by. Sporadic light contact sometimes resulted, as a degree of tactical surprise had been achieved. A variation also worked. The original company was reinserted elsewhere or returned to base camp, and a fresh unit inserted. This technique applied to watermobile operations as well. After extraction at a given beach site along one of Kien Hoa's waterways, the unit would beach again two to three kilometers from the pick-up site. A variation was to reinsert on the opposite bank.

Departure and Reentry. A rifle company on foot, after working an unproductive area all afternoon, commenced a march out of the area just before dark. However, a halt one to two kilometers away just after dark, followed by a countermarch to the area just left, was found to produce genuine surprise. Noise discipline was a prerequisite.

Results of the Campaign

In July 1969, the brigade terminated operations in Kien Hoa Province and was redeployed to the United States for deactivation. It is, then, appropriate to take a look at what the brigade left behind in Kien Hoa after operating there for nine months. Many of the results achieved were visible; others, while not readily discernible, were supported by captured VC documents which indicated the brigade's impact upon the 516th. The 516th had been hit hard repeatedly and was running out of experienced veterans. Lines of communication within Kien Hoa had been opened and improved, and, more significantly, were being used by the people. The Chet Say Canal and Ben Tre River were open and gunship escort was no longer necessary; portions of the Ba Lai Canal were similarly open. A joint US/ARVN ferry was in operation near Ben Tre on the Chet Say Canal. The road from Ba Tri through Giong Trom to Ben Tre (Highway 26) had been resurfaced along much of its length and was generally open. The effect on the populace was also noticeable: the people had become much more active; farmers increased their cultivated areas, traffic to province centers and markets increased; and a greater measure of security was generally felt. Pressure on Ben Tre, the province capital, had been relieved. Improvement of the RF/PF units in the area had been realized, though the real test for these units lay ahead, after the 2d Brigade departed.

During the period January to July 1969, documents carried by political officers of the 516th were captured; these documents from the district committees cited lack of cooperation from the people, lack of recruits, and infractions of discipline. The last item had been virtually unheard of in the 516th. A letter from a 516th political officer to a province political officer called for severe punishment of those who avoided battle. These documents, along with. other observed phenomena, indicated several possibilities: One, political control of Kien Hoa by the 516th had been seriously challenged; two, VC control of the population and ARVN military was disintegrating; three, VC leadership was attempting strong steps to recover. Letters taken from POWs also revealed that these VC had never before experienced defeat, at least not of these proportions. POWs taken during July to October 1968 averaged 24 years of age; those taken in May 1969 averaged about 15 years of age. Food procurement worsened for the VC: in February of 1969 a document taken from the Ham Luong District Committee directed each inhabitant to set aside 10 kilos of rice for main force units. This was quite unusual, as large caches of fish, rice and other foodstuffs had always been available. After March 1969, the strength of the 516th was estimated at 150 to 200, and after this time, the 516th had to rely upon local units to help with security. The 516th was no longer a force in the Mekong Delta.

Guerrilla Battalion, US Style

Colonel David H. Hackworth

By mid-1969 the 4th Battalion, 39th Infantry had set Vietnam's guerrilla-dominated Delta on fire. This battalion's achievements weren't accomplished with conventionally trained soldiers, led by conventionally oriented leaders, but by American soldiers who fought and thought like their guerrilla foes and by leaders who followed Mao's handbook on guerrilla warfare.

Since early January 1969, the battalion, known as the "Hard-core Battalion" throughout the 9th Infantry Division, had lived and fought under virtually the same harsh and demanding conditions as the Viet Cong. The troopers had become lean and hard, and had the sort of pride that comes only from sacrifice. There were no suburban luxuries like cold beer and tape recorders, for example. According to one expert on guerrilla warfare, the Hard-core Battalion had become more proficient at this form of warfare than the elite guerrilla units that they challenged daily in western

249

Dinh Tuong Province. The helicopters and airstrikes helped, but the attitude of the men was the determining factor.

Surprise, deception, mobility, imagination, cunning, and familiarity with every stream, trail, hamlet, and village within the area of operations (AO) were the characteristics of Hardcore's tactics. The battalion acquired an ability to move at night with stealth and ease, and when it struck, it struck hard. The catalyst for all of this was alertness, which came to be the cardinal requirement.

Little dependence was placed on the sophisticated machinery of modern warfare. The helicopter was viewed not as some magic panacea for winning the war, but as a vehicle to move men into battle. Ground radar, sniffers, technical intelligence devices, and countless other mechanical gimmicks which had been developed to bring a quick and easy solution to the war were used, but only as a means to an end. They weren't considered an end in themselves. The battalion's concept was that machinery doesn't win battles. Battles are won only by trained, dedicated, highly motivated men who are expertly led.

As guerrillas, the Hardcore Battalion adopted the Asian's contempt for time, and they never hurried. They were slow, careful and methodical. In strict accordance with Mao's rules of guerrilla warfare, they would fight only when victory was assured at a minimal cost in friendly casualties. The battalion's most priceless assets were its troopers, and their safety was always uppermost in the commander's mind. If an element had to attack across an open rice paddy through antipersonnel mines to take a bunkered position just to kill a few enemy, then forget it! No attack would be made. "We'll strike it hard with artillery and air, sneak to their rear and ambush them as they try to run away," would be the solution. The Hardcore Battalion didn't believe in costly frontal assaults.

This talk of safety shouldn't imply timidness or reluctance, for the battalion was bold and took risks few units would take, providing the game would be played according to their rules.

The battalion's primary tactic was the ambush. Its units operated in widely decentralized platoon or smaller formations, normally over a 50-kilometer AO. Obviously, this type of employment required small unit leaders of exceptional skill. Weak leaders were replaced. Company commanders were hand-picked, ideally had two previous Vietnam tours and possessed the ability to operate independently as guerrilla chieftains.

Company commanders trained with an Australian Infantry company for four weeks, where they learned platoon and company tactics from the finest jungle fighters in the world. In addition, all leaders (E6 and above) were required to read battalion-prepared counterinsurgency handbooks which spelled out in detail how they were expected to operate. This theoretical instruction was augmented by a minimum of two weeks on-the-job training with a proven guerrilla leader. Here the new leader learned tricks that weren't taught at West Point or Fort Benning, but which were need-to-know in order to outfox the fox.

The battalion's basic organization was drastically modified to facilitate the ambush concept. All rifle company heavy weapons platoons were converted into rifle platoons. The battalion was stripped down by eliminating extraneous equipment. The battalion's reconnaissance and heavy mortar platoons were transformed into a sniper and special action force respectively.

Each of the rifle companies was assigned a specific tactical mission. Each was given broad guidance, time to conduct needed special training and maximum latitude in developing and preparing its organization.

Company A became the long-range ambush company and was organized into two 60-man heavy platoons. Its mission was to operate on the periphery of the battalion's AO. One platoon was always deployed, while the other stood down, resting and training. The deployed platoon would normally enter the target area by helicopter several hours before dusk, as part of another company which would be assigned a target in that area. While the airmobile force, or "jitterbug," was on the ground, the heavy ambush platoon would go into hiding. After dark, the platoon would move to its first ambush site, to set up where there was evidence of frequent enemy movement.

The platoon used artillery defensive concentrations (defcons), dug deep, carefully camouflaged its positions, and conducted limited local patrolling around its base. Movement during daylight and helicopter overflights were forbidden. The ground commander moved his ambush when he had concluded that the fish would no longer bite or in concert with future battalion plans. This platoon normally stayed out six days and was picked up by helicopter after its sister element was inserted in another area. The company commander occasionally went out with a platoon to set the example and check on operations. Normally, he remained at his company base camp monitoring operations, prepared to lead the stand-down platoon or the initial reinforcement element and planning future operations.

Company C was assigned the mission of conducting short-range ambush operations. The company was organized into four identical platoons; each night three platoons would establish ambushes within 10 kilometers of the battalion firebase, while the remaining platoon would stand down.

The commanders of Alfa and Charlie companies were each assigned a general area of operations and given maximum independence and latitude. Their ambush commander in turn would conduct detailed intelligence collection, reconnaissance and other necessary troop leading procedures. Once they had selected the

exact ambush sites, they would present a detailed briefing to the battalion commander.

It wasn't long before these two commanders knew the battlefield better than their own personnel files. Most contacts were with small enemy forces at night, which were moving by sampan or on trails alongside canals. Contacts were violent and brief. Claymores and fragmentation grenades were the main weapons, and small arms were seldom used. The surprise effect was so great that the VC normally died in the killing zone without returning fire. At first light the killing zone would be swept and enemy weapons, documents and other materiel would be secured for eventual evacuation to battalion.

Both ambush companies conducted all operations by the book — air recons — rehearsals — sandtable briefings — detailed before-mission personnel inspections. The battalion staff spot-checked all stages of the before-mission preparations.

Bravo and Delta companies were organized similar to Korean war-vintage Ranger companies. These units were the guerrilla companies and rotated on operational missions. One company would stand-down at the fire support base (FSB) and serve as the battalion reaction force, while its sister unit would operate in a clearly defined AO. The areas were selected after a meticulous intelligence profile was made. Every intelligence source available to the battalion was used, from the super-secret black box in the delta-winged jet to the wrinkled brown farmer who tilled the rice paddy. When completed, the intelligence profile blinked like a neon light that pointed a bright red arrow at the enemy. The guerrilla companies conducted the same exacting pre-operation preparations as the ambush companies. Nothing was missed.

The guerrilla company normally entered its AO by a night overland march or as a last insert on a "jitterbug." When the airmobile insertion was used, the birds would return to the landing zone after the company had concealed itself in a hiding position and conduct a false pick-up. As the slicks came in for the pick-up, the aircraft doors would be open. But on lift-off they would be closed, to deceive a sharp-eyed enemy who might be observing from the distance. After dark, the company would move to its ambush sites and set up. The exact number of ambushes depended on the ground commander's estimate, based on the tired but true cliche: the enemy, terrain and weather. At first light the company would assemble, dry out from a long night of soaking in the Delta paddies, and sleep. Only outguards would remain alert and provide security.

At about 1500 hours, the company would commence checkerboarding in the direction of its next night ambush location. The rear guard platoon always would go into a "hide" location as close as possible to the "dry out" position and then sneak back as a stay-behind force. The batting average for kills by these stay-behind elements never slipped below .500.

When moving, the company always traveled along concealed routes in multiple columns, with scout elements out front. Normally, contact was with squad-size enemy forces which would easily be dealt with. When larger forces were found, the find 'em, fix 'em, fight 'em rule wasn't applied; the Hardcores had better ways. The find 'em force would draw back to a position that provided good cover, and then maximum tactical air and artillery was employed. Battalion would drop other noncommited units astride the likely enemy escape routes. Tactical air and artillery would pour in on the enemy, and the loose net would be slowly concentrated until it became virtually impossible for the enemy force to escape.

All units traveled light. Only essential equipment was taken. For the soldier this meant weapon, ammo, load-bearing equipment, poncho, rations, and air mattress. The standard 70-pound rucksack which is so popular with many US units was forbidden. Resupply aircraft weren't used and units lived off the land, just like their guerrilla opponents. Medevac was summoned only for seriously wounded. Lightly wounded and moderately sick went along with their units. Everyone realized that once a chopper came near the element, the operation was compromised, and the enemy would know exact locations and intentions of the friendlies.

Stealth was one of the main weapons of the Hardcore Battalion. Every soldier was required to memorize the rules of Rogers' Rangers and leaders were charged with their enforcement.

The sniper platoon was a 15-man element commanded by one of the sharpest lieutenants in the battalion. His command consisted of 7 two-man sniper teams of handpicked volunteers. These sniper teams received comprehensive training conducted by the 9th Division's Sniper School. They wore a special uniform, received quick promotions and had high priority on awards. In short, they were the spoiled children of the battalion commander and everyone knew it. Consequently, men fought to become snipers.

During the day, four sniper teams were employed, while two were used at night and one stood down. The day sniper teams would be augmented by three volunteers from headquarters company. This would make a five-man team: two snipers, one RTO and two security men. Each day at 1600 hours Sniper 6 met with the short-range ambush commander and the battalion commander to outline the planned sniper activity for that night and the following day. Adjustments would be made to insure that Company C's short-range ambushes and other battalion activities would be complemented by the snipers' operation. At first light, a slick, escorted by a gunship, inserted each of the five-man teams individually in a 10-kilometer area around the FSB. By dawn the teams were in a concealed position, had set up all-around security and had commenced their search for enemy soldiers. Just before dusk, the teams would be picked up and returned to the FSB. The night teams, working with starlight scopes and pink filters, would normally set up at Regional Forces outposts. Sniper 6 would select the exact sites, based on intelligence, and conduct necessary coordination with the district chief.

The special action force was an 18-man volunteer platoon composed of 12 Vietnamese-size Americans and six Tiger Scouts (former enemy soldiers who had changed to the government's side and volunteered to work as scouts). This force, operating in black pajamas, armed with Russian AK47s and other captured Communist equipment, conducted covert operations such as prisoner snatches, collection of intelligence or special reconnaissance missions. Lieutenant Colonel Trinquer's book on French Army guerrilla tactics, "Modern Warfare," served as their bible.

Jitterbug operations were normally conducted every third day by the stand-down guerrilla company. These operations were tightly controlled by the battalion commander and his staff. The day before the operation, an intelligence analysis would be made of the battalion's area of influence. District, Province, RF, PF, US Special Forces, ARVN units, higher headquarters, and the battalion's own agent net were squeezed for the last drop of information. Targets were selected and priorities assigned based upon many factors, such as target perishability, optimum blade-time utilization, location of friendly units, placement of supporting fires, and probable enemy strengths. Next, the battalion CO, S2 and S3 attended a target meeting at brigade. Here, each target was discussed in detail, and additional brigade or division targets were assigned, based on "hotter dope." By midnight the target priorities had been finalized and about 20 blue target circles would be printed on a map. At first light the command and control (C&C) aircraft and the air cavalry commander arrived at the FSB and were briefed with the Infantry CO on targets, call-signs, frequencies, pick-up zones (PZs), landing zones (LZs), unit SOPs, rearm and refuel points, and air cav recon zones.

At the designated hour the air cav troop moved to its recon zones, the C&C bird headed towards the first target and the initial lift of Infantry moved into a PZ formation. The C&C bird carried a minimum of six Air Force CS canisters. If, in the commander's judgment, the target appeared not worth striking — this would be based on lack of fresh trail activity or recent signs of enemy movement, gut feeling, and other telltale signs of the enemy — a CS canister might be kicked out, followed by gunship reconnaissance fire. If the CS and machinegun fire didn't stir things up, the target might be scratched.

If the second target looked good, a rifle platoon would be inserted. The gunships and a forward air controller would cover the platoon while it searched out the target area. If no contact was made, the C&C would move to the next target, and the Infantry at the second target would move into a PZ formation. This procedure would be followed all day and would be broken only if solid contact was made. Based on the size of the contact, Infantry troops and adequate combat support would pile on the contact to seal the enemy force. Experience gained by the Hardcore Battalion makes this axiom ring true when jitterbugging: there is a direct correlation between the number of inserts and the number of contacts made. Maximum inserts result in a high number of contacts. But great care must be taken to insure that the small Infantry force doesn't bite off more than it can handle, for it can be harshly treated by a clever enemy waiting in ambush.

The PPS-5 ground radar tracked the enemy's movement at night and was normally set up at a district headquarters, or with RF or PF outposts. This way, it could scan the deployed ambush patrols more effectively. Permanent overlays were made of all radar movement, and future ambush patrols and sniper employment were based on these overlays. The radar provided the battalion with the enemy's movement pattern. It wasn't an uncommon event for an ambush patrol to be notified, "You have 10 VC moving on the trail you are on. They are 400 meters from your position and moving in your direction." All enemy activity that wasn't moving towards an ambush position was plastered by artillery fire.

The VC closely follow Mao's dictum: "Our duty is to fight a protracted war, avoiding the enemy if possible, never engaging him unless it can be made certain in advance that it is to our advantage." As a result of this strategem, the enemy was always eager to attack a small US force that appeared an easy target.

The Hardcores used the following technique, or variations, to tempt their greedy opponent: A small Infantry force would be inserted by helicopter at last light and set up near the LZ. After dark it would move, leaving a clearly defined trail for enemy scouts to follow, and link up with one of the guerrilla companies which had carefully slipped into the AO. This trap brought results more times than not. On two occasions, multiple company-

size enemy forces struck what they thought was a weak platoon only to find a well dug-in, reinforced rifle company, which was locked and loaded. What the enemy thought was a tender lamb was instead a sinewy tiger.

The 9th Division, like most US units in Vietnam, didn't push unit training. If units were removed from operations to conduct training, then the great, misleading measurement of success — bodycount — would decrease. Most high-level commanders in Vietnam followed the rule, "The more units in the field, the higher the contact rate. Hence, more enemy kills." The weakness of this thinking is that friendly casualties are also higher, because the troopers are inadequately trained and are careless because of overexposure.

The 4/39 Infantry, being a band of guerrillas, outfoxed their division headquarters, which never caught on to their training program. Each week two platoons would slip from the FSB to division rear for a rigorous one-week training program. This program used all the assets of the division training facilities and was closely monitored by the battalion executive officer. The troopers looked forward to this week. They knew they would train hard for a minimum of 12 hours a day, but they also knew they could relax and forget about hunting Charlie for a while. The training program paid rich dividends: morale went up, casualties went down, and the battalion became a little sharper at outwitting the guerrilla.

The tactical innovations discussed here weren't played as separate musical instruments with each musician doing his own thing. They were employed in close concert with each other, closely controlled by the battalion commander. One example:

Early morning, May 21, 1969, intelligence indicated that a large enemy force was staging to the north of FSB Danger. At 0700 hours a special action force element was dispatched, with the mission "get a prisoner." Simultaneously, two battalion-controlled civilian agents were told to infiltrate the suspected enemy assembly area to determine the size and mission of the enemy force.

The agents and the SAF element were back by 1000 hours. SAF didn't have a POW to show for its efforts, but it had made contact with an enemy patrol and killed four of them. One of the KIA was the recon company commander of the 261A VC Battalion. Found on him was a map showing attack plans against a nearby RF company, including company objectives, movement routes, supporting weapons sites, and most importantly, the exact location of each assembly area for all the companies in the 261A Battalion. The agents confirmed that it was 261A and concluded that it was ready to jump off.

The Hardcore commander deduced that the attack on the RF company was of secondary importance. The enemy's objective was to frighten the people of Giao Duc, for if an RF company could be destroyed right under the nose of a US battalion, how secure was the average peasant?

The enemy's plan might have worked had the American opponent been a unit which played by ordinary rules. But this opponent was a guerrilla like himself, who cheated and read his hand, then stacked the deck.

The US battalion readied itself for combat. Holes weren't bored in the sky by helicopters circling over the target. Nor was artillery and tac air placed blindly on red dots on the map marking VC locations. Helicopters weren't hastily assembled for an ill-planned airmobile assault. The battalion knew that the enemy would be gone slick as a whistle before the lead ship set down on the LZ.

Experience had taught this lesson well. The VC can't be destroyed by conventional tactics employed by the average US battalion in Vietnam. Only guerrilla tactics augmented by US firepower can defeat the enemy at low cost.

The target was perishable. The enemy wouldn't linger long in the assembly area. He would either attack soon or slink away. He had to be baited to stay one more night. Two M41 dusters, with potent twin 40mm cannons, and a rifle platoon were moved to the RF outpost to reinforce it. It was hoped that this would cause the enemy to reassess his attack plans, thus buying time. False helicopter insertions were made along all the enemy's probable withdrawal routes, to cause him to think twice before running away into a possible hornet's nest of ambushes.

After these deceptive measures were taken to keep the bird in the cage, the following concept of operations was outlined to the commanders:

Each rifle company would be divided into two parts. Half the battalion, operating under company control, would infiltrate at dark and establish ambush positions by 0600 on May 22d. The other half of the battalion, less one heavy platoon from Company A which would be the battalion reaction force, would conduct a combat assault at first light. The combat assault force's mission wasn't to become decisively engaged, but to serve as the beater and get the rabbit running.

All preparations were carefully concealed. The battalion knew that the VC constantly observe all US installations, searching for signs of unusual activity. Harassing and interdiction (H&I) fires weren't allowed and everything at FSB Danger went on its normal merry routine.

After dark the ambush forces moved out. Long lines of ghostly columns moved silently along separate infiltration routes towards their critical blocking positions. Stealth was the key. One careless movement could blow the show.

At 0600 hours all ambush elements were in position and the stage was set to spring the trap. At 0700 hours the airmobile force was launched. Once the beaters were on the ground, the enemy reacted as if it were an aggressor force at Fort Benning and followed the scenario according to plan.

"The helicopter assault was the prop designed to cause Charlie to blow his cool," related Major George Mergner, battalion operations officer. He continued, "Lose his cool he did. The minute the first bird hit the LZ, the enemy was on the move. He was attracted to the ambush sites as if he was being pulled by powerful magnets. But the magnets were our ambush positions which had been painstakingly selected, based upon Charlie's most likely escape routes."

"I've never seen anything like it," said Captain James Mukoyama, a company commander. "The VC bounced off one ambush after another. Almost like a spinning ball in a pinball machine. Each time they ran panic-stricken into one ambush, they would lose a dozen or so men and bounce off, only to hit another blocked escape route."

All morning long the enemy tried to escape. He couldn't hide because heavy artillery fire, tac air and gunships blasted all possible hiding positions. There wasn't one inch of ground that he could use to escape this murderous fire or the probing thrusts of the airmobile search force.

By 1200 hours the enemy command structure had disintegrated. Enemy soldiers ran in every direction, pursued by fire from gunships or battalion sniper teams attached to the maneuver elements.

By 1800 hours the fight was over. All elements of the battalion had departed the battlefield except Company C, which went into a hide position after a false helicopter pick-up. That night their ambushes killed 17 VC who had hidden in the reeds all day and tried to escape under cover of darkness. Friendly casualties: two US slightly wounded. Enemy casualties: 167 KIA, seven POWs and numerous weapons captured.

This ends the story of a battalion which used radical techniques to win. Yet these techniques weren't new. Marion had used the same unorthodox tricks at Cowpens, as had Rogers against the French at Detroit. The Hardcores had simply updated the tactics of our guerrilla forefathers and given them a 1969 Vietnam twist.

From January to late May 1969 the Hardcore Battalion killed over 2,700 enemy soldiers with a loss of 26 troopers. But more important than the awful enemy losses, the western portion of Dinh Tuong Province was made secure. The people of Giao Duc identified with the government. An average of eight Viet Cong infrastructure rallied to the Giao Duc District force per week. The enemy's main force units were shattered and rendered ineffective. There was light at the end of the tunnel in one small area of South Vietnam.

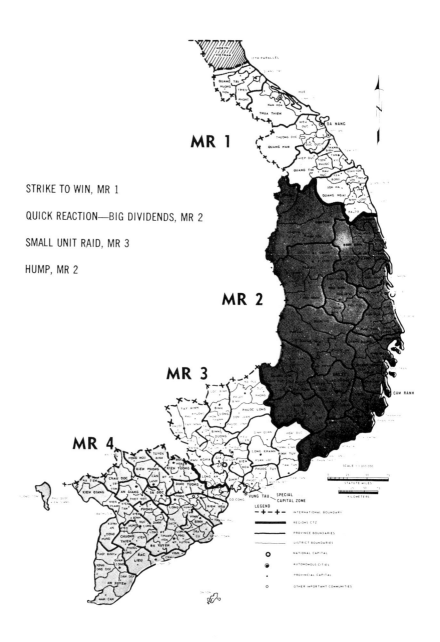

STRIKE TO WIN, MR 1

QUICK REACTION—BIG DIVIDENDS, MR 2

SMALL UNIT RAID, MR 3

HUMP, MR 2

Chapter 9

Keeping The Pressure On

Strike to Win!

Captain Fred L. Meyers, Jr.

In late July 1969, the 1st Battalion, 11th Infantry, 1st Brigade, 5th Infantry Division (Mech) attacked west from Con Thien on the southern edge of the DMZ in Vietnam. The attack began at 2000 hours with three footmobile rifle companies attacking west into AO Orange in separate zones of action.

A reserve, consisting of a rifle company minus, reinforced with one platoon of M48A3 tanks, was maintained within mutual supporting distance of the attacking companies. An additional force, consisting of a tank company minus with an Infantry platoon attached, was employed to secure the battalion base and conduct limited operations east and south of Con Thien. Extensive artillery and air support was preplanned and on call.

The enemy, in multi-battalion strength, consisted of NVA Infantry, sappers, and mortar and rocket artillery within easy striking range of both the attacking force and the battalion base at Con Thien. A good portion of the enemy force operated as guerrillas in squad, platoon and company-size elements.

The attack took the enemy completely by surprise and, after two weeks of heavy contact, the 1st Battalion, 11th Infantry terminated operations in AO Orange. More than 200 enemy soldiers had been killed and large quantities of equipment and munitions were captured or destroyed. The battalion sustained only light casualties.

This success, in the face of a numerically superior enemy, highlights the potential of Infantry units to plan and execute strike operations. Careful planning and violent execution, coupled with maximum use of all available fire support and solid leadership at all levels, were primary factors in the success of this operation.

The battalion commander allowed the companies maximum initiative in executing the plan. This freedom of action permitted the company commanders to develop situations which led directly to the lopsided success of the entire battalion. The rifle companies were the basic ingredients of this operation. The battalion commander provided necessary guidance and exploited the opportunities developed by his subordinate units.

Strike operations are highly mobile offensive operations, generally of short duration, conducted in areas controlled or contested by the enemy, which seek to seize, disrupt or destroy an objective. The object of the strike operation is destruction of the enemy. It is a combination of the five basic types of offensive operations — movement to contact, reconnaissance-in-force coordinated attack, exploitation, and pursuit.

The rifle company is usually employed semi-independently within a specific area of operations. The company commander attempts to make contact with the fewest number of troops possible. By establishing contact in this manner, the commander retains maximum initiative without unduly exposing subordinate elements. Once contact is gained, every effort is made to maintain and develop the situation.

Probing attacks are conducted to develop intelligence and weaken the enemy. If destruction of the enemy force is within the company's capability, and the commander is confident the company will not be overcommitted, a coordinated attack may be conducted. Otherwise, contact is maintained while additional forces are brought in. The companies of the 1st Battalion, 11th Infantry located the enemy, fixed him in place with probing attacks and fire support, and destroyed him. In contacts beyond the capability of a single company, the battalion commander led reaction forces in a pile-on. Then, in combination with air, artillery and armor, the Infantry attacked and destroyed the enemy.

262

In planning and conducting the operation, the company commander plans for several factors over and above normal considerations. The first of the planning factors is mutual reinforcing capability, or mutual support. Terrain, weather, enemy capabilities, and mobility are key factors in planning for mutual support. The key question is, "How long will it take to reinforce separated elements?" Selection of formations or decisions to employ platoons semi-independently requires careful analysis of the situation, as well as a realistic evaluation of the capabilities of subordinate elements in terms of leadership, training and relative combat power. After careful consideration, the company commander aggressively seeks contact by employing the company over as wide an area as possible, consistent with the situation.

As a general rule, a reserve element or reaction force is maintained. The reserve force commander is briefed as completely as possible on likely missions, and tentative plans are made to exploit situations which may arise during the conduct of the operation. Enemy capabilities are of primary concern to the reserve force commander in making tentative plans for the employment of his force.

Emphasis is placed on security throughout strike operations. The company commander maintains security through dispersion of individual soldiers and aggressive patrolling. Maximum use of observation and listening posts, ambushes, patrols, and fire support is essential to proper security. Noise and light discipline, camouflage and silent movement techniques employing arm and hand signals are equally important. Scout dogs and Kit Carson scouts can offer invaluable aid in improving security in all phases of the strike operation. Above all, every leader and every soldier must understand that the enemy will take full advantage of every crack in our security. Enemy attack is possible anywhere, at any time, under any conditions. The phrase "stay alert and stay alive" is still true.

Initially the 1/11 Infantry made a night attack into AO Orange. This attack, and subsequent night attacks and movements, completely surprised the enemy and contributed greatly to the success the battalion enjoyed. These night operations deceived the NVA .completely and aided in masking the overall tactical plan.

The object of deception at company level is to attain tactical surprise and reduce casualties. Night operations, stay-behind ambushes, deceptive use of fire support, and other techniques have proven effective in Vietnam, and are limited only by the imagination of the commander.

One aspect of security often overlooked is battlefield police. Enemy forces, especially guerillas, will use anything discarded or lost by friendly forces. Batteries, electrical devices and

munitions are particularly critical. After each stop, or before moving from night defensive positions, the company commander must take steps to insure that each platoon area is thoroughly policed. C-ration cans should be crushed and buried, paper should be burned or buried, discarded rations should be destroyed, and unserviceable ammunition, batteries, electrical devices, and other equipment should be evacuated or destroyed.

Leaders must check individual soldiers to insure that hand grenades, ammo magazines and other equipment are all properly secured to prevent accidental loss. Stay-behind ambushes should be used to take advantage of enemy attempts to forage abandoned night defensive positions.

The company commander establishes tactical control measures designed to give maximum flexibility while providing for adequate control. Ideally, these measures will increase the probability of gaining contact, while minimizing the possibility of casualties from friendly fires. Only necessary control measures are employed, and maximum independence is allowed subordinate leaders in accomplishing the mission. Tactical control measures are tied in closely to proper planning, use of available fire support and coordination with adjacent units.

The commander's primary means of destroying the enemy at minimum cost is effective use of fire support. Properly employed, fire support increases the relative combat power of the Infantry company. Individual companies of the 1/11 Infantry were heavily engaged with NVA forces on several occasions. In each case extensive tac air support and artillery was used to overpower the North Vietnamese. Preplanning provided the commanders with the extra margin of combat power necessary to win.

Strike operations begin with an attack into the area of operations, seeking to locate the enemy. The writings of Mao, Giap and others are replete with admonitions for the guerrilla to avoid combat unless certain of victory. The strike operation is intended to compel the enemy to fight when no possibility for victory exists. To accomplish this, the Infantry company commander must employ search techinques designed to ferret out the well-concealed guerrilla.

Searching for the enemy requires constant alertness by every member of the company. Anything which seems unnatural should be reported. The importance of the senses, logical thought process and accurate analysis cannot be overemphasized. The enemy is human — he sets patterns, leaves evidence of his activity and is often careless. Constant alertness and aggressive patrolling are key ingredients of a successful search for the enemy.

Prisoners are important sources of intelligence information and defectors are even more valuable. Both can provide otherwise unobtainable assistance if properly exploited. Prisoners of war and persons detained as suspects should be handled firmly but without undue harshness. To do otherwise may rob our forces of significant intelligence information.

Based on his estimate of the situation, the company commander elects to search the area of operations on either a narrow or wide front. These may be defined in terms of reinforcing time. With the narrow front search, the search elements are normally located no more than 30 minutes from the reserve platoon or other reinforcements. On a wide front, the time factor is about one hour, but may be much more depending on the situation.

Searching on the narrow front offers the advantages of good reinforcing capability and ease of control. The chief disadvantage is the decreased probability of gaining contact. This technique is used when the terrain isn't suitable for the wide search and when the enemy situation is such that the wide search isn't possible without incurring unacceptable risk.

Searching on a wide front increases the likelihood of gaining contact. Control may be difficult and reinforcing may be a problem. Immediate fire support is necessary when the company is widely separated. This technique is good against small guerrilla bands or in terrain suited for relatively easy overland movement.

Within the outlines of the wide and narrow front, there are many specific techniques and formations available to the company commander. Two stand out as particularly effective. The first of these techniques is the company base. The company commander establishes a temporary base of operations secured by a reserve element. The area around the temporary base is then divided into search areas and the platoons conduct extensive patrolling in "cloverleaf" fashion out to about 1,000 meters. Normally, the platoons and squads drop their heavy equipment at the base and conduct the search unencumbered. This technique is characterized by a fixed base, centralized control of search elements and a centrally located reserve or reaction element.

Coordinated routes and tactical control measures will help reduce the possibility of casualties from friendly fires and insure a good search of likely areas.

Immediate fire support is available if the company employs its organic mortars. If not, primary reliance is placed on artillery fire support and variations of this technique are numerous. One of interest is the use of the company base in "movement by bounds."

In this technique, the company moves periodically, establishing temporary patrol bases along the direction of movement. Small patrols are sent out to clear the flank areas and secure the area forward of the company. The company searches the area and secures its route of movement at the same time. The point patrol may remain to secure the site of the next temporary base until

the flank cloverleafs are completed and the company moves forward. Once the company reaches the point security element, the process is repeated. The patrols are usually squad-size and contact, if gained, is made by squads, leaving the remainder of the company free to maneuver. Early detection of ambushes, base camps, boobytrapped areas, and enemy troop concentrations is likely if this technique is properly employed.

Another concept involves the use of separate platoon zones of action. When required to cover a large area in minimum time, the commander may assign platoon zones. Platoons are employed abreast in assigned zones of action about 1,000 meters wide. A rifle company employing this technique may be deployed on a front about 3,000 meters wide. A detailed search of an area isn't possible, but indications of enemy activity will be uncovered and may increase the possibility of gaining contact. This technique is characterized by widely separated elements, limited reinforcing capability and the requirement for immediate artillery fire support. There is no fixed base and all elements normally move simultaneously. Separate zones of action are suitable in areas of light enemy activity and where terrain limitations aren't severe. It is a good technique for searching low ground or stream lines straddling a center ridge line. In this situation, platoons search the low ground to each flank of the ridge or finger while a center element searches the ridge itself and maintains a terrain advantage in the event the elements on the low ground gain contact. The company commander is afforded a good deal of flexibility and has a good chance of making contact.

Many techniques are available in addition to the two mentioned here. Variations in standard formations are numerous. Boxes, diamonds and lines, as well as other formations, are commonly employed with good results. All fall within the general guidelines of wide and narrow front. Selection of the specific formation to be employed is at the discretion of the company commander, platoon and squad leaders. Rarely, if ever, can anyone select the appropriate formation or search technique without being present on the ground. The view from a helicopter is radically different from the view on the ground. Tentative plans should be made, based on aerial reconnaissance, but flexibility must be maintained.

Without a doubt, the single most important ingredient of a strike operation is good leadership. Initiative, courage, leadership by example, professional concern for mission and men, and efficient management of resources are essential to the success of the Infantry company conducting strike operations. The good guy officer or NCO literally kills his men with kindness. Leaders at all levels must establish high standards and take all necessary measures to insure the standard is met.

Unfortunately, there are many combat examples which show that poor leadership results in needless casualties and lost opportunities. Dirty weapons, poor battlefield police and poor security all reflect inadequate leadership. In strike operations, it is normal for elements to be separated from their parent headquarters. Consequently, the highest standards of leadership must be maintained if the elements are to survive and win on the battlefield.

The strike operation is a primary means of destroying the enemy in counterguerrilla war. It contributes to the political-military objectives of a counterrevolutionary war strategy by depriving the enemy of the military means of achieving his goal.

The strike operation is an offensive operation designed to find, fix and destroy the enemy. When you strike, strike to win!

Quick Reaction — Big Dividends

Major Herbert H. Hameister

For Company B, 123d Aviation Battalion, it was just another mission. They had been conducting an area reconnaissance in the southern portion of the 11th Infantry Brigade's operational zone for the past several hours and were presently reconning 515 Valley, a well-used infiltration route from the mountains to the coastal lowlands.

Suddenly, there was a heavy burst of automatic weapons fire from the ground and one of the light observation helicopters be-

269

gan plummeting out of control. It crashed in a thickly wooded draw. The three crew members were extracted by another aircraft operating in the area.

Word of the heavy weapons position was immediately sent to the 11th Brigade tactical operations center and a quick assessment of nearby friendly units was made. Company D, 1st Infantry was conducting a combat sweep in the foothills 5,000 meters to the east. The intervening terrain was fairly open and two hours was the estimated time for reaching the downed helicopter. Company D received the order to move.

Company C also was operating in the lowlands and was very near a cleared pickup zone. The company commander was given a warning order for a combat assault. Lift helicopters were scrambled for the movement of the company's 98 men to a landing zone just north of the suspected enemy position.

The lift aircraft, coming from several different locations, joined up enroute and Company C's first nine-ship-lift was soon airborne. Seventy minutes after the observation helicopter was hit, the first lift of Company C landed in the area.

Although spontaneously planned and quickly executed, the tactical plan for eliminating the enemy position and securing the downed aircraft was sound. Since two hours was the estimated overland travel time for Company D, it was planned that both companies would move simultaneously through parallel attack positions and conduct the assault together.

Company C would sweep the high ground to the west of the draw, with Company D utilizing the same tactics on the east. Each company was to eliminate any resistance on the high ground and then turn downward into the draw towards the final objective — suspected machinegun emplacements.

Two events occurred to prevent the plan from reaching fruition. Company D made contact with an estimated platoon of NVA after having moved only 1,200 meters. They never did get to the machinegun positions. Company C's move, however, was ahead of schedule due to the rapid reaction of the aviation units involved. They arrived at their attack position nearly an hour early. That left Company C alone on the northern end of the draw to conduct the attack.

To take maximum advantage of the element of surprise, only two airstrikes were used and these were to the flanks of Company C. Artillery support was available, but was not used because it would slow down the swift combat assault.

Approximately 300 meters from the enemy heavy weapons positions, Company C began taking small arms and automatic weapons fire. Two helicopter gunships provided suppressive fire while the 1st and 2d platoons began to fire and maneuver against the enemy position. Using all of the company's organic firepower, the assaulting Infantrymen finally overran the position.

Having pushed to the far side of the position, the Infantrymen secured the area and began a thorough search of the position. Captured enemy equipment revealed that they had overrun a heavy weapons company of an NVA battalion.

Two Russian-made 12.7 mm (.51 caliber) antiaircraft machineguns and one SKS rifle were captured. One of the machineguns had been dismantled and hastily hidden in nearby brush; the other was still in position. A total of 22 NVA were killed; three US soldiers lost their lives.

There were four contributing factors to the success of the operation. Each factor played a significant role and had that factor been missing, the operation probably would have failed.

The first was the teamwork between the two aviation units and the Infantry. Aircraft for the lift were not immediately available and quick, accurate coordination had to be accomplished. Once specific aircraft were targeted for the mission they were launched, pilots were briefed and rendezvous effected while airborne. In the meantime, Company C was preparing for the move, securing the pickup zone, organizing for the lift, and briefing personnel on the change of mission.

Secondly, when it became apparent that the second company would not be available for the assault, additional measures were taken to secure the flanks of Company C as it moved forward. This security was provided by the Air Force, which struck at the high ground to the east and west of the attacking company. Enemy positions in these areas were neutralized and Company C was able to concentrate its main effort on the enemy to its front.

The third factor is one which plays a large part in virtually every successful engagement of the war — aggressive leadership and violent execution. When the second company became engaged in another action, the battalion commander made a quick estimate of the situation and then pressed the attack with only one company. The small unit leaders led by example and the men responded by vigorously attacking the position and annihilating those who chose to remain and fight.

And finally, the largest contributing factor was rapid reaction. Had the attack been characterized by slow, methodical and deliberate tactics, the enemy would have had ample time to react, either attacking or withdrawing. Seventy minutes, however, was all the grace period allocated to him, and this proved to be insufficient time for him to react. From the moment the observation aircraft went down until his position was overrun, the enemy was pinned down by either gunships, airstrikes or small arms fire.

The timely, decisive and violently executed assault caught the enemy unawares and led to the complete destruction of the heavy weapons company.

Small Unit Raid

Major Wayne A. Downing

SAIGON — A late afternoon attack caught surprised Communist soldiers at the dinner table Saturday as GIs backed by air and artillery strikes ransacked an enemy supply complex 25 miles northwest of Saigon.

At least 50 of the Reds were killed in two hours of fighting. No Americans were hurt, U.S. military spokesmen said.

This news item, tucked away on page six of a newspaper, tells little of the actual events of a rarity in the Vietnam war — the perfect raid. The story began in early June when a routine sweep operation through a hamlet uncovered four Viet Cong concealed in a well-camouflaged bunker. The prize catch of the group was the head of sub-region training, a Viet Cong senior captain. A member of the Viet Minh since 1947 and educated in North Vietnam's military schools, the senior captain proved to be a willing source of top-level intelligence information.

Initially ignored in the attempt to gain information from the senior captain was a Viet Cong private who was a member of the enemy rear service group which supplied the three Viet Cong main force regiments operating in the area. This low-level guerrilla had little information that could be readily used. However, as an afterthought, he mentioned his unit's resting places during the hours of darkness.

The division military intelligence detachment began surveillance of the areas mentioned. Detailed studies of aerial photographs revealed heavy trail activity around two bamboo huts on the western edge of the Hobo Woods. This information, combined with past activity in the area, recent intelligence reports, and further interrogation of the source, indicated that 15 to 20 men from the rear service group slept in the huts nightly, normally arriving between 1630 and 1730 hours and departing at daylight for the security of the dense underbrush.

Ten days after the capture of the prisoner, all information and intelligence concerning this activity was sent to the US brigade operating in the area. The brigade commander, along with the S2 and S3, analyzed the information and decided that it merited an immediate response. Based on past US operations in the area, the known habits of the enemy and the combat assets available, the decision was made to conduct an airmobile raid on the target about one hour before early evening nautical twilight (EENT). Since 10 days had already passed, it was not essential to conduct the raid that evening. If the guerrillas were going to leave the area, they probably would have done so earlier.

The brigade commander and his operations officer flew to the Infantry battalion within whose area of operations the target was located. With them they took a complete packet of photographs, maps, prisoner readouts, and all available intelligence about the enemy unit and the area. The raid was to be conducted the next evening. Therefore, detailed planning had to begin immediately.

Support made available to the battalion commander included one assault helicopter company (AHC), including nine lift ships, a command and control (C&C) aircraft, a smoke ship, and a heavy fire team of armed helicopters. Also available were one strike light fire team (LFT), a forward air controller (FAC) flying an armed OV10, and the direct support of four batteries of artillery (two light, one medium, and one heavy). As guidance, the battalion commander was instructed to consider destroying the target houses with gunship fire prior to the insertion of the Infantry. He was to insert the Infantry no later than 1800 hours and extract them by 1915 hours. All agencies were warned against any un-

usual aerial activity over the target area at any time prior to the conduct of the operation.

The battalion commander decided that one lift of nine ships carrying 54 Infantrymen would comprise the assault element. To achieve surprise and maximum shock action, the two target huts were to be destroyed by the strike LFT prior to a four-minute artillery preparation and the ensuing airmobile assault.

Once on the ground, the company minus would split into two platoons, with one platoon attacking each target house and searching the surrounding woodline to the east and northeast. At EENT the company minus would be extracted to a fire support base.

After the initial planning phase, the battalion conducted detailed coordination with the S3 of the direct support artillery battalion, the assault helicopter company, and the team leader of the strike LFT. One of the key elements of the plan was the immediate destruction of the target houses. The LFT leader was thoroughly briefed on the mission, with aerial photographs and a circuitous overflight of the objective area. The ground unit's complete scheme of maneuver and fire support also were discussed in detail.

A thorough artillery prep was a must for this operation. To insure this and to tie in the fires of the gunships with the artillery, a scheduled prep was planned on known and suspected antiaircraft positions, bunkers and trenches in the area and along the flight path into and out of the area. In the preceding four weeks three aircraft had been shot down and numerous others had received fire from the area to the northeast of the target. This region had to be neutralized.

As a result of the planning and coordination, the following sequence of events was established:

1755 Strike LFT destroys target houses in one pass
1756 Four-minute artillery prep commences
1800 Troops land in objective area
1900 Extraction of troops from objective area

The battalion commander and his S3 planned to control the operation from the C&C ship. In addition, the LFT, the FAC and the AHC would operate on the same UHF frequency to minimize traffic on the battalion command set.

On cue from the S3, the light fire team rolled in on the target at precisely 1755 hours and on the initial firing pass completely obliterated both targets, resulting in five NVA soldiers KIA. The team leader observed several enemy break and run and rolled in on a second unscheduled pass resulting in three more KIA. Ten seconds after the trail gunship broke from its run, the artillery prep commenced with devastating effectiveness.

Adhering to the time schedule, the combat assault element touched down on the landing zone about five seconds after the last artillery rounds impacted. The Infantry disembarked from the helicopters and obtained three quick kills as they raced to the assembly areas on the edges of the landing zone. Supporting gunships from the AHC reported and engaged 15 to 20 enemy attempting to flee to the southeast during the insertion. The strike LFT and the armed OV10 quickly joined the fight and for the next 20 minutes engaged the fleeing enemy in the wide open rice paddies to the southeast of the objective.

Realizing the enemy was not prepared to stay and fight from his bunkers and was attempting to flee the area, the battalion commander immediately ordered all available artillery fires to set up a "wall of steel" to block escape routes to the east and south-

east. Additional gunships were requested. One of the additional light fire teams placed minigun fire on about 10 VC running into a hut. After devastating rocket fire was placed on this hut, six of the surviving enemy fled to another. The lead ship then took out this hut with three pairs of rockets and the remaining two enemy limped to the next hut to the south. The wingman destroyed the last hut.

The ground troops swept through their objectives and confirmed the earlier gunship kills. The sweeping Infantry killed one bunker-protected Viet Cong as he attempted to transmit on a Chinese radio. During the sweep the Infantry captured 10 members of the rear service group and a recon party from a Viet Cong main force regiment.

The combined action of the sweeping Infantry and the gunships flushed more VC into the open. Obviously caught by surprise in a formerly safe haven, the VC madly attempted to flee the area. Taking advantage of a favorable gun-target line, the gunships continued to engage targets of opportunity while the artillery was "walked in" on enemy locations.

One incident typifies the effect of this massed firepower. Three enemy — receiving rocket, 40mm grenade and minigun fire — were observed racing toward a hut. As they reached their haven, one Cobra gunship hit the hut with a pair of rockets, and the three VC again broke and ran into the open. Simultaneously, a 155mm artillery round landed in their midst, resulting in three more enemy KIA.

At 1915 hours the Infantry company minus, with prisoners, captured weapons, documents, and materiel, was extracted by the AHC. Two follow-up airstrikes at 1930 and 1945 hours produced three additional KIA and five large secondary explosions.

In 75 minutes, 1,200 rounds of mixed artillery, five light fire teams, one armed OV10, and 54 aggressive Infantrymen accounted for 56 enemy KIA, 20 AK47 rifles, 10 RPG launchers, 1 RPD light machinegun, a Chicom radio, and 10 enemy soldiers captured.

The violent exploitation of credible and current intelligence information produced a successful operation. The operation was built around surprise — the operational techniques of the implementing battalion were tailored to hit the enemy when and where he least expected it.

Detailed prior planning was the key to the success of the operation. Close coordination between maneuver commander and the various fire support agencies produced overwhelming, effective firepower at the critical time and place. The plan was followed exactly, especially during the crucial first five minutes when the gunship and artillery fires achieved the initial surprise and destruction and the Infantry gained entry into the objective area.

Once the troops were on the ground, the commander was able to direct the massive fires available to him to destroy the maximum number of the enemy. The maneuver elements were directed to areas to exploit this firepower and take advantage of the resultant enemy confusion.

Command and control was nearly perfect throughout the operation. From the C&C ship, the commander was able to control his maneuver elements and all supporting aircraft. Sitting next to him, the artillery liaison officer delivered firepower at the time and place desired. The commander of the AHC, flying the C&C aircraft, was able to pass essential information such as target description, artillery air data, and holding patterns to other supporting aircraft on UHF, thus easing the amount of traffic on the battalion command net.

The entire operation was a model of combat efficiency and effectiveness — a goal constantly sought and seldom achieved.

Hump

Captain Bardon Blizzard, Jr.

"Damn, I'm glad that's over!" was the feeling of every man in Company B, 3d Battalion, 12th Infantry, 4th Infantry Division on this cold, wet January day. During the past four days, Company B had humped 16 kilometers in some of the roughest terrain in Military Region 2. Initially, their mission had been to search and clear a portion of VC Valley—a well-known enemy stronghold—and the surrounding cliffs. VC Valley is situated in the Central Highlands to the east of Pleiku and Camp Enari, the 4th Division base camp.

The preparation phase of the operation was completed at Plei Lim, a small outpost just south of Camp Enari. This phase included

279

the final briefings and replenishment of the basic load. After a final inspection, everyone was placed in aircraft loads and situated on the pick-up zone (PZ). The airlift was to be accomplished with 12 Hueys (UH1s), working in two separate flights. The PZ was an old fixed-wing airstrip, and Company B was to go out last. At 1100 hours the helicopters arrived to lift Company B, and with them came a pathfinder team to control the PZ. First platoon, company headquarters, 3d platoon, 4th platoon, 2d platoon, and a portion of the battalion mortar section all departed the PZ with no major difficulties. The landing zone, a large open field on a plateau, had not been preped and was cold. By 1300 all elements were prepared to move into the valley, except the mortar section and its security element, a portion of the battalion recon platoon that had been lifted in after B Company to provide security.

As Company B prepared to move down a long steep finger into the valley, the company commander began to feel uneasy concerning his mission. He had been instructed to put his entire unit on the valley floor, which was only 400 to 600 feet wide. Once in the valley, the company would be completely enveloped by steep, rocky cliffs 100 to 200 feet high. Security from atop the rocky cliffs was to be provided by Company A on the east and Company C on the west. The only fire support that could reach into the valley was the 81mm mortar section that he had just left. As the 3d platoon, the lead platoon, started into the Dak T'Mal Valley, the company commander called the battalion S3 to insure the other units were in place. He was advised to, "Drive on."

A strange feeling, instinct, or whatever you want to call it, told him not to get himself into an "untenable position." At that point, he directed the 4th platoon to set up on top of the west cliff of the valley. From there the platoon was to support by fire the remainder of the company as it entered the valley. The 3d platoon and the company headquarters moved down to the valley floor. Once there, a landing zone was prepared to evacuate two soldiers who had injured themselves during the descent. The 2d platoon was to move across the valley floor and then scale the cliffs on the east side, to provide flank security. The 2d and 3d platoons were to link up and then move up the valley.

By 1700 the 3d platoon and company headquarters had cleared an LZ and were awaiting the arrival of a medevac helicopter. The 1st platoon was halfway across the small canyon; the 2d and 4th platoons were still in their previous locations. Just then the artillery forward observer's radio-telephone operator yelled, "Hey Six, there's Alfa Company!" He pointed to the cliffs on the east side. At that moment all doubts as to whether or not that was an element of Company A were erased. The newly observed group opened fire with two light machineguns and several AK47s. Immediately, two men were wounded and several items of equipment

were hit. As the firing continued, the company commander called the 4th platoon and directed them to fire onto the enemy location. The 1st platoon had started up the east wall of the canyon and the 2d platoon was instructed to reinforce the 4th. Simultaneously, a call for artillery fire was sent by the artillery FO to the direct support artillery battery and the company's mortars. The battalion commander was informed by his S3 that B Company was in contact with an estimated VC platoon supported by two light machineguns and a 61mm mortar. The battalion commander shifted priority of fires to Bravo, and requested a light fire team of helicopter gunships and tac air. Gunships were on station in 15 minutes, but no tac air was available.

By 1730 the situation had deteriorated greatly. The artillery battery was unable to place rounds on the target due to the steepness of the valley walls. Likewise, the 81mm mortar section was having difficulty because they had been given an incorrect location by the battalion S3. As a result, the only fire support available to Bravo's commander was from the 2d and 4th platoons firing across the valley at the enemy positions. The 3d platoon had little cover and couldn't maneuver because of the enemy fire. By now the 1st platoon was about halfway up the east wall, and hadn't been detected by the enemy. As the firefight continued, the 4th platoon expended about half its basic load and the 2d platoon was directed to replace the 4th in its support-by-fire role. Once the switch had taken place, the 4th platoon was to prepare a night defensive position for both platoons, under the control of the 4th platoon leader. A continuous volume of fire was to be maintained while the exchange took place. The 2d platoon was to continue suppressive fire until the gunships arrived.

At 1745 the light fire team arrived on station and was directed on its first approach by the company commander. All company elements had marked their locations with smoke except the 1st platoon, which was nearing the top of the east wall. As the gunship made its first strike, the pilot checked fire and pulled out hard to his right. Bravo's CO was advised that a platoon of Company A was about 400 meters east of his target on the gun-target line, and that he couldn't fire because of safety requirements. There they sat with darkness moving in, the 1st platoon deployed and ready for a flanking attack on the enemy, and no outside fire support. The battalion commander ordered Company A to withdraw its element immediately. By 1755, the gunships were cleared to start their strikes.

At 1810 one of the Cobras had completely expended its ordnance and the other was down to a half-load of rockets and fuel. At that point, Bravo's commander directed the 1st platoon to attack, utilizing supporting fire provided by the 2d platoon, while placing the remaining Cobra in a standby status on station. The 1st platoon leader was given full control of all supporting fires when the actual assault began. As the 1st platoon maneuvered against the enemy, the volume of enemy fire quickly decreased and the enemy began to fade into the jungle. He left behind large quantities of small arms and 61mm mortar ammunition, pieces of bloody clothing, and used combat dressings, but he made good his escape.

By now it was dark, and the 1st platoon was instructed not to pursue the retreating enemy. Bravo's CO had the remaining gunship, and a newly arrived Cobra light fire team try to locate the retreating enemy from the air. Finally, the situation cooled enough to get the medevac into the 3d platoon's LZ and evacuate the five injured and wounded personnel.

Even though it was dark, the platoons were completing their night security measures. Defensive concentrations were registered to within 50 meters of the fighting positions before listening posts were sent out and the remainder of the security measures were implemented. Around 2230 all elements reported that they were secure and reported their ammunition and weapons status to the company commander. During the fight about half of the company's basic load had been expended, and seven weapons damaged or destroyed. A request for resupply of these items was sent to battalion over the admin-log net. Company B was to be resupplied by 0730 the following morning, provided the helicopters were available and the weather cooperated.

By first light the weather had started to deteriorate, and battalion advised the company that because of high winds and limited visibility, the aircraft were grounded at Camp Enari. At 0800, without being resupplied, Bravo started up the valley with one platoon on each flank on the high ground, and two platoons in the valley clearing from the river bed up the sides. Around noon the company stopped and sent out local patrols to conduct a recon of a bald place on the side of a cliff. In an area about 400 meters north of the bald spot, on the valley floor, a patrol found half a wing of a fighter aircraft. Further investigation revealed that it was part of an F4 that had been lost almost two years earlier, and had never been located. After a two-hour search for any major parts of the fuselage or any evidence of the pilots, the unit continued up the valley. No enemy contact was made during the remainder of the day and the resupply of ammunition and weapons wasn't received.

Day three in the valley began with a light rain and very poor helicopter weather. The resupply was again cancelled, and at 0730 Bravo was on the move. By now the rain, cold, and little or no significant findings, coupled with all the climbing up and down, was taking its toll on the morale of the unit. Everyone was starting to feel as though everything had been against them from the start. Then the company commander was called to the point element and the crowning blow was struck. There, directly ahead

of them was a 60 to 80-foot high waterfall, and it was the only way out of the steep part of the valley without backtracking five kilometers. Now here was a problem! The only thing that saved the day were the two 100-foot climbing ropes carried by each platoon. While two soldiers scaled the face of the cliff, the CO maneuvered the other two platoons on the high ground into positions to provide local security. By now it was 1400, and the first two squads were scaling the waterfalls. As the climbing continued, people slipped and fell into the water below, others looked just plain scared, and before long everyone had started to laugh at one another. The longer the climbing continued, the funnier it got until everyone had had his "turn in the barrel or on the ropes." This apparent disaster had turned into a shot in the arm for company morale. Once everyone was out of the valley, three platoons linked up on the high ground on the eastern wall and the 4th platoon remained on the western side.

Beyond the waterfall the valley floor widened to about 500 meters and the walls weren't as steep or rocky. Night defensive positions were established around 1730, with three platoons on the eastern wall and the one platoon on the western wall. While reporting the location of the company's night defensive positions, the CO asked about being resupplied. By now everyone was down to ham and lima beans, date pudding, and ham and eggs. Resupply was becoming a must proposition if B Company was to continue its mission at the required rate of movement. Again, resupply was promised at first light if the weather was agreeable. The night was quiet, with little or no activity other than the tigers and monkeys playing outside the perimeter.

Along with resupply on the fourth day came the order to consolidate the company and prepare for a 15-kilometer air assault. Bravo Company was to have a PZ cleared by 1000, and then stand by to be lifted. After all of the platoons arrived on the east side of the valley, the supplies were distributed, the basic load replenished, and the PZ prepared. Now there was nothing to do but wait. Just before noon, the battalion commander informed B Company that no aircraft would be available for their lift until 1600, if at all that day. During the slack time another detailed briefing of the air assault was completed, including the allowable cargo load, load number, the cross-loading of key weapons, load sequence, and the ground tactical plan at the LZ.

After the briefing was completed and the platoons were organized for the move, everyone except the security element flaked-out or read mail, because this short respite would soon be over. The next phase would be just as hard — the 1,000-meter-high mountains were their next terrain objective. The hump goes on, with its daily boredom and little or no significant findings. Just step after step, and rain . . . . . rain . . . . . rain.

1970

DISENGAGEMENT AND REDEPLOYMENT

The year began with a low level of ground action which continued, with few exceptions, until March. From a military point of view, Vietnamization was moving forward on schedule in some areas and ahead of schedule in others.

Although there were 112 enemy violations of the TET truce, compared with past years, Tet of 1970 was quiet. In March, President Nixon announced the fourth increment of redeployment. The troop cutback would be more than 50,000.

On April 30, American units shouldered aside a screen of jungle and plunged into Cambodia to seek out and destroy the enemy's border sanctuaries while simultaneously capturing suspected weapons and ammunition caches.

In regard to the offensive, President Nixon announced that he was temporarily widening American involvement in Vietnam in order to shorten it. He repeatedly emphasized that there would be no firm and permanent U.S. military presence in Cambodia. The offensive was designed to weaken enemy striking power and U.S. forces would thus be able to safely continue disengagement and withdrawal.

Task Force Shoemaker slashed into the once-sacrosanct Fish-hook area, while American-advised and supported South Vietnamese troops continued a four-pronged drive on the tactically important Parrot's beak. In early May, elements of the 1st Cavalry Division (Airmobile), the 11th Armored Cavalry Regiment and the 4th Infantry Division captured several large base complexes. One enemy supply and communications complex was so large, officers of the capturing 1st Cavalry Division called it "Bunker City."

Huge munitions caches, the largest of the war, were unearthed at the "City" and enemy heavy equipment was destroyed. ARVN troops turned in remarkable performances. By the last week in May, ARVN troops had captured more than 100 tons of munitions.

By mid-year the NVA strategy began to change toward protracted guerrilla warfare. It was an austerity plan of battle designed to minimize casualities and cost, to pit maneuverability and surprise against the fearsome firepower from air and ground attacks of the Allies.

Decreasing activity on the battlefield was reflected by low friendly casualty figures and stepped-up redeployment of U.S. forces; South Vietnamese military elements assumed the major burden of combat.

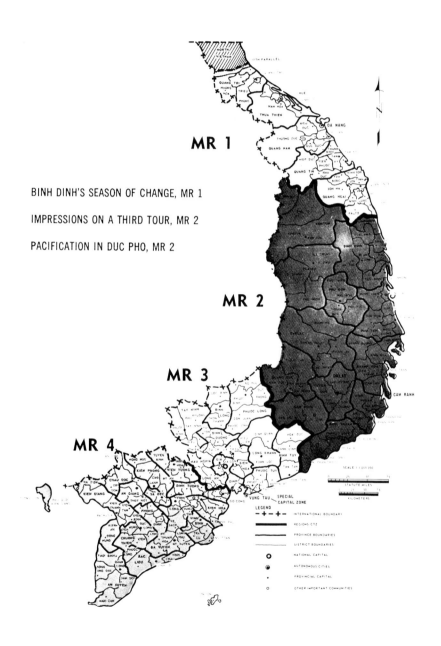

BINH DINH'S SEASON OF CHANGE, MR 1

IMPRESSIONS ON A THIRD TOUR, MR 2

PACIFICATION IN DUC PHO, MR 2

MR 1

MR 2

MR 3

MR 4

CAM RANH

VUNG TAU SPECIAL
CAPITAL ZONE

LEGEND
—+—+— INTERNATIONAL BOUNDARY
━━━━ REGIONS CTZ
──── PROVINCE BOUNDARIES
──── DISTRICT BOUNDARIES
◉ NATIONAL CAPITAL
◉ AUTONOMOUS CITIES
• PROVINCIAL CAPITAL
○ OTHER IMPORTANT COMMUNITIES

Chapter 10

Vietnamization

Binh Dinh's Season of Change

First Lieutenant James F. O'Brien

The nature of the Vietnamese war, like the seasons, has changed as time has moved along. This is the season of pacification, and it may well represent the solution sought by soldiers and statesmen in Southeast Asia ever since the end of World War II.

Pacification has as many interpretations as there are interpreters of the word. Generally speaking, it involves the destruction of the Viet Cong infrastructure by the government of South Vietnam, supported and supplemented by US military forces.

Today, Phu My District in Binh Dinh Province is a showcase of the pacification effort throughout the republic. Phu My had been under the rule of the Viet Cong longer than anyone cared to remember. Hardly a family was to be found that didn't have one or more members active in the guerrilla movement. These people had fought as Viet Minh against the French and their hatred of Saigon was legendary. All they had known for the past 30 years was occupation and exploitation by an endless parade of politicos, promising peace and prosperity and bringing terror in the night and taxation at every turn.

These shadow governments came and went, but the terror and poverty continued at the hands of the new group of rulers. The one element of relative stability and security was the Viet Cong, with promises of land for all and dreams of a better life. Husbands, sons and fathers willingly invested their lives in expectation of the day when they could stand free, as no man's peasant.

Against this setting, the 173d Airborne Brigade initiated Operation Washington Green in April of 1969. The mission was the pacification of Binh Dinh Province. The region was divided into battalion-size areas of responsibility; Phu My District was assigned to the 1st Battalion (Airborne), 503d Infantry.

This was a totally new and not easily digested mission for the troops, who had carved their reputation at Dak To, Kontum, Hobo Woods, War Zone C, and the Iron Triangle. The tactical SOPs, they would be guided by, would have been impossible to employ three years earlier and would have been scorned as idealistic by many an Infantryman.

The battalion commander collocated his tactical CP with the Phu My District headquarters. This was done so that he and the district chief — the military and political leader in Phu My — could work side by side in the pacification effort. The military forces under the district chief's command were the Regional Force companies (RFs) and the Popular Force platoons (PFs). These troops are similar to our own National Guard.

The concept of collocation, as viewed by the battalion headquarters, was extended to all rifle companies and platoons. As the program progressed, this was extended even further to individual squads. The emphasis in Operation Washington Green was on combined operations and training of the RFs and PFs. The US elements lived and worked in the same semi-permanent locations as the Vietnamese. Daily instruction was given by the Americans, covering basic rifle marksmanship, care and cleaning of weapons, map reading, land navigation, artillery adjustment, first aid, radio procedures, and virtually every subject needed for the development of a well-trained and disciplined soldier. Continuous patrols and ambushes were conducted by the Americans with the RFs and PFs along, in a "learn by doing" campaign.

Phu My District is a large, fertile lowland bordered on the north, south and west by mountains and on the east by the South China Sea. The lowlands are densely populated and rich in rice harvests. The Viet Cong operated out of the mountains, which afforded easy access to the lowlands for resupplies of food and to the lifeblood of any guerrilla movement — the people. Their recruiting and resupply took place at night; during the day they would stay in the safety of their base camps in the hills.

Their escape routes were made secure by the most devastating weapon in the enemy's arsenal — the boobytrap. Phu My District was saturated with every type of boobytrap, ranging from "toe-poppers" to 155mm artillery rounds. The vast majority of the 1/503d's casualties were from these devices. Their physical dam-

age was equaled by the psychological effect. Once tripped, there was a feeling of complete helplessness; except on rare occasions, there was no visible enemy to strike at. Even more frustrating was the common knowledge that some of these devices were emplaced by the civilian population, the object of the entire pacification program.

The natural instinct of the paratroopers was "to close with and destroy the enemy," granting him no quarter. But they were to find that the pacification effort called for the proverbial patience of the Orient, as well as their own Western aggressiveness. Instead of heliborne assaults into the rugged mountain terrain, they were placed in semi-permanent compounds in the lowlands. All free-fire zones were abolished. Artillery fires were restricted by new rules of engagement that forbade high explosive impact within 1,000 meters of any populated area. This all but eliminated any close-in artillery support in the lowlands.

Initially, relations between the RF/PF soldiers and the Americans were far from idyllic. The RFs and PFs were poorly trained and disciplined, and showed a marked reluctance to leave the security of their compounds. The Americans felt impatient with the restrictions placed on them and, angered by the inevitable booby-traps, were eager to make contact with the elusive shadow that was Charlie. Company commanders, platoon leaders, platoon sergeants, and squad leaders — trained and honed to a fine edge for combat — found that they had to develop new skills as diplomats, instructors and civil affairs consultants.

The Vietnam conflict has highlighted the importance of the small unit leader, but never has his role been more influential than in the pacification program. As the program progressed and in order to attain as complete a saturation of the district as possible, the rifle platoons were further broken down to their squads, each of which was located at a different RF/PF compound. One can immediately see that the control problem arising from such dispersion is a tactician's nightmare. Very often, young and inexperienced noncommissioned officers were the ranking American troops in these positions, and their Vietnamese counterpart was a second lieutenant. It is to the credit of these young men and their instructors at the Fort Benning Noncommissioned Officer Candidate School that, for the most part, they met this challenge with the decisive leadership and maturity of men many years their senior.

The majority of ground operations conducted in the lowlands were of the cordon and search variety. The tried and proven method of operation was to have the American troops provide the cordon and/or blocking element and have the RF and PF units, assisted by the National Police Field Force (NPFF), conduct the search of homes and interrogation of suspects. These procedures insured identification of the effort with the government of Vietnam, rather than with a foreign power. The population was naturally more at ease and cooperative with their own countrymen. These operations, along with extensive ambushing, served to cripple the Viet Cong infrastructure in the hamlets by severely limiting their access to their lifelines — the people. The enemy was hurt badly, even though he still enjoyed relative security in his mountain hideaways.

By January 1970, the RF and PF troops had progressed to the stage where they were ready to assume more of the lion's share of lowland security. The 1st Battalion commander then instituted a new concept in combat operations in Phu My District. The enemy, from his vantage points in the mountains, could easily detect any significant troop movement in the lowlands. The situation called for small elements that could maneuver undetected to catch the VC in their own backyard. The dispersion of the battalion and the months of relative autonomy in the numerous semi-permanent compounds were to pay off in a manner which was never anticipated back at the start of Operation Washington Green.

And so, the Hawk team was conceived. It consisted of six men who were lifted deep into the mountains by helicopter. They remained for four days at a time, hunting for Charlie. Once contact was made, it was maintained until the enemy was destroyed or broke contact himself. Often these teams were augmented by the presence of a trained sniper who could drop a target at ranges in excess of 500 meters.

Months of training the RFs and PFs had sharpened the skills of each soldier in the battalion to the point where the trooper who couldn't read a map, utilize a compass correctly or effectively adjust artillery fire was the exception rather than the rule.

The Hawk concept was utilized gradually at first, with many skeptics anticipating disaster. Its success far exceeded anyone's expectations. The guerrillas were denied access to the lowlands by extensive patrolling and ambushing, and were being driven from their mountain sanctuaries by the relentless Hawk missions. Enemy casualties and equipment losses soared as never before.

Decimated, demoralized and starving, Charlie began to return home from the war, as the Viet Cong turned themselves in under the Chieu Hoi or "Open Arms" program. After months of hiding in the hills, they found their native hamlets changed drastically. Schools had sprung up throughout the district and US Army engineers were converting footpaths into a network of thoroughfares that would make vehicular traffic possible to any point in Phu My. But the most significant development was in the people themselves. Though the people were far from avid supporters of the government of Vietnam, they could see that there was no future at all for the Viet Cong. The VC were unable to provide for themselves and had nothing whatever to offer them. Families convinced sons, fathers and husbands to return home under the Chieu Hoi program and refused to be coerced into supplying their "neighbors from the North" with needed rice and medical supplies.

The Communist cause in Phu My suffered terribly in a period of one year. These people who had lived under Communist rule for so long were not becoming avid democrats; they were merely realizing that for the first time in a quarter of a century they were living without terrorism, exploitation or the threat of starvation from interminable taxation.

Phu My District and the progress of pacification there might seem to be a dream come true. This is not the case. The enemy has been hurt there and hurt badly, but he is not through yet in Phu My District. He will be back in strength to try and recapture that which for so long was one of his bastions. The progress of the RF/PF soldiers, and the relative security and prosperity of the populace are going to make it that much more difficult for Charlie to find a new home in Phu My.

The success realized in Phu My District attests to the fact that the hope for the future of an independent and free South Vietnam is becoming a reality — a reality that can survive on its own merits. The role of the American Infantryman in the determination of that future has never before been so complex or demanding. Yet future historians will attest that the Infantryman's role has never before been so rewarding or far-reaching in its impact.

Impressions on a Third Tour

Captain Joseph W. Moore

Just a few notes on some of the changes I've noticed while starting the third month of my third tour in Vietnam.

Pacification is the mission of Company B, 2/503d. We have an AO three by five kilometers wide, half mountains, half valley with several scattered hamlets. About 1,000 lowlanders and rice farmers live in the area. But there are only 18 young men in the entire area. They are Chieu Hoi returnees. We are in Phase II of pacification.

The 692d RF Company (Vietnamese) is collocated with Bravo. The idea is to train, motivate and prepare the RF company to take over when we leave. As phony as this may sound, it's working.

Captured documents reveal the following:

"Presence of US and RF troops in the hamlet areas are making it difficult to procure rice and supporters will not rally. Sympathizers are dwindling and popular support is at an all-time low. The mountains are no longer a sanctuary. The US and RF troops are penetrating and locating base camps in the Tiger Mts. by use of squad and platoon reconnaissance in force. US troops choose to fight under all circumstances, and will insanely pursue us into the mountains."

The above paints a rosy picture; however, the documents and local intelligence also reveal the following:

"US troops clumsy and vulnerable to boobytrapping and mining. US troops discard munitions and valuable equipment. US troops give C-rations to children and villagers for services rendered. C-rations are a valuable supplement to the VC daily ration. US troops sleep on ambush, set up RTO watch only. Radios give away ambushes by noise of the receiver of the PRC-25 radio. US radio security bad, easily monitored and broken with Panasonic transistor, portable radios. Reaction time for US fire support weapons and air-artillery-mortar is very slow. Ineffective in most cases. US troop movement easily telescoped by use of our intricate early warning signalling systems throughout the hamlets."

None of the above mentioned are new tricks or shortcomings. If the individual US soldier goes as long as a month without any significant contact, he will become complacent, relax, and the VC will move in. The VC, for the most part in our hamlet AO, don't choose to fight. They are seemingly back into Phase II of guerrilla warfare. Their main function seems to be improving or trying to sustain the Viet Cong infrastructure. Collecting rice, an occasional small unit attack, harassment and interdiction of US and RF camps, take place for the most part to show the local population that they (NLF) are still able and effective.

All tactical operations by Bravo are conducted at night. The stationary ambush is out. We ambush only targets of opportunity or on intelligence info. Four to five-man stay-behind ambushes in the hamlets have proven effective. Roving patrols are effective but must have **aggressive** leadership. The hand grenade (frag) is the principal weapon to break contact with. When making contact at night, answer the call with frags, look for cover (temporary), then pursue, all night if necessary. Of course, during encounters in the hamlets, immediate action drill in the form of small arms is out during the initial contact.

Almost all spotting of VC movement is done by the use of hawk teams (company recon) or wildcat teams (battalion recon). For the most part, spotting has been of small elements of VC crossing the valley or skirting the mountains. Reaction time is too slow, seldom effective and the VC seem to disappear. Bravo has found one solution to this problem: increase the company recon team to seven men, four of whom are a trained caliber .50 machinegun crew. The remaining men are ammo bearers. This technique is most effectice. The gun is used on semi-auto as a sniping weapon, effective up to 2,000 meters — very taxing on the company recon, but we hear few complaints because of the kills achieved.

We have a fire support problem because of our rules of engagement. The first round must be 1,000 meters from any friendly element and at least 600 meters from any known hamlet. The fire is brought to within 600 meters of the troops in 200-meter increments and below that range in 50-meter adjustments. In order to get night defensive targets registered, the troops must be off the gun-target line by at least 300 meters. The earliest illumination round I ever received during contact was 14 minutes after the initial request.

Transportation — we have made it known to the hamlet people that on rare occasions helicopters leave the CP empty. Even though a daily manifest is maintained on a first come, first served basis, the hamlet chief has the last say as to who goes. This hasn't cost Company B or anyone else a dime and it's been the most effective way of winning the minds of the hamlet people.

One day per week is allocated to the hamlet defense — barbed wire details, cutting brush, police calls, burning trash, etc. This is the opportunity to have the US troops and RFs work side by side with the people. Care must be exercised not to offend the people with our hurry up and complete the job attitude.

Medcaps must take place daily by the company and platoon medics. Always take a village elder along and agree wholeheartedly with him. If the villagers are dirty, make them go wash before treating them even for a headache. The medic now goes through the hamlet and by coincidence everyone is bathing and

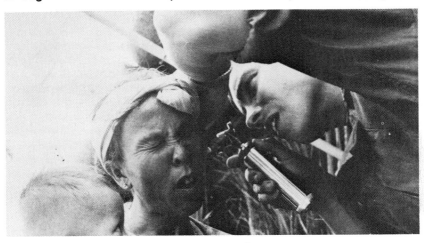

lining up. Treat all with patience, and if you're sure that nothing's wrong, prescribe an APC.

Two Chieu Hoi's have resulted from US soldier - children relationships in the past week.

Keep the troops in combat gear during pacification. Troops have a tendency to become lax. Even platoons operating as far as four kilometers away may move about with as few as seven magazines in a bandolier, one or no frags, no water, no water purification pills, no first aid dressing and on one occasion a squad leader was without a compass and map. Troops become familiar with the platoon AO and begin taking chances by discarding equipment. Use all equipment as it was intended. This includes the AN/PRC-25 radio with backpack and accessory bag.

Pacification demands good strong leadership down to the fire team level. Ambushes and roving patrols three kilometers away from the platoon and company CP are conducted with four to five men. The fire team has got to be good.

The key to preventing complacency and boredom is training,

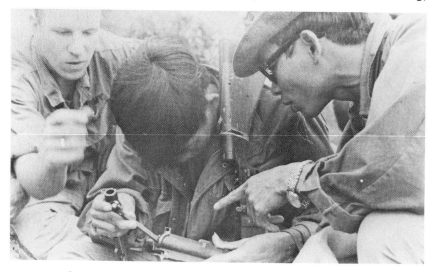

weapons firing, alerts, missions demanding physical stamina, constant day and night patrolling, checking out the most minute indications of VC in the area, hard work (trenches, bunkers, brush cutting, etc.) and tactical defense and demolition training. Make squad leaders and fire team leaders call in admin and resupply choppers, using proper radio and navigational procedures. Take PT in the form of sports and make everyone participate.

Whenever possible have the interpreters, Kit Carson scouts and platoon leaders give a half-hour to one-hour class on the Vietnamese language; only useful phrases. Use a poncho for a chalk board and scrounge up a piece of chalk.

Pacification is new to me and certainly new to the troops. It's harder than the old days of search and destroy. It demands more and is more taxing on the men. Maturity, intelligence, tolerance and stability is demanded of the troops in addition to the training they receive.

You guessed it, I'm out of paper. Good thing, too, because I'm getting sleepy. Maybe this is all old stuff, not very colorful, but that is the way it is.

Pacification in Duc Pho

Captain Boyd Harris

The VC in northern Duc Pho District of Quang Ngai Province were nearly at wit's end. It was known that C219, the Main Force VC company in the area, was down to three regulars who were last seen near Duc Pho City trying to recruit teenage boys into their ranks.

Pacification, that peaceful word, had brought the VC to this sad state of affairs. They had to do something against pacification and they knew it. They had tried sniping, mortaring and selected acts of terrorism to destroy the pacification effort, but to no avail. The VC were desperate and they concocted a bold plan that came within a hair of killing the US and Vietnamese leaders of the pacification program. The VC plan embodied the elements of intrigue and ingenious subversive warfare that they are famous for.

Prior to pacification, the area around Duc Pho had been largely controlled by the VC. The men who were now in the government and the PSDF (People's Self-Defense Forces) had, in earlier days, supported the VC to one degree or another. Many had relatives or friends among the VC.

The target picked for the attack by the VC was the command post compound, which protected an important hamlet on QL 1, a highway in the center of the pacification area. The forces inside the CP compound were one Vietnamese Popular Force (PF) platoon, 20 PSDF personnel, one US rifle platoon, one US mortar platoon, and the US company commander and his headquarters. The VC figured if they could annihilate this compound they could destroy the heart and credibility of the pacification program. Since the VC couldn't take this compound by attack from the outside, they would try from the inside.

The first part of the VC plan was to persuade one of the young PSDFs to turn traitor. They promised him 1,000 dollars for his services. This PSDF soldier had been nicknamed "Speck Four" by the Americans who lived in the hamlet because he always wore Specialist 4 stripes. The US troops had liked his friendly attitude and nobody would have dreamed of suspecting him. Speck Four's mission was to talk to the other PSDF soldiers and convince them that the VC were eventually going to come back in power. The farms, property and lives of the PSDF wouldn't be worth a plugged nickel if they didn't help the VC. On the night of the VC attack, the PSDF were to attack the forces in the CP compound from the inside by throwing grenades and explosives into the bunkers. The VC platoon would then enter the compound through a break in the wire made by Speck Four and would destroy the Vietnamese and US forces.

The leader of the PSDF threw a hitch into the VC plan when he decided that he was willing to take his stand against the Communists, regardless of the danger involved. He told the assistant hamlet security chief about Speck Four's plot. This security chief, a man named Khooi, was one of the best fighters in any country's army. He understood VC intrigue and had a little cunning of his own. The part of the VC plan that Khooi disliked the most was that, just prior to the main VC attack, Speck Four and one other hired killer were to assassinate Khooi. The VC wanted Khooi dead in the worst way, because he had gained the confidence and respect of the people and was also responsible for the death of many VC.

Rather than foiling the plan immediately, Khooi decided to let the VC and Speck Four think that everything was fine. The night of the attack came and the trap for the VC was ready. Khooi positioned himself in a place where he could catch Speck Four cutting a passage in the concertina wire for the other assassin and the VC platoon. Speck Four appeared at the wire and out of the darkness came the assassin, with the VC platoon not far behind. Khooi captured the assassin and Speck Four, and the VC platoon was greeted with a hail of small arms fire, LAWs, 81mm mortar fire, artillery, and gunships. Unfortunately, enemy casualties were unknown. One thing was of interest though. The assassin was Khooi's half-brother!

What caused the VC to attempt this desperate scheme? How had pacification hurt the VC? How was it organized? Before pacification, the countryside and its people were controlled by the VC. Only the population of Duc Pho City was controlled by the government. The VC had been able to coexist satisfactorily with Vietnamese and American units. The Vietnamese Regional and Popular Forces rarely left their triangular compounds, and the roving American units were dealt with using classical guerrilla doctrine. Tragedy for the Viet Cong began about four months prior to their final attack, when Vietnamese and American forces pooled their talents and resources in a successful program of pacification.

Three Vietnamese Regional Force companies, four Popular Force companies, the PSDF, and one American rifle company formed the pacification force. Their mission was to destroy the Viet Cong, the VC infrastructure, and to gain control of the population in an area approximately 8,000 by 4,000 meters. Unfortunately, the complete mission wasn't accomplished in four months; however, approximately 250 VC and NVA were killed or captured, about 50 weapons were taken and about 30 VC and VCI rallied to the government.

Among the Hoi Chanhs were one province-level propaganda chief, a village-level woman cadre who was responsible for the death of 1,000 people, and several other high-level VC cadre. A VC captain in charge of intelligence for three districts had been killed by a Vietnamese/US ambush patrol. He was carrying documents, plans and maps that proved to be of great importance.

The pacification force operated from six compounds along an 8,000 meter stretch of QL 1. Each compound contained a minimum of one PF platoon and one American squad. Continuous operations were run from these bases and, when necessary, the entire force could be massed against one objective. The working relationship between the Americans and Vietnamese was based on mutual respect and friendship. This mutual respect at all levels was the keystone of successful Allied operations. Training and small-scale operations began immediately and gradually increased as the troops and leaders gained confidence.

Training was organized and conducted at platoon and squad level, with Vietnamese and US troops training together. Emphasis was placed on the fundamentals of Infantry tactics, immediate action drills to stress teamwork under fire, ambushes, and counterguerrilla techniques. The Vietnamese were particularly useful in teaching Americans how to search hamlets, read trail signs and understand VC tactics. The Americans found that the Vietnamese troops needed training in individual weapons, demolitions, battle drill, and the use of artillery and gunships. Both nationalities developed an understanding and compassion for each other that hadn't existed before.

One of the main missions of pacification was to gain the support of the people. The peasants in the area had always supported the VC, with a little friendly persuasion from the guerrillas' AK47s. It's easy to talk about winning the hearts and minds of the people, but it becomes difficult when the VC are pointing guns at those people. Therefore, it was essential to provide security for the people by isolating them from the VC. In pursuit of this goal, the population was moved into hamlets along QL 1, where they could be separated from the enemy base areas. This was an unpleasant jolt to the people, but the reasons were explained and it was an easy walk to their fields. Control of the people is one vital key to success in revolutionary war. The people were the VC's source of food, supplies, manpower, and intelligence.

Elections had been held just prior to the beginning of this pacification program. With the security provided by the Allies, the elected officials were able to live and work in their hamlets for the first time in many years. Previously, they would have been assassinated by the VC who had governed these same hamlets. Sure, Americans or South Vietnamese might have been there in the daytime, but the VC were there at night and that is what counted.

Of course, our main mission was to kill the enemy, and that involved good planning, tactics and operations. It was important to get the Vietnamese leaders to do as much of the planning as possible. Initially, American leaders had to take the initiative, but after a few successful operations the Vietnamese leaders planned and executed more and bolder missions. The principle of using combined forces, Allies fighting side by side, was always followed. At first, a patrol would normally be half-Vietnamese and half-American, but after a month the Vietnamese were content to have one or two Americans with a radio, in case they needed gunships or artillery.

All types of counterguerrilla tactics and techniques were used against the VC. Day and night patrolling, ambushes, dawn and night illuminated cordan and searches, airmobile assaults, and combinations of the above were all used successfully. The most lucrative operations were well-placed ambushes and cordons which moved into position under the cover of darkness. The VC had excellent observation techniques in the daytime but movement at night normally achieved surprise. By hindering the VC's night movement, the pacification forces cut his lifeline of resupply, liaison, taxation, and intelligence.

One of the most successful operations resulted from intelligence received by the village security chief that there was a VC platoon in the northeastern part of the pacification area. The security chief, the Vietnamese commanders, a US battalion S3, and a US company commander planned an operation to hit the VC. The US company commander asked for and received the help of a sister company in the battalion.

The plan called for three blocking forces to move before dawn into areas east, south and west of the objective. All blocking forces would move at night to avoid VC observation and achieve complete surprise. Then, at dawn, there would be a 10-minute artillery bombardment to rattle the VC and start them running. It was thought they would try to escape to the north, along a river and into several wooded areas. Six strategic LZs were picked on this escape route and after the artillery the Allies would combat assault into these LZs. Gunships would be on hand during the entire operation.

Dawn came and the plan went like clockwork. The VC threw their weapons into the river and commenced to run in all directions. Six VC ran into the blocking forces on the east and strategically Chieu Hoied. Eight VC were killed by gunships and Infantry, while 19 were captured from hiding places under the water, near hooches, etc. Two of the captured were identified as C219 regulars and the rest as village guerrillas. Some documents, grenades and VC equipment were taken.

This operation wouldn't have come about except for the excellent intelligence net the village security chief had developed as a result of the confidence the people had gained in pacification. Also, the excellent cooperation and coordination between US and Vietnamese forces was vital to success. Two US companies, one Regional Force company, and three Popular Force platoons were used on this operation.

Pacification is and will continue to be of great importance in Vietnam. Company grade officers will be working extensively with the Vietnamese and this challenge can be extremely rewarding. Units with a pacification mission have a much more challenging assignment than US units operating alone. Through coordination, cooperation, mutual respect, and friendship, this company commander and his platoon and squad leaders exerted a great deal of influence on the training, operations, confidence, and performance of the Regional and Popular Force Vietnamese units.

Success in this type of operation with the Vietnamese is based on counterguerrilla and revolutionary warfare strategy and tactics that are taught in military schools. However, success is also largely based on human relations and emotional intangibles between American and Vietnamese leaders and soldiers, and the Vietnamese people themselves. These relations and the manner in which military leadership relates to them are not so easily taught. They are based on being open-minded, having a fair regard for all segments of humanity and abandoning the prejudices that limit a man's potential in working with his fellow man.

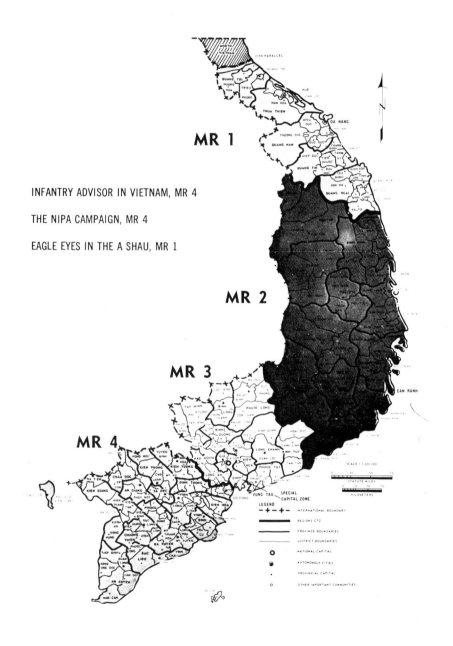

INFANTRY ADVISOR IN VIETNAM, MR 4

THE NIPA CAMPAIGN, MR 4

EAGLE EYES IN THE A SHAU, MR 1

Chapter 11

The Varied Scene

Infantry Advisor in Vietnam

Captain Ronald D. Bowen

The policy of Vietnamization of the war in Southeast Asia is aimed at placing the burden of the combat effort upon the Republic of Vietnam Armed Forces. Shouldering a fair share of this burden are the basic units of Vietnamese combat power, the ARVN Infantry battalions. As this trend continues, the role of the US advisor with these units very likely will become the most effective residual US influence upon the outcome of the Vietnam conflict. In this light, then, it seems critical that the mission, organization and equipment of these advisory teams be monitored, reevaluated and modified, if necessary, to insure compatibility and effectiveness in meeting the needs of the

Vietnamese combat effort. But still more important, as the new demands of a changing advisory mission are defined, is the question concerning the US Infantryman as a future advisor: Can he measure up to his new job?

In considering the validity of these assumptions, it seems appropriate to first select a specific area of Vietnam as an example and generally evaluate the effectiveness of the ARVN Infantry and US advisory teams. At the same time, changes in ARVN and advisor effectiveness, results and basic concepts are extremely relevant in future planning. Hopefully, this information will provide the basis for conclusions concerning our advisory effort in Vietnam.

The Military Region 4 area of Vietnam, made up of the Mekong Delta, is especially suited for our purpose of discussing the advisory effort. The Delta, approximately 26,000 square miles in area, contains a majority of the Vietnamese population and is the foundation of Vietnam's agricultural economy. Stretching southward in a low fertile plain from the branches of the Mekong River to the tip of the Ca Mau Peninsula, the Delta contains about 9,000 square miles of land presently under rice cultivation. For these and many other reasons, the Mekong Delta-MR 4 area has been recognized by Allied and Communist forces alike as an area of critical importance to the determination of Vietnam's future.

For a variety of reasons, however, the Mekong Delta has not been the scene of intense combat and huge troop concentrations that have been the case in the northern areas of South Vietnam. Allied forces have never been committed there in a degree comparable to the Central Highlands or the Saigon-Cholon area. The Delta has remained, for the most part, what is sometimes referred to as "ARVN's war" since the combat effort there is almost totally an effort undertaken by Republic of Vietnam Armed Forces.

The US advisory effort, while present in all areas of Vietnam, is probably best represented in the Military Region 4 area. In the Delta, the effectiveness of the advisory effort is reflected in combat results to a more significant degree than anywhere in the country.

Within the MR 4 area, three ARVN Infantry divisions are deployed, totaling 36 Infantry battalions. While not constituting a majority of the combat forces in the Delta, these battalions, due to their mobility and firepower, represent a sizable portion of Vietnamese combat power in that area. For this reason, these battalions and their advisory teams seem to present a valid example in considering the present and future importance of the advisory role in Vietnam.

Through a combination of factors, including American military aid and US military advisory assistance, some rather dramatic changes have occurred in ARVN during recent years. A discussion of these changes and simultaneous changes in the advisory effort may provide some valuable guidance for future application.

The equipping of ARVN Infantry with the M16 rifle in early 1968 was a significant change that resulted not only in increased firepower for the units, but also provided the impetus for an aggressive esprit which has greatly increased combat effectiveness. The weapon's size and characteristics greatly pleased the ARVN Infantrymen and the M16 has proved highly effective in almost every phase of ground combat. In the same vein, the deployment of additional supporting artillery has provided support firepower to a degree never before known by the ARVN soldier.

Probably the most significant change in overall ARVN effectiveness, however, has been the relatively recent availability of helicopter support to permit the highly aggressive, fast-moving and effective airmobile assault. This change, along with resulting changes in tactics and attitudes, has been the single most important step forward for the ARVN military forces. Through the added flexibility, mobility and firepower of the airmobile assault, the effectiveness of the ARVN Infantry battalion has been almost doubled.

Other less dramatic changes can be seen in the increased emphasis on combined arms and combined service operations. Especially on the many waterways of the Mekong Delta, the Vietnamese Infantryman often gains increased mobility and firepower by combining his own unit with the assets of the US or Vietnamese Navy. These combined operations become more common and more effective as the Vietnamese train and equip their Navy and Air Force personnel with recently turned-over US equipment.

Still another change in the ARVN has resulted as the traditional role of the Infantry battalion in the protection of cities has been reduced. The protection of Rural Development cadre in critical locations has been assumed by the Regional and Popular Forces. This action has freed the maneuver battalions to perform more effectively as highly mobile, aggressive combat units.

These changes have had one significant result in the ARVN Infantry: the gaining of much-needed confidence. This confidence has begun to show not only in the enlisted combat Infantryman, but also, and more importantly, in their leaders. This perhaps will prove to be the most significant change of all.

While these changes have been taking place in the Vietnamese military, certain corresponding changes have been necessary in the US advisors. Combat support, mainly in the way of Army and Air Force aircraft, has been provided the Vietnamese at an increasing rate. Tactical air support, aerial surveillance, and troop and equipment transport have been requested by the Viet-

namese and have been provided to the maximum limits of US capabilities. At the same time, vast training programs exist to allow a future Vietnamese take-over of these activities, with results already evident in the areas of aerial surveillance, airmobile operations and tactical air support. The changes in the US advisory role have resulted in a change in the basic concept and mission of the Infantry advisor. As the ARVN units receive more and varied US support, the advisor must now become the instructor in the use of these combat tools, with the mission of eventually effecting a change-over of these tools into Vietnamese hands. A good example is the control of helicopter support used in airmobile operations. With the increasing presence of Vietnamese Air Force (VNAF) helicopter units in the country, the control, prior coordination and tactical responsibility for use of this airmobile package now shifts from the US advisor to the Vietnamese commander. It is then most important that the advisor prepare the ARVN commander, through instruction and exemplary performance, to assume this role.

The reality of this change in mission is evidenced by the change in the title of the advisory team to combat assistance team. These CATs are located at the battalion, regiment and division levels and have proved highly effective. While they may retain much of the mission of the former advisory teams, they have taken at least one additional step in the right direction by omitting the term "advisor," which in itself conveyed to the ARVN a lack of ability and need for advice. While the presence of US personnel is still required with ARVN units in order to obtain certain types of US combat and logistic support, the change in terminology and mission of the old advisory team is an important step toward Vietnamization of the war.

US Infantrymen assigned to combat assistance teams with ARVN Infantry battalions now have a responsibility that has not previously received the required emphasis. In addition to previous-ly desired qualities of tact, proper attitude, tactical knowledge and patience, the "combat assistant" must place a much greater im-portance on professionalism in performance of his duties. In the past, the guidelines for the advisor have been "anything that will get the job done." This attitude, applied to tactics, use of equip-ment and general combat readiness, was generally successful because of the well-known American traits of flexibility and in-genuity. But methods and habits derived from this type of attitude are not always in accordance with established doctrine and cer-tainly are not recommended for use by personnel with much less familiarity and experience with new tactics and equipment.

The Vietnamese military has been the recipient of ever-growing volumes of new military weapons and equipment. It is therefore most important that they receive instruction, guidance and live-fire examples of the basic, proper methods of employment of these combat tools. To begin with the short-cuts that seem to work so well for the Americans before learning the fundamentals and basic doctrine might prove very costly to the ARVN leadership in the long run. The US combat assistant must remember that there might not be another American there at the end of his tour to be briefed on the half-way efforts that will get by on the battlefield. Instead, his ARVN counterparts could be left without knowledge of the proper methods and fundamentals: in short, holding the bag.

As an example of the dramatic changes that have taken place in the advisor's role over the period of about one year and as a possible aid to predicting future advisor roles, let us consider a large-scale operation into the U-Minh Forest of the Mekong Delta, as it was conducted in December 1968, and compare it to one that might have taken place in December 1969. For the U-Minh I operation, as we will designate the 1968 operation, massive prior coordination was required to conduct a division-size operation that had been rare, if not almost unknown, to that point. To this force were added Vietnamese Rangers, Regional and Popular Forces, armored cavalry, Vietnamese Navy, and National Police. Then from American assets were added US Army helicopter troop lift, medevac and aerial reconnaissance support, US Air Force B52 tactical air support and cargo transport, US Navy riverine and naval gunfire support, and advisory teams with almost every Viet-namese unit in the operation.

The ARVN Infantry battalion advisor found himself with no small job in coordinating and directing the ground employment of these many and varied US assets while staying abreast of the changing situation within his ARVN unit. His time was well spent in directing armed helicopter strikes and acting as a ground con-troller at landing and pick-up zones. Medical evacuation by US helicopters and coordination with US resupply helicopters were other tasks performed by the advisor. The advisory team also directed US Army surveillance aircraft, coordinated with US forward air controllers for tac air employment and worked directly with US Navy and US advisors to the Vietnamese Navy for employment of those assets. To be sure, the US advisor with the ARVN Infantry during the U-Minh I operation had more than enough to do and probably did not place a great deal of emphasis on the idea of setting a professional example as an instructor to the Vietnamese. The idea that the ARVNs, within a short time, would be assuming most of the advisor's duties was little more than wishful thinking.

Now let us consider Operation U-Minh II, with basically the same task organization, mission and operational concepts. What did our newly designated combat assistance teams do during this operation? First of all, the division-size operation is no longer a stranger to the ARVN Infantry. Commanders were more experienced at large-scale operations and advisors were not as involved in prior planning and coordination. A sizable portion of the airmobile support for the operation was provided by new ARVN Air Force helicopter units, to include a part of the medevac and resupply responsibility. A few VNAF armed helicopters have completed training and provide fire support. All of these airmobile assets were controlled directly by the ARVN ground commander. More VNAF aircraft and pilots were on the scene to provide aerial reconnaissance, forward air control and tac air support with direct control by the ARVN commander. A much smaller amount of naval support was provided by the US Navy and ARVN coordination with his own naval forces required little or no help through advisory channels.

In our example, the US Advisor, as a necessary element to the ARVN Infantry battalion, was becoming much less a necessity than ever before.

As we observe the advisor or combat assistant today, his role as a forward controller of US assets is fast coming to a close. His relative worth can be quickly observed in a very big way—the ARVN effectiveness in the employment of the combat tools formerly handled by the advisor.

The US Infantryman on the ground with his ARVN counterparts must perform his new mission to insure that the proper example is set, the correct instructions given and the proper use made of the newly gained ARVN assets.

The effectiveness and professionalism of present and future advisors and combat assistants will not be difficult to evaluate. The ARVN's success in fulfilling its missions in areas like the Mekong Delta will reflect, in no small way, whether the US Infantrymen who serve as assistants to the ARVN commanders can uphold the Infantry tradition and once again "measure up to their job."

The Nipa Campaign

Major Joseph Costa, Jr.

Denial of cover and concealment has been recognized as an essential facet of successful counterinsurgency operations. At the present time in Vietnam this is most dramatically displayed in the massive and well-publicized Rome plow operations. Such operations are indeed impressive and, in conjunction with defoliation operations, have deprived the enemy of many square miles of cover in the Republic of Vietnam.

However, both Rome plow and spray defoliation operations have some serious limitations which preclude their use in the flat wet stretches of the Delta. The former relies on heavy engineer equipment which cannot be employed across the flooded paddies. The latter depends on chemicals which are simply unemployable in the populous agricultural farmlands of the Delta. The problem of removing foliage in the Delta requires another method. Here, as elsewhere, the lush vegetation is a haven for the Viet Cong. The thickest vegetation consists of the lowly but fast-growing nipa palm tree, which lines virtually every waterway.

The VC recognize the concealment value of this plant and normally forbid the local farmers to cut the branches for home construction. To further discourage incursions, the larger patches are often boobytrapped. A favorite tactic is to place signs warning of boobytraps whether or not they exist. This serves to discourage even close approach to the patches. From the enemy viewpoint, these measures have worked well in the past. Not only local civilians but also government troops have a strong natural inclination to avoid these areas. As elsewhere in Vietnam, the troops are very boobytrap-conscious. In such an environment the local Vietnamese commanders have begun the massive task of eliminating these patches by the arduous and simple method of hand cutting.

The procedure varies little from district to district, although the progress may vary greatly as seen from the air. A platoon or company will secure the area to be cut. If enemy presence is suspected, artillery, gunships or airstrikes may precede the operation. Organic unit weapons are only of limited value in such preparation, although their firing provides a psychological boost to the participants. Additionally, such fires may detonate boobytraps in the growth.

After the patch is secured, a careful search is made of the perimeter to spot tripwires. Then the cutters go to work. Cutting nearly always is done along one edge of the patch at a time. Cutters never work toward one another from opposite sides, as there may be an ensuing firefight if the enemy is trapped inside. A dispersal of five to seven meters is advisable in case a booby-trap is detonated. The most commonly encountered boobytrap is a hand grenade rigged with a tripwire or vine creeper. Due to its

destructive force, the enemy seems to prefer the US M26 grenade for this purpose.

The cutters may be either soldiers or local civilians impressed for this purpose. The local civilians may often have a detailed knowledge of these palm patches, to include the whereabouts of boobytraps and bunkers. As everywhere, hard intelligence from a rallier or POW can be invaluable.

When a bunker is discovered, all cutting stops immediately. The cutters withdraw and the accompanying security force takes over. Such bunkers in the Delta are usually quite well camouflaged and may be invisible from a distance greater than five meters. Normal procedure is to take cover and call out to anyone inside the bunker to come out and surrender. If the bunker is engaged by fire, the M79, hand grenades, demolition blocks, or the M72 LAW may be used. There are very few instances in this war of such bunkers being engaged by flame weapons since these bunkers are not usually as formidable as those in the hardwood forests further north. The exterior is usually constructed of thick mud slabs and well garnished with live vegetation. However, many are sturdily built of "imported" materials and many include planking, metal sheeting, chunks of masonry, and even pierced steel planking. They are often flooded, due to the low elevation. This flooding, combined with the frequent boobytraps, makes searching a slow, hard process. Frequently, the Viet Cong will accept the erosion caused by submersion and bury weapons and ammunition below the waterline in hopes they will be overlooked.

If a boobytrap or tripwire is spotted, almost the same procedure is followed. The cutters withdraw to a safe distance and the security force dismantles or destroys the boobytrap. Obvious paths and foot trails are favorite locations.

After a bunker or boobytrap has been neutralized, the cutters resume work. Strangely, the US standard-issue machete does not appear to be favored for this work. The long blade makes too large an arc and may contact a tripwire. The short heavy-bladed knives found in most farm houses seem better suited.

After a patch has been cut, the sun is allowed to dry the cuttings for a week or 10 days. Then the troops usually return and set fire to the dry palms, after the local farmers have been permitted first choice to refurbish their huts.

Unfortunately the nipa palms don't give up easily. A second or third cutting, far easier than the first, may be necessary before the palm dies out. The final result is well worth the effort. Deprived of cover and concealment in these patches, the VC have only one alternative. They must hide in farmhouses. Their visibility thus increases significantly. At this point they become highly vulnerable to the relentless patrolling that should accompany the nipa cutting compaign. In fact, two interdependent features of the pacification effort are constant nipa palm clearing and aggressive patrolling.

In the highly pacified districts, the progress is readily apparent from an aircraft. The dense nipa patches, which elsewhere cover up to a third of the landscape, are gone. With their removal there is far less need for the harassing and interdiction fires. The countryside is far cleaner and more open in appearance. To be sure, such results have their cost. In one battalion, over half the casualties suffered in a three-month period were during nipa palm cutting operations. Nevertheless, this transformation is a vital part of the counterinsurgency effort in the Delta. The nipa campaign may be one of the most successful efforts of the war.

Eagle Eyes in the A Shau

First Lieutenant William J. Brownsberger
First Lieutenant James L. Smith

At 0813 hours a Ranger team from Company L (Ranger) 75th Infantry, 101st Airborne Division (Airmobile) was inserted into a six kilometer-square area in the southeastern portion of the A Shau Valley. The landing zone was reported green by the aircraft commander of the insertion helicopter.

The insertion aircraft and the Cobra gunship that covered the operation rejoined the command and control helicopter which was circling several kilometers to the north of the team's location. Radio communication was established between the team and the operations officer. The team leader informed the operations officer that when the team exited the aircraft they were required to jump approximately eight feet due to the vegetation and that the Kit Carson Scout had injured his ankle. The team was instructed to prepare the scout for extraction and again the insertion aircraft and the Cobra gunship returned to the team's LZ. The extraction was completed at 0822 hours with the use of ladders. The ladders had been placed on the insertion aircraft in case the team or a team member required extraction immediately after insertion.

The flight again reformed to the north of the team, where final instructions and communication checks were made by the team and the operations officer. The flight then started its return to Camp Eagle. The time was 0828 hours.

At approximately 0835, the team reported one signal shot 50 meters to the west of their LZ, along a ridgeline overlooking their infiltration site. At that time the team halted its movement to the southwest and set up a defensive perimeter in anticipation of an enemy sighting or contact. It has been the experience of Company L that a technique used by the enemy to locate a Ranger team immediately after insertion was to have all enemy elements in the immediate vicinity of the LZ fire a series of signal shots. This notified all enemy elements of the presence and general location of the team. The signal shots were then generally followed with a combat/recon patrol from one of the enemy elements that observed the team's insertion.

With negative sightings by 1100 hours the team again began its movement to the southwest. By 1830 it had moved a total of 800 meters, doglegging to the northwest once it had reached the ridgeline that overlooked the LZ.

At 1000 hours on the second day, the team discovered a two-foot wide trail on the ridgeline. The trail showed very recent use and six US-made smoke grenades were found nearby. The team moved cautiously along the ridgeline and continuously monitored the trail. By nightfall it had moved nearly 600 meters and had heard approximately 15 rifle shots in the immediate vicinity.

On the third day the team had moved only 100 meters from their overnight halt position when they found themselves on the perimeter of a large, freshly cultivated enemy garden plot. Before the team had a chance to retrace their steps, they received small arms fire from two enemy soldiers located on the opposite side of the field. The enemy fire was ineffective and the team quickly broke contact without returning the fire. The time was 1030.

The team withdrew into the triple canopy of the jungle and moved to the northeast, again doglegging their direction of movement. After several hundred meters of slow and deliberate movement, the team circled around to monitor their back trail and set up security. They reported via radio to the Ranger company TOC that a contact had been established, but they could continue their mission. The team reported that the enemy were observed carrying AK47s, web gear and wearing gray uniforms. At 1330, the company commander and operations officer gave additional instructions to the team from their command and control aircraft and also received a full situation report from the team leader.

The following day, the team doglegged their direction of movement and observed their back trail, moving often with several hasty perimeters set to the right and left of their back trail. The fourth day of the mission yielded negative results or sightings.

On the fifth and final day of the patrol, the team moved from their overnight halt position toward their intended extraction LZ. Upon reaching the LZ they set up a defensive perimeter. It was 0930. At 1045, the team observed two enemy soldiers 20 meters from their perimeter. The team engaged the enemy with small arms fire and fragmentation grenades and, in turn, received a heavy volume of fire. The team had initiated fire on the point element of an estimated squad-size enemy element. They radioed immediately for support and a Cobra gunship and LOH were diverted to the team's location. This pink team was over the team's position five minutes after the call was received by the Ranger TOC. The pink team had been on visual reconnaissance of the A Shau Valley to the north of the team's reconnaissance zone.

The aircraft commander of the Cobra gunship requested another pink team to relieve his team on station and a section of Aerial Field Artillery (AFA) was requested.

The Ranger team continued to receive sporadic probes and small arms fire while the pink team and AFA fired around their perimeter. The team continued to return small arms fire for nearly one hour, and several bodies were observed by the LOH to the southwest of the LZ. The team had suffered no casualties during the contact.

When the enemy probe had subsided, the team was directed to another landing zone to their north. The team's movement to the

alternate landing site was monitored by the command and control aircraft and pink team on station. The section of AFA continued to place suppressive fires southwest of the initial contact site. The Ranger team was extracted at 1355.

The full effect of the mission and lessons learned, as analyzed by the officers of Company L, indicated that once a team has been inserted no attempt should be made to extract an individual from the area. If an individual must be extracted, then the entire team should be extracted, and the mission should be delayed or cancelled until a new LZ can be located and the entire insertion conducted again.

The chance contact with the two enemy on the third day of the mission might have been avoided if the patrol had utilized the cloverleaf technique to search the area near their overnight location. One of the more successful means of movement for a Ranger team is a series of doglegs that enables the team to monitor its back trail.

This type of movement allows the team to search the area surrounding their overnight position. The team is also in an ambush position should the enemy attempt to follow their trail. During the daylight hours security should be placed on the trail leading directly into the team's location.

The flexibility of the Ranger team, and the method of insertion and movement are limited only by the ability and imagination of the officers and NCOs in charge. Effective leadership and training produce an element which can see without being seen — the mission of the Rangers.

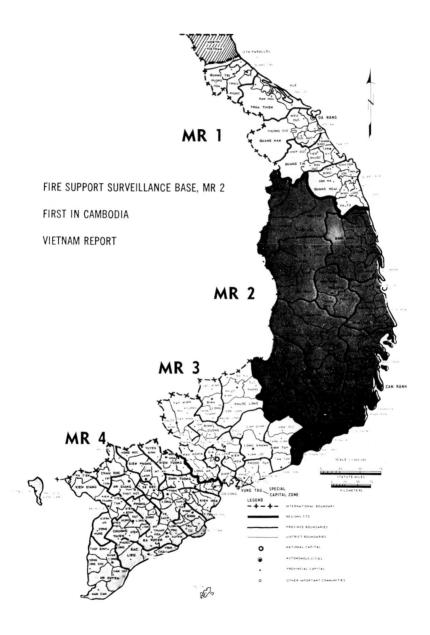

FIRE SUPPORT SURVEILLANCE BASE, MR 2

FIRST IN CAMBODIA

VIETNAM REPORT

MR 1

MR 2

MR 3

MR 4

CAM RANH

VUNG TAU   SPECIAL
            CAPITAL ZONE

LEGEND

-+-+- INTERNATIONAL BOUNDARY

REGIONS CTZ

PROVINCE BOUNDARIES

DISTRICT BOUNDARIES

○ NATIONAL CAPITAL

◉ AUTONOMOUS CITIES

· PROVINCIAL CAPITAL

○ OTHER IMPORTANT COMMUNITIES

SCALE 1:1,000,000

STATUTE MILES

KILOMETERS

Chapter 12

The Changing Tide

The Fire Support Surveillance Base

Lieutenant Colonel Jack B. Farris, Jr.

Shortly before daylight on the morning of August 29, 1970, a North Vietnamese Army battalion entered the 506 Valley in northern Binh Dinh Province. They entered from the south and marched confidently along the road toward the rich rice producing area of Hoai An District, where they were to occupy mountainous base camps while conducting operations against district forces and replenishing their supply of rice. As the battalion moved up the road, the rear of the column was suddenly hit by a barrage of 4.2-inch and 81mm mortar fire. Not initially realizing that their movement was being observed, the enemy battalion moved on, until minutes later the head of the column was shattered by barrages of 105mm howitzers, and 4.2-inch and 81mm mortars.

By now it was obvious to the enemy that his movements were being watched, so he fled in groups of twos and threes to the obvious safety of the mountains to the west of the valley floor. However, as he fled, artillery, mortars, and quad .50 machinegun fire pursued and blocked his routes of withdrawal. At first light, a reaction force of cavalrymen from the 173d Airborne Brigade began a sweep of the valley floor. Blood trails leading west into the high ground proved the accuracy of the indirect fire, and the enemy had been unable to remove all his dead and wounded. The cavalry troop found six enemy KIA and captured one wounded enemy, one AK47, one 60mm mortar, one courier pouch, and numerous items of individual equipment that had been discarded by the fleeing enemy.

The helicopters of the air cavalry troop attempted to regain contact with the disorganized force but were unable to locate it. They confirmed that trails led into the mountains and that individual equipment and sacks of rice were scattered along these trails and in the mountains. On September 3d, a wounded enemy soldier, captured in the mountains near the 506 Valley, confessed that the toll in enemy dead and wounded had been great. A wounded rallier on October 2d said that his company XO had recently died from wounds sustained during the march up 506 Valley, and on October 13th still another rallier admitted that he too had been wounded during the same action.

How badly was the NVA battalion hurt in this engagement? The fact that there was not a single significant action conducted by this battalion in Hoai An District after August 29th indicates that it was hurt severely. This blow against the enemy was dealt by only a small group of paratroopers from the 3d Battalion, 503d Infantry on a fire support surveillance base (FSSB) in the northern portion of 506 Valley. The following narrative describes the intelligence situation and concept of an FSSB.

Evaluation of the enemy situation in and around the 506 Valley in August 1970 indicated the importance of the valley to the enemy, not only as a close-in base area, but as a principal route of travel seldom interdicted by Allied forces. The valley is a natural, easily traveled corridor. It provides easy access to the north from the Suoi Ca Valley through My Trinh Village, a traditional resupply base. It is the only high-speed north-south route in the area that is not under South Vietnamese control. There are also east-west routes leading through the valley from the Crow's Foot and Base Area 226.

Between June 1 and August 11, 1970, elements of an NVA artillery battalion, a sapper battalion, an NVA regiment, and local VC units from Hoai An and Phu My Districts were reported to be in this valley. Many of these units were in base camps around the valley floor and on the mountain slopes surrounding the valley.

Recon teams were inserted into the valley to substantiate what was known about enemy movements and to locate trails on the ground. After 45 days of patrolling, positive identification of these trails was made, enemy traffic was recorded and analyzed, and construction of the FSSB began. The FSSB was conceived as a total interdiction base which would integrate sensors, radar and other target acquisition means with a family of direct and indirect fire support systems.

Every commander has wished at one time or another that he had more troops with which to accomplish his mission. Today's modern arsenal of weapons and target acquisition systems provides unlimited opportunities for the commander to employ the enonomy of force principle, thereby freeing his ground troops for other missions. The FSSB was an economy of force measure employing a target acquisition system and immediate fire support in an interdiction mission.

The basic component of a FSSB is the unattended ground sensor. The sensors are planted in strings and have several important advantages: The operator is able to determine the direction of movement, the size of the force and the length of the column. However, before permanent sensors are emplaced, a temporary sensor field is implanted to confirm information on enemy movements. Wherever confirmation is obtained, permanent sensors are installed. Accurate information on the enemy's movement is now provided by the sensors. Once the direction of movement is determined, mortars and artillery can plan fires on a predetermined sensor further along the string, ready to fire when that sensor is activated.

A mix of sensor types is used to eliminate erroneous readings and verify readings for more accurate intelligence data. The basic sensor is seismic and if used alone could be of questionable value. So acoustic and magnetic sensors were mixed in the sensor strings to produce more valid data. NVA soldiers talk while they move and their conversations can be monitored by the acoustic sensors. Voices around the sensor indicate a positive target (and a boost to operator morale). The magnetic sensor will detect weapons and other metal equipment carried by troops. The three types of sensors complement one another and their mix provides confirmation of enemy presence in the sensor field. The sensors were planted by air and by hand (hand-planted sensors are preferred since their exact location is known and they can be positively concealed). Precise location provides for accurate registration of fires and the capability to relocate and recharge the sensor.

An essential component of a FSSB is the PPS-5 radar. The PPS-5 is able to cover that part of the kill zone not monitored by sensors. It confirms readings provided by the sensors and maintains contact with the target after it leaves the sensor field, providing polar coordinates of the target, the number of personnel and direction and rate of movement. Mortar and artillery fire can be accurately adjusted by radar during hours of reduced visibility. Since most targets are engaged at night and sensors may make erroneous readings, the PPS-5 is an integral, complementary part of the system.

The TVS-4 Night Observation Device and a set of 20-power

naval binoculars provide another means of confirming and maintaining contact with targets. Since all sensors require line of sight to the fire support surveillance base, visual contact is possible with the area around the sensors. Use of each target acquisition

means — sensors, radar, and optic devices — provides positive identification and contact with the target until it leaves the kill zone.

Once a target is acquired and confirmed, it must be engaged immediately. The primary weapons of the fire support surveillance base are the organic mortars of the Infantry battalion. The 4.2s and 81s are responsive, can maintain a high rate of fire, and can be quickly shifted as the target moves about the kill zone. The 105mm howitzer is an excellent back-up weapon and the firecracker round is particularly effective.

Registration of mortars and artillery on all sensor fields is required to insure effective engagement of the target. Data must be preplanned, updated regularly, and made available to each gun, since time is of the essence. All sensors are numbered to provide easy reference to gun data already plotted. A quad .50 machinegun provides a direct fire capability to engage targets near close-in sensors, canalize enemy movements and engage him as he flees the kill zone. The psychological effect of the quad .50 is an added bonus.

Organization of an FSSB provides for rapid reaction to confirmed targets and adequate base defense. Located in the TOC, the nerve center of the base, are the monitoring device, radar scope, and optic devices. Collocation of target acquisition means insures rapid comparison of readouts and confirmation of targets. The mortar FDCs are also located in the TOC, which facilitates instant dissemination of data to the guns. Information is quickly and freely exchanged between all elements, permitting rapid acquisition, confirmation, and engagement of targets.

The action on August 29th occurred shortly after the construction of an FSSB, and proved the validity of the concept. As the enemy column entered the valley, the southernmost sensor began activating and continued to do so for about 20 minutes. A sweep by the PPS-5 confirmed what was suspected — an enemy column was moving north in the 506 Valley. The decision was to engage the rear of the column in hopes of getting a second try at the head of the column. The rear was hit with mortar fire and, as expected, the remainder of the column marched on.

The radar continued to track the enemy, and additional sensors began activating. By this time the night observation device had picked up the activity. As the head of the column activated a predetermined sensor, it was halted in its movement by 105mm howitzer, 4.2-inch mortar, and 81mm mortar fire. After this concentration, the PPS-5 and night observation device confirmed that the enemy was fleeing to the west. Quad .50 fire pursued the fleeing enemy and mortar fires blocked his escape to the west. Contact was not lost until the enemy left the kill zone for the safety of the mountains. This is a vivid example of the FSSB in action, using all of its resources to bring fires to bear on the enemy. Sensors, radar, and optic devices identified and confirmed the target; mortars, artillery, and quad .50s engaged it; and radar and the night observation device maintained contact with the enemy until they left the kill zone.

After the FSSB was established, its capabilities were used to complement the battalion's saturation ambush operations in 506 Valley, an added advantage not anticipated. Successful saturation ambush operations require that the ambushing element infiltrate into the area undetected, which is possible only during the hours of darkness, and that the ambush be established as an offensive weapon along a known enemy trail. It is not a night defensive position, and members of the ambush must think offensively.

Ambush positions in 506 Valley were set up along sensor fields capable of detecting enemy movement toward the ambush. The FSSB could then provide the ambush commander information concerning the number of enemy, direction, rate of march, and possibly the disposition of enemy elements in the column. This early warning and information about the approaching enemy gave the ambush commander time to alert his entire force and determine how best to ambush the column. The number of enemy and their disposition in the column was of particular importance. With this knowledge, the ambush commander was able to initiate his ambush when the maximum number of enemy were in the kill zone. After initiation, the fire support surveillance base was able to determine the direction of flight of any surviving enemy, pursue them by fire, or alert other ambush elements to maneuver and cut off the enemy retreat.

Operation of the FSSB incorporated increased psychological operations. The theme was "Chieu Hoi or be killed by the demon of death." A leaflet depicted a traditional Vietnamese demon living in the 506 Valley. The narrative stated that the demon "sees all movement in the valley and will kill all intruders." Thousands of these leaflets were dropped in and around the 506 Valley. As added impact to the leaflets, broadcasts were made from the FSSB addressing groups of enemy soldiers detected in the valley. They were told that the demon was watching, and to convince the enemy of this fact, their movements were described in detail. As mortar rounds slid down the tubes, they were told the demon was going to strike. After the intial impact, the enemy was told there was no hope of escape. If he attempted to flee, the mortar fired. Maximum effort was made to capitalize on traditional Vietnamese fears and superstitions. The psyops campaign produced two ralliers who stated that the enemy was uncertain of what is taking place in the "valley of death."

What accounts for the success of the FSSB in the 506 Valley? First, a detailed study was made of the valley to determine the enemy's habits and routes of movement. This was followed by insertion of recon teams and of temporary emplacement of sensors to confirm routes of enemy movement and the feasibility of these routes being monitored by sensors from the FSSB. Only after definite confirmation of enemy routes of movement were more permanent sensor strings planted along the valley floor. This detailed analysis conducted prior to the permanent emplacement of sensor fields avoided haphazard scattering of sensors along the valley.

Second, the PPS-5 radar and optic devices were used to confirm sensor readouts and to permit continuous contact with the target until it left the kill zone. These devices also provided for the adjustment of mortar and artillery fire during hours of reduced visibility. Sensors alone were not the answer.

Third, immediate fire support was available to instantly engage targets. All these assets were brought together in a TOC, under one commander, fully integrating the entire system. The fire support surveillance base concept, as employed by the 173rd Airborne Brigade, proved to be an effective and reliable means of eliminating enemy resistance in the 506 Valley.

First in Cambodia

Staff Sergeant Ron Renouf

The long line of helicopters dropped onto the landing zone as the Cobra gunships circled, ready to surpress enemy fire. This was similar to the countless number of other combat assaults the men of Company C, 2d Battalion, 7th Cavalry, 1st Cavalry Division (Airmobile) had made before—with one difference. When the lead Huey set down in the clearing and Specialist 4 Terry Hayes jumped onto the ground, the 1st Cavalry was ready to meet the enemy on a new frontier—in Cambodia.

Throughout the Vietnam war, the US had adhered strictly to a policy that Cambodian soil was off-limits. The enemy saw this as an advantage and was using the Cambodian jungle along the Vietnamese border as a sanctuary for troops and supplies. The border between Cambodia and Military Region 3 of South Vietnam is marked by two prominent geographical features; the Parrot's Beak to the south and the Fish Hook farther north. These two extensions of Cambodia into the heart of South Vietnam had for years allowed the enemy to mass men and supplies only 50 miles from Saigon. The 1968 Tet Offensive against the South Vietnemese capital originated in these areas. In an address to the nation on April 30, 1970, President Nixon announced that attacks were being launched to clean out the enemy sanctuaries on the Cambodian-Vietnam border.

As President Nixon announced his decision to attack NVA ammunition caches and other enemy sanctuaries, joint ARVN-US task force elements moved across the border. Chosen to participate in the attacks were elements from the 1st Cavalry Division (Airmobile), the 25th US Infantry Division, the 11th Armored Cavalry Regiment, and various other line and support units. Along with these American units were approximately 40,000 South Vietnamese troops.

On D-day the men of the 2/7 Cavalry, 1st Cavalry Division built Fire Support Base X-Ray, the first artillery firebase in Cambodia. X-Ray was named for the base where the 1st Cav's first major battle in Vietnam took place in the Central Highlands during the 1965 Pleiku Compaign.

Other units quickly moved into Cambodia's Fish Hook to reinforce the operation. D-day plus one brought Charlie Company, 2/5 Cavalry to X-Ray. The following day the 1st Battalion, 5th Cavalry combat assaulted into the northern sector of the Fish Hook, setting up FSB Terri Lynn. The 1/12 Cavalry established

Fire Support Base Evan on D-day plus three, followed by the remainder of the 2/5 Cavalry on D-day plus four.

Completing the first week, D-day plus six, two additional battalions of Skytroopers smashed into Cambodia northwest of Song Be and established firebases north of Phuoc Long and Binh Long Provinces. The Skytroopers moved out from the bases to search for enemy sanctuaries. The new units were the 2/12 Cavalry at Fire Support Base Myron, and the 5/7 Cavalry at FSB Brown.

Even before the Cavalry's ground troops were in Cambodia, the Cobras and LOHs of the 1st Squadron, 9th Cavalry were in the air, watching for signs of enemy activity. They spotted plenty of movement, mostly Communists rapidly retreating from the contact area. Time after time the hunter-killer teams swooped down on the fleeing foe, accounting for many of the enemy killed by the Cavalry in the operation. The pink teams also spotted enemy complexes that contained huge stores of supplies.

On May 2, 1970, helicopters of Bravo Troop, 1st Squadron, 9th Cavalry, found a major NVA military installation, soon to be nicknamed "The City." It consisted of more than 300 buildings, complete with all-weather bamboo walkways winding through the complex.

The 1st Battalion, 5th Cavalry was inserted four kilometers north of the complex area. Charlie Company deployed and swept toward the huge military installation. Refugees, flooding Highway 7 near FSB Terri Lynn in an attempt to escape North Vietnamese forces, confirmed the location of the installation and further described it as a major supply depot.

Charlie Company moved out of the LZ and down Highway 7 toward the suspected enemy complex. Leaving the road, they entered extremely heavy underbrush, slowing movement to a crawl. Overhead, a light observation helicopter from Bravo Troop circled and called directions to the troops below, leading them toward the gigantic complex.

That first night, Charlie Company set up in their night defensive position (NDP) less than a kilometer from the installation's perimeter. The undergrowth below the triple canopy jungle was so dense that it took the company the entire following morning to move the final kilometer to the complex.

As the troops of Charlie Company approached the edge of the gigantic base they received light AK47 fire from two of the enemy bunkers. This fire was quickly silenced by grenades.

The complex was three kilometers long and one-and-a-half wide. The buildings were bulging with arms and ammunition. In the first 24 hours of the search of the complex, Charlie Company discovered four bunkers loaded with .51 caliber ammunition, one building full of weapons ranging from an old flintlock to shotguns and new SKSs, 15 .30 caliber antiaircraft machineguns complete with wheeled carriages and extra barrels, and six cases of 9mm machineguns with drums and magazines.

Uncovered later were many 60mm mortars and ammunition, crated 120mm mortars, repair kits for numerous types of weapons, two bunkers of 57mm recoilless rifles complete with mounts, two bunkers of explosives, detonation cord and shaped charges, and medical supplies. Many of the weapons were still packed in cosmoline, a protective grease. Also discovered in "The City" was what appeared to be an elaborate NVA rest and recuperation center, complete with a swimming pool.

Meanwhile, tankers from the 2d Battalion, 34th Armor interdicted Highway 7 in the southern portion of the Fish Hook.

Patrolling the area around their CP, the armored vehicles overran countless enemy bunkers that the troops methodically destroyed. As the enemy fled, scores of Cambodian refugees packed the highway to the tanker's position. These refugees were loaded aboard Chinooks and Hueys and moved to the main refugee processing point at An Loc, Vietnam, near the headquarters of the task force.

The 1st Cavalry's other initial Cambodian assault, north of Phuoc Long and Binh Long Provinces, also had spectacular results.

While on a routine scout mission, a helicopter pilot spotted three 2½-ton trucks loaded with troops in complete NVA field uniforms. The trucks were engaged and destroyed. Learning of the discovery, Lieutenant Colonel Francis A. Ianni, commanding the 2/12 Cavalry, sent Delta Company to make a combat assault into the contact area. Delta Company landed 500 meters north of the site and moved south, engaged two individuals, but lost their blood trails in the jungle. Two platoons began sweeping the area. Fifty meters across the road they made contact with an estimated 40 to 50 enemy soldiers. The company broke the ambush by forming an assault line that scattered the enemy. The company renewed the sweep and found several small caches before setting up an NDP. The enemy hit the NDP that night in groups of two to three, moving toward the perimeter from all sides. During the night, Charlie Company and reconnaissance platoons of Echo Company entered the area and joined Delta Company for a sweep of the area the next morning.

Nicknamed "Rock Island East," after an arsenal in Illinois, the supply complex contained 40 to 50 individual caches, stacked six feet high on 20 by 15-foot pallets hidden in the jungle and sometimes covered with brush. The pallets were 20 to 30 meters apart on alternating sides of the trail. The cache contained millions of .51 caliber rounds and thousands of mortar, recoilless rifle and rocket rounds. Large quantities of rifles, grenades and other equipment were also found.

Attention remained focused on the region north of Phuoc Long and Bing Long through the rest of May, as most 1st Cavalry units moved into that area and activity declined in the Fish Hook. Elements of the 5th Battalion, 7th Cavalry were the first to make significant munitions finds in the area when they encountered a well fortified NVA storage complex built into a hill 26 miles northeast of Song Be.

The fight for the hill began when Bravo Company spotted headlights disappearing over the distant hills. As they moved through the valley toward the lights, determined delaying tactics by the enemy slowed the advance to a crawl. The Skytroopers spent the night at the foot of the hill and started the assault the next morning. After a day of fighting, the Skytroopers owned the hill. They found 12-foot deep bunkers cut on all sides of the hill. At the bottom of each bunker a drainage system kept the supply pallets—stacked high with weapons and ammunition—dry.

This cache and others found in the area yielded hundreds of tons of rice and salt, and thousands of weapons and rounds of ammunition. Munitions and food were not the only items found. Alpha Company, 1st Battalion, 8th Cavalry captured 380 hammocks, 1,000 pairs of socks, 900 leather belts, and 500,000 buttons.

A Presidential Order established a 21.7-mile limit of advance into Cambodia for American troops. The ARVN had no such limitation set on their advance. The ARVN sweep went from Tay Ninh, Vietnam across the border to Svay Rieng, through Kompong Trabek, northward by way of Trey Veng, to the Chup Rubber Plantation, and then back into South Vietnam.

As the last US forces withdrew into Vietnam, the ARVN remained in Cambodia to establish a buffer zone between the Communists still operating in Vietnam and their supply sources.

By the end of the Cambodian operation, the allied units had achieved phenomenal success. By the time the last American unit had withdrawn, the NVA-VC supply system in the area had been crushed. Captured equipment included: 19,337 individual and 2,499 crew-served weapons; 1,768 tons of ammunition and 41 tons of explosives; 29 tons of communications equipment; 55 tons of medical supplies; 18 tons of gasoline and oil; 6,877 tons of rice; and 432 enemy trucks.

The enemy lost more than supplies during the operation In Cambodia. US intelligence sources indicate that the enemy lost more than 11,000 troops killed in action. This compares with 337 American dead and 1,524 wounded for the entire campaign. The month of May also produced over 1,300 enemy ralliers in Military Region 3. High ranking military officials estimated it would take the enemy months, perhaps more than a year to recover from these staggering losses.

This operation would, according to President Nixon, "permit the Vietnamization Program to forge ahead, unimpeded. By the time the enemy forces are able to rebuild, if they do, the Vietnamese Army will be strong enough to handle the situation by itself, enabling us to continue withdrawing our soldiers from Vietnam."

Vietnam Report

Colonel Lawrence L. Mowery

As the Vietnamization program proceeds on course, US operations in Vietnam have entered a new phase. In essence, forces of the Republic of Vietnam now operate along the Cambodian and Laotian borders, while US units concentrate their operations in or near populated areas. American forces now direct a majority of their efforts towards pacification and providing training assistance to the Army of the Republic of Vietnam (ARVN), Regional Forces/ Popular Forces (RF/PF) and Peoples Self-Defense Forces (PSDF). The impact of this changing mission for US units is significant: it reflects the increasing progress of Vietnamization, but at the same time presents new challenges to the American soldier and his training.

Effect of Vietnamization on Combat Operations

Small unit operations continue to be stressed throughout Vietnam, with emphasis on company-size and smaller operations. ARVN units are now being assigned their own areas of operation and conduct unilateral operations using US-provided combat support as required.

The tempo of direct involvement by US forces in combat operations varies by military region. In Military Region 1 (the Military Regions were formerly known as Corps Tactical Zones), US units are directly opposed by NVA forces, and frequent contact occurs. In Military Regions 2 and 3, on the other hand, the US effort is directed against small NVA and VC operations and involves the capture of enemy caches and disruption of his lines of communication. With the exception of the 1st Cavalry Division's area of operations, ARVN forces are deployed along the border. US forces, operating from base camps or fire support bases, conduct air assaults of company-size or smaller to locate enemy caches and block infiltration routes.

Night operations continue to be characterized by platoon and squad-size ambushes employing the mechanical ambush technique. Air and ground emplaced sensors are being successfully employed by US units for target acquisition and detection of enemy movement.

The continued emphasis on small unit operations has placed a premium on effective leadership at platoon and squad level. Shortages of junior officers and senior NCOs sometimes result in platoons being led by E6s and E5s, who in most instances are graduates of the Noncommissioned Officer Candidate Course.

All US units have introductory training programs in effect for newly arrived personnel. Still, there are several areas where training shortfalls exist, including the following:

- Marksmanship, technique of fire control and distribution of fires. There are still too many instances where enemy elements are sighted or contacted without any tangible results. US small unit leaders are failing to insist on aimed, semi-automatic fire, which has proven its worth many times in Vietnam. As a result, units are conducting marksmanship training during stand-downs.

- Land navigation. Tactical maps of Vietnam are frequently inaccurate, making it essential that land navigation training emphasize use of the compass, intersection and resection techniques, artillery and mortar fire, and aerial observers to pinpoint unit locations.

- Mechanical ambush techniques. Junior leaders and enlisted personnel arriving in-country are generally unfamiliar with this type of ambush, which is being employed extensively by all US units. Junior leaders must be trained in how to plan, emplace and execute the mechanical ambush. This instruction is presently being presented by the Infantry School, but graduates who have received this training are just beginning to arrive in-country.

• Mine and boobytrap detection. Complacency and lack of alertness by US personnel, combined with enemy ingenuity, continue to result in unnecessary casualties from boobytraps. We still take too many casualties from enemy mines and boobytraps.

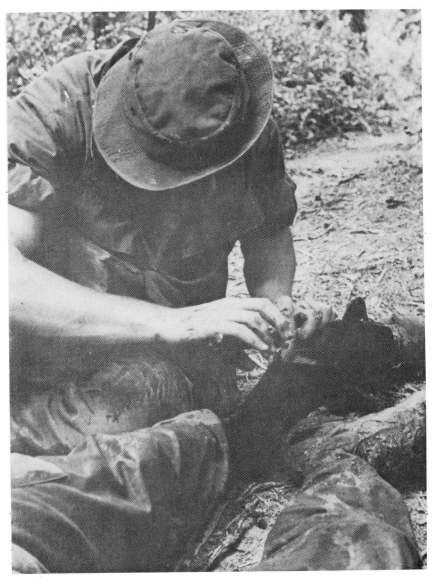

• Reporting of information. Intelligence information about enemy activities isn't being reported in a timely manner in too many instances. What may appear to be of no consequence at small unit level becomes significant when reported to higher headquarters, where it is combined with information from other sources. There is an unfortunate tendency for US units to wait for higher headquarters to pass information down, when the reverse should frequently be the case.

• Communications security. The NVA and VC for years have listened to our communications. Our communications security has been greatly enhanced by the mandatory establishment of secure nets and the introduction of the CIRCE wheel encryption device in the summer of 1970. Strong command emphasis and introduction of the CIRCE wheel have brought about the disappearance of the locally developed codes which the enemy was reading with relative ease.

• Litterbug syndrome. The continuing problem of battlefield police by US personnel allows the enemy to obtain material used to fashion mines and boobytraps, as well as foodstuffs.

As a result of a January 1970 liaison visit to Vietnam, where many of the same problems were noted, the Infantry School has adjusted and intensified its instruction in these areas.

Role of the Advisor

The increased role of the US advisor to ARVN and territorial forces has produced an important change in our training requirements. The redeployment of US forces and the ARVN assumption of areas of operation along the border has resulted in large unit operations by ARVN forces, conducted over extended periods of time.

As ARVN forces have relocated to border areas, the RF/PF role in providing security to local areas has become more significant. Most US personnel on orders to Vietnam as advisors attend the Military Assistance Training Advisor course at Fort Bragg and possibly the Foreign Service Institute at Arlington, Virginia. But many advisors lack recent experience with troops and their knowledge of tactics, techniques and equipment presently in use by US and ARVN units is deficient. They need additional training in areas such as airmobility, ambush techniques and night observation devices.

As the US role in combat operations diminishes, certain inherent problems develop. Senior American commanders point to the transition required to turn the principal combat role over to the Vietnamese armed forces as rapidly as possible. US commanders who have been trained and oriented toward a fighting role have adjusted successfully to this revised mission, and positive emphasis is being applied in-country.

Performance of Junior Leaders

Graduates of the Infantry Officer Advanced Course are seldom assigned to company command positions. They are normally on a second tour in Vietnam and, because of a shortage of field grade officers, are usually assigned to a staff position or as battalion XO. IOAC graduates commented favorably on their course at the Infantry School, but recommended additional instruction on race relations, drug abuse and STANO (surveillance, target acquisition, and night observation) techniques. These items are all presently emphasized in the IOAC program of instruction.

Junior officers who had recently graduated from the Infantry Officer Basic Course or Officer Candidate School were sometimes criticized by senior commanders for a general lack of "knowledge to detect and courage to correct." The decentralized nature of small unit operations prohibits company commanders from providing the mature personal guidance required. Our lieutenants are good, but they could be better, particularly in those areas of training shortfalls described above.

Graduates of the Noncommissioned Officer Candidate Course were given high grades by all commanders. Although many of the NCOC graduates aren't prepared for the initial shock of combat leadership, their confidence increases with time, particularly after their first contact is made with the enemy.

G1/S1 Considerations

Commanders have placed considerable emphasis on rifle company "foxhole strength" to help compensate for a shortage of 11B Infantrymen. It has been said, with some truth, that a unit is lucky to have two experienced personnel in a rifle company — company commander and first sergeant. A large number of platoons are being led by staff sergeant (E6) and sergeant (E5) graduates of the NCOC program, because of a shortage of senior NCOs.

Because of inadequate numbers of Infantry lieutenants, many rifle companies operate without an executive officer. Those that use an XO employ him to command the company rear and supervise logistics missions. Battalion XOs normally command the battalion rear in base camp, control base defense and supervise administrative and logistic operations. Brigade executive officers are generally found at the brigade base camp, acting as deputy installation coordinators and base defense commanders. They also supervise brigade logistic and administrative operations.

Infantry second lieutenants arriving in-country are generally assigned to a line company. However, in exceptional cases, they may be assigned as support platoon leader, battalion communications officer or assistant battalion staff officers. Less than two percent of the Infantry second lieutenants in any division are initially assigned to positions other than platoon leader.

Racial incidents have occurred among US personnel, despite the best possible leadership. The main problem in units which have had racial problems has generally been a lack of communication. To bring problems to the surface before incidents occur, all units have formed Human Relations Councils, with results of meetings being promptly furnished to commanders.

To minimize racial tensions, US units have initiated a program geared toward increased understanding of the problems and conflicts inherent in racial problems. The Human Relations Councils seek to recognize, acknowledge and conduct frank discussions of all potential problem areas. The introduction of race relations instruction in courses for leaders at the US Army Infantry School promises to help considerably in reducing racial tensions.

Disciplinary problems reported by commanders normally involve refusals to go to the field, insubordination, possession of marijuana, sleeping on guard and AWOL. Effective leadership is succeeding in holding these cases to a minimum.

In the case of drug abuse, there has been no impact on combat operations from use of drugs. The discovery of drugs is generally difficult in Vietnam because of the large number of different drugs available and the many forms in which they appear. Where drugs, such as marijuana, are found in the possession of individual soldiers, the "chain of custody" involved in handling the drug evidence is extremely difficult because of the widespread deployment of tactical units.

To control the drug problem, divisions are employing mobile training teams of criminal investigators, military police and legal personnel to visit units and brief junior leaders and NCOs on the appearance and characteristics of marijuana and other drugs, the proper methods for conducting a search, and the.importance of maintaining the chain of custody. Most divisions have organized a drug suppression council, which encourages users to come forward voluntarily under an Amnesty Program. The user is given assistance without fear of punishment, which includes an interview with the division surgeon, establishment of a buddy system with a respected friend of the user, and continued counseling sessions with the commanding officer, chaplain and surgeon. These sessions help to solve difficulties which may arise, and aid toward evaluating and encouraging the individual's success in breaking the drug habit. All commanders in Vietnam suggested increased emphasis on the drug problem in Infantry School leader courses.

G2/S2 Considerations

There has been a noticeable change in the tempo and type of enemy operations as a result of the Cambodian operation. In

Military Regions 2 and 3 particularly, contacts with the enemy have been reduced to infrequent engagements with small carrying parties in search of food and other supplies. In Military Region 1, with its close proximity to the DMZ and Laotian border, there has been little change in the nature of the enemy's activity. Strong enemy forces are positioned in MR 1 and are capable of launching battalion and regimental-size attacks against US and ARVN forces in the area.

In general, NVA and VC operations are characterized by small unit attacks from a few men up to platoon-size. The enemy uses indirect fire weapons and occasional sniper attacks against key allied installations. In MR 1 and 2, the principal NVA objective is to infiltrate the lowlands and disrupt the pacification program. The enemy continues to exploit the carelessness of US forces by retrieving abandoned and discarded munitions, equipment and other materials.

Since the Cambodian operation, relatively few enemy prisoners have been captured, reflecting the reduced tempo of operations. Those PWs captured in the northern provinces are generally in good health and have evidenced good morale. Prisoners taken in MR 2 and 3 reflect poor health and morale. Most prisoners are uncooperative at first and lie when answering questions, usually out of a fear of being killed. After a few days, when they realize

that they are actually out of danger, they become more cooperative and truthful.

US forces have arrived at common intelligence indicators of the presence of an enemy base camp. These include:

- Heavy trail usage.
- Secondary trails branching out from main trails.
- Streams near large trails.
- Boobytraps along trails.
- Refuse left by the enemy (he can be guilty of this, too).
- Pigs, chickens, cows, and water buffalo in the area.
- Well-tended cultivated crops.
- Signs of wood cutting.
- Cultivated fields in a sparsely populated area.
- Large quantities of drying or stored rice.

Effective liaison has been established by US intelligence personnel at brigade and battalion level with Vietnamese District and Province Intelligence and Operations Coordination Centers (DIOCC, PIOCC). The pattern of liaison varies with individual units, but generally includes enlisted liaison personnel who operate on a 24-hour basis using AN/PRC-25 radios and periodic visits by US brigade and battalion commanders to the DIOCC and PIOCC.

In terms of collecting information about the enemy, the most valuable agencies have been US maneuver battalions, air cavalry troops, document readouts, and PWs. Information about the VC political infrastructure generally comes through the DIOCC, because its area of responsibility is small enough for effective coordination between the village and district chiefs. Where DIOCCs haven't been established, a combination of sources — maneuver battalions, PWs, documents, hoi chanh ralliers, and agent networks — has proven important in providing intelligence about the enemy infrastructure.

The M3 airborne personnel detector (people-sniffer) is receiving increasing command emphasis as an intelligence technique. People-sniffer results are carefully checked with other information, and airstrikes, artillery or troops are then committed against the more lucrative enemy targets. The primary effectiveness of the M3 detector has been in pinpointing areas of enemy activity, rather than in providing specific targets.

Another area receiving increased command emphasis is the use of STANO equipment, particularly sensors. Planning and execution of sensor operations varies from unit to unit. Some units employ sensors for the sole purpose of target acquisition and then place indirect fire on single activations. Other units coordinate sensor information with other intelligence about enemy movements and then develop ambush plans, acquire targets for indirect weapons based on an overall pattern analysis or enhance the security of their firebases and base camp.

344

G3/S3 Considerations

The primary offensive role of US Infantry units in Vietnam today is to search for and locate enemy forces, using elements which range from fire teams to company-size forces. Once the enemy has been located, emphasis is placed on employing maximum firepower — artillery, tac air and B52 strikes where ap-

propriate — on his troop concentrations. To exploit the results of firepower, troops are inserted, if needed, to seal off escape routes and close with the enemy.

In the 1st Cavalry Division (Airmobile), for example, the primary role of Infantry units is reconnaissance — to locate enemy caches, neutralize base areas, interdict lines of communication, destroy enemy forces, and advance pacification and Vietnamization. Heavy reliance on firepower, particularly artillery, aerial field artillery (formerly known as aerial rocket artillery), and tac air, continues as a principal means of enemy destruction. However, the majority of the 1st Cav's contacts are meeting engagements and ambushes initiated by friendly forces. In fact, the 1st Cav, as of late fall 1970, had not encountered any large enemy forces since the Cambodian operation.

In all units, Infantry closes with the enemy for the purpose of fixing and destroying him. A preponderance of firepower, not assault, is the technique used. When the enemy is sufficiently neutralized, Infantry sweeps the area of contact and mops up.

At the same time, however, limitations have been placed on the expenditure of artillery ammunition. Operators haven't been hampered, but commanders and staff at all levels have had to be more precise in their planning and execution.

The size and frequency of airmobile operations in MR 2 and 3 has decreased since Cambodia. In most cases of squad or smaller unit insertions, artillery preparatory fires aren't used. However, aerial field artillery (AFA) and gunships are habitually employed to support smaller insertions, and artillery preps are reserved for larger combat assaults.

As part of the pacification program, all units evidenced increased emphasis on elimination of the VC infrastructure. In the 173d Airborne Brigade, for example, the tendency has been to shift from an emphasis on pacification alone to a simultaneous destruction of the enemy infrastructure. Mobile training teams are used to conduct combined operations with RF and PF units in the populated lowlands and deny local VC access to pacified hamlets. Combined cordon and search operations seek to identify

and capture members of the VC infrastructure. Eagle flight operations, using an airmobile reaction force, are conducted with RF intelligence squads from subsector headquarters. The eagle flights attempt to locate and identify VCI agents such as tax collectors, operating during the rice harvesting and woodcutting seasons.

Night defensive positions are used by all US maneuver units during field operations. Platoon-size NDPs are most common, although company-size positions are used during periods of increased enemy activity.

Firebases have become austere again. Strictly enforced guidelines and command emphasis have standardized the amount of construction and barrier material used in firebase construction, and the quantity of artillery ammunition located at any one base is also under stringent control.

To avoid enemy ground fire, US aircraft have adopted effective evasion and deception techniques. Nap of the earth flying during visual reconnaissance and resupply missions makes enemy fire less effective. Emphasis has been placed on panel markers instead of smoke to mark landing zones during resupply flights and avoid advance notice to the enemy of an aircraft's approach. When firebases are being resupplied under fire, smoke screens are used to conceal incoming aircraft and secure voice communication is employed whenever possible during air assaults and resupplies. The most commonly encountered enemy antiaircraft weapons are small arms, .51 caliber machineguns, and 12.7mm, with occasional .37mm, antiair fire.

To provide aviation support for ARVN units, the 1st Aviation Brigade and airmobile divisions have been tasked to furnish aircraft. For example, the 101st Airborne Division (Airmobile) provides the 1st ARVN Infantry Division with a daily package of command and control ships and UH1H utility aircraft. If a particular ARVN regiment requires additional assets for an operation, the necessary aircraft are furnished the appropriate US brigade, which then coordinates with the ARVN force to support the operation. The ARVN commander becomes the air mission task force commander, assisted by the US commander. The system is working well and is developing considerable airmobile competence among ARVN commanders and troops.

The role of antitank weapons in a non-armor environment is worth mentioning. With the exception of the 1st Cavalry Division, all US units have turned in their 106mm recoilless rifles; the Cav employs the 106 on its jeep mount for convoy and reconnaissance missions. Individual antitank weapons such as the M72 LAW are being used against fortified positions, troops in the open and enemy snipers. LAW is generally transported by individual riflemen, with one LAW per fire team being average. In its antipersonnel and antisniper roles, LAW is being effectively employed with a tree-burst technique. Using cannister rounds, LAW has come in handy in firebase security, and the 90mm recoilless rifle is also used occasionally in firebase defense.

As a general rule, junior leaders still need more training in land navigation techniques. Many maps in Vietnam aren't accurate enough for precise navigation, and junior leaders require additional practice in resection and intersection. Air assaults present

a special problem of reorientation before moving out from the landing zone, because it is easy to lose one's sense of direction after the helicopter flight.

G4/S4 Considerations

There appears to be room for improvement in training junior officers and NCOs in supply techniques while they are still in the CONUS training base. Methods used at battalion level for transporting and stocking supplies is one area requiring additional emphasis. We need to stress the concept of a forward trains area and a fire support base combat trains area. Rigging external loads for the UH1 and particularly the CH47 helicopter is another important area.

Commanders reported that junior officers require additional training in conservation of our equipment resources, promptly evacuating damaged or unserviceable equipment to the rear, operator maintenance, and property accountability. All of these areas are receiving current command emphasis in Vietnam.

The litterbug syndrome must be controlled. The major step to reduce combat littering is the use of sumps and the burning of C-ration boxes and other discarded paper items. Emphasis is being placed on field sanitation, control of littering, policing as-you-go, backhauling at the earliest opportunity, and traveling as light as possible. Prior to closing out a firebase, a thorough police of the area is conducted, to prevent items from falling into enemy hands and becoming potential boobytraps against us.

Summary

These are only the highlights of the changing nature of Infantry operations in Vietnam in the fall of 1970. Where in earlier years the battalion-size combat assault was standard, this is no longer the case, because the enemy doesn't present battalion-size targets any more. From one end of the Republic of Vietnam to the other, the key words are "pacification" and "Vietnamization," and the American Infantryman has adjusted to these new missions with flexibility, understanding and professionalism. The job is being accomplished in the highest traditions of the US fighting man.

349

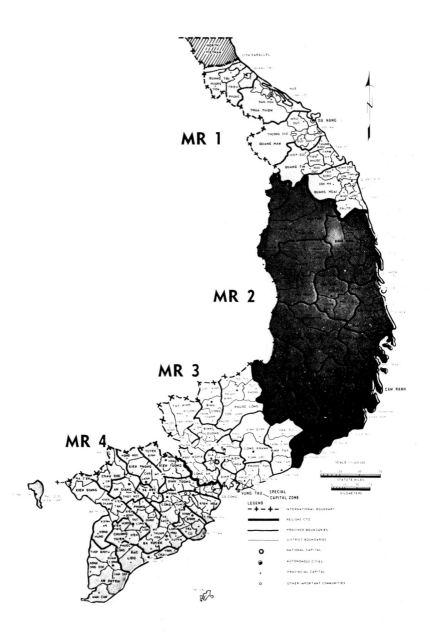

MR 1

MR 2

MR 3

MR 4

DA NANG

CAM RANH

VUNG TAU SPECIAL
CAPITAL ZONE

LEGEND

—·—+—·— INTERNATIONAL BOUNDARY

———————— REGIONS CTZ

———————— PROVINCE BOUNDARIES

———————— DISTRICT BOUNDARIES

◎ NATIONAL CAPITAL

◉ AUTONOMOUS CITIES

· PROVINCIAL CAPITAL

○ OTHER IMPORTANT COMMUNITIES

SCALE 1:1,000,000

STATUTE MILES

KILOMETERS

1971-1972

Reflections

LTC Albert N. Garland, USA (Ret.)

The redeployment of United States ground combat units continued at a steady pace during 1971, and more than 100,000 U.S. soldiers left South Vietnam for home.

In January, the U.S. Special Forces turned over control of the last of its border camps in the central highlands to the Army of the Republic of Vietnam (ARVN) thus marking the end of their five years of operations from those camps.

Most of the 1st Cavalry Division (Airmobile) was gone by the end of April, as were the 2d Brigade, 25th Infantry Division (the last major unit of that division still in South Vietnam) and the bulk of the 11th Armored Cavalry Regiment.

These were followed later in the year by the 1st Brigade, 5th Infantry Division; the 173d Airborne Brigade, which had been, in May 1965, the first major Army ground unit sent to Vietnam; all but one brigade of the 23d (Americal) Division; and the 3d Brigade, 101st Airborne Division (Airmobile).

By the end of 1971, only one division-size U.S. ground combat unit remained in South Vietnam: the 101st Airborne Division (-) at Phu Bai. And that unit, too, was gone by mid-March 1972.

During 1971, ARVN units did most of the fighting on the ground, as they had been doing since the official beginning of the Vietnamization program in June 1969. They continued to receive massive air (both Army aviation and Air Force), naval, and logistic support from the United States. The remaining U.S. ground combat units assumed responsibility for the security of their assigned base areas, the pacification program, the upgrading of the South Vietnamese territorial forces, and for conducting combined operations, when and where possible, with ARVN units. (Until it left Vietnam early in 1972, the 101st Airborne Division conducted most of these combined operations. It was linked with the ARVN 1st Infantry Division in Operation JEFFERSON GLENN, which lasted from September 1970 to October 1971, with time out for Operation LAM SON 719.)

The U.S. advisory effort continued to receive increased emphasis during the year as more and more war-making equipment was given to the ARVN under the Project ENHANCE program. During the summer of 1971, the headquarters of the various U.S. Field Forces were deactivated and became Regional Assistance Commands, demonstrating the increasing reliance the U.S. Army was placing on its advisory efforts and on improving the capabilities of the various ARVN units.

Allied forces also began to withdraw from South Vietnam in 1971. The Thai Black Panther Division, which had been in Vietnam since 1968, was withdrawn in two increments, the first during July 1971, the second in February 1972.

By November 1971, all Australian and New Zealand units were gone, and in December, the first of the South Korean Army ground combat units began leaving for home. (South Korea ranked next to the U.S. in the number of troops sent to Vietnam. At the peak of its effort in 1968, South Korea had the equivalent of 22 maneuver battalions, some 50,000 soldiers, on the ground. Its major combat units were the Capital "Tiger" Division, the 9th "White Horse" Division, and the 2d Marine "Blue Dragon" Brigade.)

U.S. infantry units did take part in one major combat operation in 1971: Operation LAM SON 719, which lasted from 30 January to 6 April. This was a four-phase operation during which ARVN forces invaded lower Laos to disrupt a North Vietnamese Army (NVA) buildup by doing as much damage as they could to NVA logistics installations and infiltration routes.

The final plan called for the reinforced 1st Brigade, 5th U.S. Infantry Division during Phase I (code-named Operation DEWEY CANYON II) to occupy the Khe Sanh area, to clear Route 9 as far as the Laotian border, and to clear ARVN troop assembly areas and forward artillery positions. At the same time, the 101st U.S. Airborne Division was to fire artillery into the A Shau Valley as a diversionary tactic.

U.S. ground units and advisors with the participating ARVN units were prohibited from crossing into Laos, but U.S. Army aviation units were not. In fact, the bulk of the helicopter support needed by the ARVN units was furnished by the supporting U.S. units, particularly the 101st. U.S. Army artillery units and U.S. Air Force formations were also tasked to support the ARVN effort, while the 26th U.S. General Support Group supported both U.S. and ARVN units.

DEWEY CANYON II began on 30 January 1971 and met immediate success. The 5th Infantry Divisions's soldiers secured Khe Sanh and the surrounding area on 1 February, and by 5 February, they had reached the border where the brigade deployed a cavalry task force along Route 9 to screen the movement of the ARVN units that followed.

The ARVN units committed to the cross-border operation moved into their assembly areas to prepare for the operation's succeeding phases: the attack into lower Laos, the exploitation to destroy the NVA operational bases and supply installations, and the withdrawal.

DEWEY CANYON II went extremely well against only scattered NVA resistance, although the 1st Brigade did come under attack several times before LAM SON 719 ended two months later. (The entire operation cost the 1st Brigade 489 men, of whom 55 were killed, 431 wounded, and 3 missing.)

Phase II began early in the morning of 8 February when an ARVN combined infantry and tank force crossed the border along Route 9. The crossing was followed almost immediately by a flight of U.S. air cavalry helicopters, which soon took the lead to cover the main ARVN effort. Heavy fighting raged along Route 9 in lower Laos for the next 60 days.

When it was all over, U.S. Army helicopter units had flown almost 46,000 sorties in support of the ARVN units in Laos at a cost of 82 helicopters destroyed. U.S. Army units, all told, suffered 1,402 casualties during LAM SON 719: 215 killed, 1,149 wounded, and 38 missing. ARVN units counted a total of 7,683 casualties, of whom 1,549 were killed.

For the remainder of 1971, all of 1972, and until the cease fire agreement between the warring countries was signed on 27 January 1973, the major U.S. Army effort in South Vietnam was in support of the Vietnamization program. By the end of 1971, U.S.—supplied war material for the Republic of Vietnam Armed Forces (RVNAF) had reached huge proportions: 855,000 individual and crew-served weapons, 1,880 tanks and artillery pieces, 44,000 radio sets, and 778 helicopters and fixed-wing aircraft.

Numerous new ARVN units were activated and all ARVN units received some of the most modern equipment the U.S. had to offer, including the TOW missile system. But at the same time, the number of U.S. military advisors to ARVN units began to decrease, because the U.S. felt that the Vietnamization program was succeeding. Thus, advisors were withdrawn from all ARVN infantry battalions and their numbers were reduced at the regiment and the division levels. All told, in June 1972, there were fewer than 5,000 U.S. advisors on duty with ARVN units.

As the U.S. ground combat units left Vietnam, they turned their bases over to ARVN units. Thus, the Cu Chi base, which had been occupied by the 25th U.S. Infantry Division, was taken over by the ARVN 7th Infantry Division and other units; the Lai Khe base, the Forward CP of the 1st U.S. Infantry Division, was taken over by the ARVN 25th Infantry Division; the Chu Lai base, the American Division, by the ARVN 2d Infantry Division and some logistics units; and Eagle base, near Phu Bai, the 101st U.S. Airborne Division (Airmobile), by the ARVN 1st Infantry Division.

On 30 March 1972, though, before the number of U.S. advisors was curtailed, NVA forces launched their long-expected summer offensive—the *Nguyen Hue* campaign. At the time, only 69,000 U.S. soldiers were in South Vietnam and they were responsible only for local security duties near their base areas.

Before the NVA offensive ended in September, with heavy losses on both sides, the Vietnamization program had been severely tested. Although they initially suffered crushing defeats, the ARVN forces battled back and, with massive help from U.S. Army aviation units and from U.S. Air Force and U.S. Navy elements, regained most of the ground they had lost. U.S. Army advisors played a key role in directing the various U.S. fire support elements.

The ARVN units that were directly involved in throwing back the various NVA thrusts lost a great deal of equipment and, as a result, the U.S. military headquarters in Vietnam began its Project NOW to replace those losses in the shortest time possible. The re-equipping and re-training processes were accomplished in near-record time.

As the NVA offensive ground to a halt, the last major U.S. ground combat units left Vietnam for home. In May and June 1972, the 3d Brigade, 1st Cavalry Division (Airmobile) and the 196th Infantry Brigade departed. They were followed in August by the 1st Battalion, 7th Cavalry, which for several months had been operating as Task Force GARRY OWEN, and by the 3d Battalion, 21st Infantry, the last U.S. infantry battalion to leave Vietnam. The latter had first arrived in Vietnam six years earlier, in August 1966.

In January 1973, when the cease fire agreement was signed, the

ARVN counted some 450,000 soldiers in its ranks. It had 171 infantry battalions, 22 armored cavalry and tank squadrons, and 64 artillery battalions, plus numerous support units. Regional and popular force units made up half of this number; they were mainly responsible for the protection of hamlets, villages, and important government installations.

On 28 January 1973, the day after the cease fire was signed, U.S. military strength in South Vietnam stood at 23,000. The cease fire agreement also marked the end of the U.S. military advisory effort, and within 60 days all U.S. military advisors had been withdrawn from the ARVN units. Too, by the terms of the agreement, the headquarters of the Military Assistance Command, Vietnam (MACV) ceased to exist.

But since some sort of U.S. military headquarters was needed to continue the U.S. military assistance program and to supervise the technical assistance the RVNAF still needed to complete the goals of Vietnamization, the U.S. organized the Defense Attache Office (DAO) Saigon. Consisting of 50 military people and 1,200 civilians, DAO Saigon did not expect to be in business for more than a year. By then, it was hoped the RVNAF would be in a position to take care of themselves.

Reflections

Not since the Philippine Insurrection in the early years of the 20th century had the U.S. infantryman found himself fighting in such an alien environment against such an elusive, determined, and cunning foe. And there were other similarities as well.

Both were small unit wars—platoons and companies—and they both placed a high premium on individual and small unit discipline and on such things as jungle craft, perseverance, initiative, physical conditioning, morale, and esprit. Both also required the infantryman, even as he fought, to administer to the needs of a civilian population and to support indigenous forces.

But if there were certain similarities between these two wars, there were also many differences. In fact, in many respects the war in Vietnam was unlike any other war in history.

One of the major differences was in the widespread use of the helicopter, which was the most significant advance of the Vietnam War. Even in World War II and the Korean War, infantrymen did not have it, and this airmobility added a new dimension to his operations: It greatly extended his area of control and permitted him to react to opportunities more quickly, to change plans even while he was in the air, and to shift to new areas on short notice. This meant that the terrain no longer necessarily restricted his operations.

The infantryman in Vietnam could also employ a wide variety of more powerful weapons than ever before. In addition to the M16 rifle, he had and effectively used the M60 7.62mm machinegun, the M79 40mm grenade launcher, the M203 40mm semiautomatic grenade launcher mounted on an M16A1 rifle, the M1911A1 .45 caliber automatic pistol, the XM 21 7.62mm sniper rifle system, the M2 .50 caliber machinegun, the M72 66mm LAW, and the M28 81mm mortar. In special situations the infantryman also made effective use of 12-gauge shotguns, XM174 40mm automatic grenade launchers, and M19 60mm mortars.

The infantryman's basic weapon—the M16 rifle—did come in for a good deal of criticism, particularly in 1965 and 1966. Many soldiers claimed it had to be cleaned too often, that it manfunctioned too frequently, and that its ammunition was not dependable. Unfortunately, the M16s that were being issued during those early years of fighting in Vietnam were not, in fact, good weapons, and the rifle thus acquired a bad reputation from which it has never fully recovered.

But major modifications were made to the rifle and to its ammunition, and the M16 soon became recognized by those who were knowledgeable on the subject as an excellent weapon for an infantryman to use in a jungle environment. Even before the last U.S. infantry unit was withdrawn, the M16 had proved to be a dependable rapid firing weapon.

Improvements in communications were truly significant and were of untold value to all commanders. For example, a brigade commander in Vietnam could talk to all of his platoon leaders, and division commanders could count on having almost as many hot lines as they wanted, on secure voice radios and on instant communication up the chain of command, down to every tactical unit, and across to other units, to other services, and to Allied forces.

VHF radio relay was the backbone of the communications network in Vietnam, and multichannel VHF connections extended from brigade to battalion level, and even farther down. Artillery batteries supporting infantry battalions were allocated patch-through circuits from these radio relays, and alternate routes and backup systems were used extensively during tactical operations.

The tactical operations center of the 1st Infantry Division was typical of how much communications had improved since 1941. In Vietnam that installation had 35 sole-user circuits that ran from the corps (field force) to terminate in the operations center. During World War II, by contrast, only four channels ran from corps to division, and in the Korean War, the use of eight channels from a corps to a division was standard practice.

In Vietnam, too, it was common to have 32 channels to a single combat brigade. And airborne command posts were used extensively, with radio consoles installed in UH-1 helicopters. Airborne radio relays were also used.

To go along with his new and more powerful weapons, and his extensive communications network, the infantryman also had sensors (acoustic, magnetic, and seismic), target acquisition devices, and night observation devices, combined with automatic data processing equipment. All of these represented a major advance in military systems management at the battalion level and higher.

Despite all the progress in weaponry, communications, and the like, the infantryman's age-old tactical principles did not change. In Vietnam, the infantry units conducted a mobile defense for more than five years. Although they fought from fixed bases, they used almost purely offensive tactics in doing so.

Contact with NVA forces was usually made either by battalions or by smaller units. Having found an enemy force, an infantry commander habitually called on overwhelming reinforcements and firepower to defeat that force. Artillery units and U.S. Air Force tactical formations gave him magnificent support and pointed up again the value of good, solid combined arms training. Mechanized infantry units proved to be versatile, effective, and well-suited to the type of low-intensity warfare that the Army encountered.

The infantryman's adaptation to the countrywide nature of the war evolved through a process of trial and error. Success was not always clear-cut; control of the population was often in doubt; and victory or defeat usually lay at the grass-roots level after the maneuver battalions had done their work.

But the frequent changes of leaders at company, battalion, and brigade levels—a six-month command tour was the norm—had its effect on the Army's operations. Critics felt that a commander was just getting a real feel for his unit when he had to turn it over to another commander. They suggested that the soldier in the ranks, who had to spend a full year in a unit before he could turn his job over to someone else, did not appreciate a change in commanders for no apparent reason and felt betrayed when he was turned over to someone else. This, the critics charged, led to refusals to obey orders, to the heavy use of drugs by some soldiers, to racial incidents, and to a general lack of communication between the leaders and the led.

To the Army, the solution to these problems could be found in effective leadership. Accordingly, human relations councils were started in most units to handle racial problems; drug suppression councils were organized in the divisions to encourage drug users to present themselves voluntarily for treatment under an amnesty program; and the number of hours of instruction in such subjects was increased at the Army's service schools.

There were other leadership problems, many of which are discussed by Colonel Lawrence L. Mowrey in Chapter 12. For example, as Colonel Mowrey points out, infantry captains who were recent graduates of the officers advanced course at Fort Benning were seldom assigned as company commanders as they should have been. Instead, because there was a shortage of field grade officers in Vietnam, these captains—many of whom were on a second tour in Vietnam—were usually assigned to battalion and brigade staff positions.

This meant that junior infantry officers, few of whom were experienced, had to command the companies. At the same time, many of the same companies also suffered a serious shortage of experienced noncommissioned officers. This was a problem that was never completely solved. The Army, because of its other commitments, simply did not have enough people to do any more about the problem than it did.

The U.S. advisory effort, too, suffered from a shortage of trained and experienced personal. Too many advisors lacked recent troop experience and their knowledge of the tactics, techniques, and equipment used by the ARVN was deficient. Many advisors did not take firm stands in dealing with their counterparts and few ever recommended that unsatisfactory ARVN commanders should be relieved. In fact, many U.S. advisors were guilty of spending too much time trying to be good buddies with their counterparts at the expense of their mission. (A good account of how one U.S. advisor looked at advisory duty can be found in Captain Ronald D. Bowen's piece in Chapter 11.)

The infantryman in Vietnam carried on the infantry's traditions of ingenuity, imagination, and flexibility. He accomplished all that was asked of him. And like those infantrymen who had fought a savage guerrilla war in the Philippines for six years between 1900 and 1906, he came home to a less than warm welcome. His war, like theirs, ended on a quiet but somber note.